1992

The Social Environment

The Social Environment

OPEN SYSTEMS APPLICATIONS

by

Patricia Yancey Martin
Gerald G. O'Connor

Florida State University

Longman
New York & London

The Social Environment: Open Systems Applications

Longman Inc. 95 Church Street, White Plains, N. Y. 10601

Associated companies:
Longman Group Ltd., London
Longman Cheshire Pty., Melbourne
Longman Paul Pty., Auckland
Copp Clark Pitman, Toronto
Pitman Publishing Inc., New York

Senior editor: David J. Estrin
Production editor: Louise M. Kahan
Text design: Steven August Krastin
Cover design: Steven August Krastin
Text art: J & R Services
Production supervisor: Eduardo Castillo

Library of Congress Cataloging-in-Publication Data

Martin, Patricia Yancey.
    The social environment: open systems applications by
Patricia Yancey Martin, Gerald G. O'Connor
        p.   cm.
    Bibliography: p.
    Includes index.
    ISBN 0-582-29014-7 (pbk.)
    1. Social service—United States.   2. Social systems.
3. Organizational behavior.   I. O'Connor, Gerald G.   II. Title.
HV91.M316 1989   87-36148
361.3'0973—dc19   CIP

ISBN 0-582-29014-7 (pbk.)

3 4 5 6 7 8 9 10 AL 9594939291

To Nellie, Odell, Andy, Melissa, Matt, and Joey
and To Joyce, Sean, and Amy

Contents

Preface

The ability to perceive, conceptualize, and assess social systems is a necessity in a rapidly changing and complex world. This book—which represents a decade of study, teaching, and learning—is our contribution toward that end. We hope our readers will gain a better understanding of the social environment in which social workers and social work practice are embedded.

In the mid-1970s at The Florida State University, we first applied Open Systems Theory (OST) principles in a course required of both undergraduate and master's degree students in social work. This task was more formidable than we had anticipated. Most of the literature of General System Theory (GST), the parent of our version of Open Systems Theory, seemed to apply to biological rather than social systems. Unlike biological systems, social systems are disorderly, loosely organized, and rarely governed by obvious principles or rational goals. Social systems can change in more fundamental ways than biological systems can. We always believed, however, that we could apply OST principles to social systems, and this book demonstrates, we hope, that we were right. As our understanding of General System Theory grew, we increasingly focused on the theme of openness and its consequences. This theme emphasizes the linkages between social systems and their environments, the primacy of social process, and the potential for fundamental change. We trust that our book is true to these principles, as we understand them to be.

Portions of the text are published elsewhere. Chapter 5, on professional–client dyads, is a reworked version of a 1980 paper ("A Critical Analysis of Power in Professional–Client Relations") that appeared in *Arete* (Vol. 6,

Spring 1981, pp. 35–48). Chapter 7, on small groups, appeared in 1980 in *Small Group Behavior* ("Small Groups: A General System Model," Vol. 11, May 1980, pp. 145–174). Portions of Chapter 8, on social welfare organizations, have appeared in three articles, including two in *Administration in Social Work* in 1980 and 1987 ("Multiple Constituencies, Dominant Societal Values, and the Human Service Administrator: Implications for Service Delivery," Vol. 4, Fall 1980, pp. 14–27, and "Multiple Constituencies and Performance in Social Welfare Organizations," Vol. 11, 1987); and one in the *Journal of Sociology and Social Welfare* in 1980 ("Multiple Constituencies, Differential Power, and the Question of Effectiveness in Human Service Organizations," Vol. 6, No. 7, 1980, pp. 801–816).

We have many people to thank. For three years, we co-instructed the Open Systems Theory course with a colleague, Shimon Gottschalk, who taught us about communities and reminded us often of the inherent tensions between individual liberties and social, or collective, order. We thank Shimon for his contribution to our understanding and absolve him of responsibility for any misinterpretations we have made. Linda O'Neall drafted the original version of the upside-down staircase in Chapter 2 (Fig. 2.1); we are in her debt for this useful way of representing the concept of hierarchy. We thank Michael Austin, our colleague in the 1970s, for encouraging us to develop a course on Open Systems Theory and suggesting that we send our manuscript to Charles Guzzetta, then editor of Longman's social work series. Chuck Guzzetta helped us gain a review and contract with Longman, Inc., and for this we are grateful. Betty Etzler, Peter Iverson, Courtney Elliott, Joseph Hodge, Michael Smith, and Waldo Klein helped us teach the Open Systems Theory course and gave us useful suggestions that we tried to incorporate in the text. Etzler and Iverson, along with Herman (Hi) Resnick of the University of Washington, Tina Howard Hancock of the University of South Florida, Ken Kazmirski of the University of Central Florida, and Mona Schaly of Colorado State University, adopted earlier drafts of the manuscript and gave us suggestions for improvement and encouragement to proceed.

Mary Harvey, our typist and good friend, is thanked for her never-failing optimism, grace, competence, accuracy, and speed. Secretarial staff in The Florida State University School of Social Work who helped us include Sheila Samson, Sherry Bradford, and Nancy Holladay. Colleagues who either co-taught the OST course with us or lectured to our classes include James P. Love, Walter LaMendola, and John Alderson. We thank them for their help. David Estrin, senior editor at Longman, has been a champion friend, cheerleader, nudger, and guide. Without his belief in us, and his patience, we could easily have given up. We appreciate the editorial assistance that Joan Heggen, Elfin Moses, Anne Humphrey, and Jan Wells gave us. Finally, we thank the hundreds of students who waded patiently through earlier drafts of the manuscript and taught us as much, if not more, than we taught them.

Our families and friends believed in us even when we stopped believing in ourselves. For their encouragement, support, and love, we say thank you, thank you, thank you.

SUGGESTIONS FOR USING THE BOOK

This text has many uses for social work educational programs and practitioners, as well as professionals in other human service fields. Instructors and students in social work courses on Human Behavior and the Social Environment will find it a useful complement to material on personal or individual development. Additionally, the text can serve as primary text in courses that focus on the social work profession *qua profession* or on a *system's orientation*. Programs that view system's theory as their organizing framework can use the text to establish a conceptual core or base upon which to build. Additionally, the text overviews the major practice arenas of the profession. Social work courses that focus on practice with individuals, families, groups, organizations, and communities will find it helpful as an orienting framework and practice guide. Finally, professionals in other fields will find our holistic and dynamic conception of the social environment instructive. Nurses, mental health counselors, job placement specialists, family therapists and related professionals will find that our conception of the social environment helps them make sense of a complex, and seemingly chaotic, world.

To the Instructor

This text is appropriate to all levels of higher and adult education and we offer some suggestions on its use.

At the undergraduate level, we recommend that instructors focus on Chapters 1, 2, and 5 through 9. Chapters 3 and 4 can be skipped without depriving those who are interested primarily in our depictions of the social environment. (Chapter 3 addresses philosophical questions of greater interest to scholars than to many practitioners and Chapter 4 builds on Chapter 3.) Those parts of Chapter 4 that deal with the history of systems theory are useful to undergraduates, however, as is the overview of predominant theories-in-use by social workers. Chapter 2 presents the basic concepts of Open Systems Theory, essential material for all readers. Students will find it helpful to read Chapter 2 more than once. We recommend that Chapter 2 be read early in the course, again at mid-term, and a third time near the end of the course. If the instructor prefers, Chapter 2 can be assigned in conjunction with the first Applications chapter (i.e., Chapter 5) rather than *before* the latter is read.

At the master's degree level, we recommend that instructors focus on Chapters 1, 2, 4, and 5 through 9 (skipping, if anything, Chapter 3). As with undergraduates, reading and re-reading of Chapter 2 will be helpful. Chapter 4 presents a brief history of systems theory in social work and a review of other major theories-in-use by social workers. Since systems theory remains popular within the profession, today's social workers should be informed about its history and philosophical compatibility with other theories. MSW students can benefit from Chapter 3 but we recommend that it be assigned, along with Chapter 4, later rather than early in the academic term. The Applications chapters will orient students to the issues that Chapters 3 and 4 pose.

At the doctoral level, the entire book is useful. Chapters 3 and 4 summarize, in relation to Open Systems Theory, the major philosophical debates in modern social work. Arguments for or against logical positivism make more sense if we understand that some people view social reality as a hard, external facticity that can be studied with natural science methods whereas others see it an illusive ephemerality that exists only in the human consciousness. Chapters 5 through 9, the Applications material, can serve as a review and update for advanced graduate students who have returned to school after an absence and need an overview of major issues and literature in the field.

Social work practitioners and professionals in other fields will find Chapters 1, 2, 4 and 5 through 9 most useful. Chapter 2 is essential for understanding basic OST concepts and principles and Chapter 4 presents a useful historial perspective. As noted earlier, Chapters 3 and 4 can be assigned out of sequence without loss of understanding or continuity on the reader's part.

To the Student

To gain the most from this text, students must relate the concepts that are explained here to the world that they know, experience, and observe. Many Open Systems Theory concepts have unusual names and may at first seem obscure. As familiarity and understanding increase, however, students will realize that the content is more familiar than they first thought. We believe that it is worthwhile to take the trouble to learn OST terms and organizing principles because of their utility for the professional social worker. An Open Systems Theory perspective will enable the student who invests to perceive the world more accurately and understand it better. Additionally, it will provide him or her with better skills for problem diagnosis and intervention with a variety of social systems and heightened awareness of the levers for social action and change.

Patricia Yancey Martin
Gerald G. O'Connor

PART ONE

Open Systems Theory–
An Introduction

Chapter 1

The Social Environment: American Society and Social Work as Social Contexts

Many people look about them and see confusion. Mass society, with its anonymous cities, impersonal high-rise buildings, and reliance on the media (especially television), is experienced by many people as alienating and isolating. Chaos and mystery seem to triumph over order, reason, and purpose. Cynicism and a sense of futility overwhelm the individual who tries to understand a world that seems to lack meaning. The increasing reliance of Americans on professional therapy to handle crises and life-course changes suggests that life is neither simple nor easy.

Another perspective is that people fail to see the order that lies behind much that they observe. Events seen as chaotic may be predictable to those with the conceptual tools to understand them. High crime rates in central cities may be consequences of high-density population and high unemployment, not indicators of the urban dweller's inferiority or the social fabric's decay. Murder and assault may result from rapid social change that makes neighbors strangers and undermines feelings of commonality and mutual support. The ability to conceptualize modern life, including how things mutually influence each other, is a necessary skill in today's changing and complex world.

Americans do not understand their society. Emphasis on the individual— individual rights, individual freedom, individual opportunity, and success— discourages them from seeing the impact of the social context on their lives. They resist the sociological generalizations that child rearing, family life, and leisure preferences are affected by their social and economic backgrounds. They deny the impact of class, religion, ethnicity, race, gender, age, marital status, and other influences on their actions and beliefs. Some Americans leave their families and communities and "go it alone" even though the paths they follow are shaped by these very influences. In their zest to embrace individualism, they toss the baby out with the bathwater and deny the value of tradition and contextual influences on their lives (Bellah et al., 1985).

THE SOCIAL ENVIRONMENT

This book is about the social environment. *Social* means people: When people share a common locale and culture and interact with each other over time, this is called a *society*. The *environment* is the context that people live in. The *social environment* is the social context in which people live and act, both individually and collectively. Individuals are both embedded in and separate from the social environment. The social environment is *constructed* by individuals and groups (organizations, communities, etc.) in interaction with each other. It encompasses the cultural, economic, political, religious, indeed all aspects of everyday life.

Social environment has a general and specific meaning. As a general term, it refers to American society as a whole. As a specific term, it refers to particular contextual settings: for example, families, communities, factories, treatment groups. Both meanings are used in this book, but the Applications section employs mostly the second meaning.

Social environments predate individuals and shape their perceptions and actions. Social environments can be created deliberately; existing ones can be framed anew and changed. In presenting an Open Systems Theory account of the social environment, we try to promote understanding of the environment as it exists antecedent to and independently of individual persons. We hope also to point out possibilities for creating new, alternative environments. The social environment's duality (1) as a preexisting and enduring context and (2) as emergent and changing context is a central theme of this book.

OPEN SYSTEMS APPLICATIONS

The subtitle of this book is "Open Systems Applications." Open Systems Theory (OST) is the conceptual framework used to communicate and illustrate the social environment. Open Systems Theory is a general theory that emphasizes the dynamic relationship between social systems and their environments and between social structure and social process. Throughout the book, OST is used to help readers understand the multiple, and often conflicting, social contexts in which they live. The particular contexts include: (1) the professional–client dyad, (2) the family, (3) the small group, (4) the social welfare organization, and (5) the community. The family and community are informal or existential contexts (Gottschalk, 1975) with diffuse, as opposed to specific, goals. The professional–client dyad, the treatment group, and the welfare organization are formal social contexts with specific goals and intended results. While these do not exhaust all varieties of social context, they represent the majority of types encountered by social workers in their daily work.

SOCIAL WORK AND OPEN SYSTEMS THEORY

Like modern society, social work is complex and changing. It is oriented to the alleviation of many social problems, and its domain seems continually to expand (O'Connor and Waring, 1981). Over 90,000 Americans are members of the National Association of Social Work (National Association of Social Work News, 1983). About 400,000 Americans are employed in general social service work and one-half of these are estimated to be professionally trained (U.S. Bureau of the Census, 1982). Social work's emergence as an organized, distinct profession (or semiprofession; Toren, 1969) has occurred in the twentieth century basically as a result of the trend in developed nation-states to address problems associated with urbanization, industralization, and modernization through formal and official, as contrasted to informal and unofficial, means (Offe, 1984; Skocpol and Ikenberry, 1983; Cates, 1982).

Social work's growth and changes in task and domain over the past half century are dramatic, yet social work theory and research have had difficulty keeping pace. Theoretical perspectives are numerous, and little consensus exists between caseworkers who subscribe to Freudian psychology versus social learning theory or between caseworkers and community organizers. Many social workers have more in common with non-social-work associates than with social workers in other types of jobs or work settings. A caseworker in a mental health agency may identify more with mental health aides, psychologists, and psychiatrists than with community organizers (Miller and Fiddleman, n. d.). This militates against communication and sharing of knowledge across social work's fields of practice and modalities. It also weakens efforts to present a unified front to the world. Finally, and more seriously, it prevents the accumulation of knowledge that could lead to a general theory of intervention and change (Briar and Miller, 1971).

Open Systems Theory, in addition to explaining the social context, can be useful to social work in other ways. It provides *a general framework for organizing other theories* about different aspects of the social world, for example, about individual psychology, family dynamics, treatment group structure, organizational change, and policy implementation. Social work's complexity stems, in part, from the multiple theories it relies on to account for all the phenomena with which it is concerned. If OST can help simplify and clarify the morass of competing theories that are taught to social workers as guides to practice, it will serve the field well.

OVERVIEW OF CHAPTER 1

As noted above, society is complex. Factors that have contributed to its complexity—industrialization, urbanization, modernization, and individualism—are discussed below. To illustrate our nation's complexity, information is presented on the personal and family circumstances of Americans in the 1980s. Crime trends and urban and rural differences are examined, and changes in the social work profession over the past decade are reviewed. Evidence on the varied tasks, contexts, and activities of practicing social workers documents social work's diversity and underscores the need for a framework that can explain, orient, and integrate.

MODERN LIFE AND ITS ORIGINS

Life is fast-paced, complex, and changing. The hegemony of a few values, norms, and mores that formerly constrained the actions of family, neighbor, friend, and stranger has given way to a variety of competing standards. Informal social controls like those described by Sinclair Lewis in his novel *Main Street* have weakened (or vanished) in cities and towns across America today. They seem to have been replaced with a "live and let live" philosophy. It is difficult to make *a priori* assumptions about people's motives. Competing explanations exist for every so-called fact. In her book *Out on a Limb*, Shirley MacLaine (1983) claims that aliens visit earth and humans have reincarnated souls. Although scientists and theologians probably reject her claims, MacLaine is able to bring her views to the attention of millions through television, radio, and the press. She has found, furthermore, a receptive audience among many who read or hear her ideas. In today's high-technology world, proponents of even the most farfetched views can get their message out to a wide audience. Through satellite television, they can literally reach around the world. Perhaps most importantly, they have a presumed right to "do their thing." The reign of a few clear standards, norms, and ideas seems to be a thing of the past.

What has produced the demise of narrow, explicit behavioral standards and legitimated, or at least allowed, so much diversity? Most explanations focus on the effects of industrialization, urbanization, modernization, and the rise of individualism.

Industrialization

With the advent of the factory system in the early stages of capitalism, work became separated from family and home. Whereas father and mother previously worked at home (in the fields, around the children), the invention of the factory system and the organization of work at a central site under the control of employers changed the family and family-work arrangements dramatically (Sokoloff, 1980; Martin, Seymour, Courage, and Godbey, and Tate, 1988). Wives, mothers, and daughters of the poorer classes were sent by husbands and fathers into the mills as common laborers while better-off (upper middle class) women were forced into idleness and economic dependency as they remained at home with no productive or apparently useful work to do (Cott, 1977; Degler, 1980). The role of the family in the lives of its members changed and the influence of formal organizations increased (Marglin, 1976; Hall, 1987). As this occurred, informal controls over the family members' behavior were replaced with the formal controls of work organization and urban life.

As the United States became industrialized in the nineteenth century, millions of Europeans immigrated in search of work and a better life. The United States is a nation of immigrants. Hundreds of nationalities and ethnic groups have come here since the arrival of the first colonists from England. Over a million Africans were brought here against their will as part of the slave trade before the Civil War. The nation's change from agrarian and rural to industrial and urban was greatly accelerated by the Civil War, which destroyed the plantation and agricultural system that had predominated in the South and elsewhere prior to that time. Betwen 1900 and 1914, the beginning of World War I, 12 million to 13 million immigrants, the majority from Europe, swarmed to America's shores and were absorbed by the burgeoning industrial cities of the Northeast and Midwest. Industrialization led to the development of a national market that, in time, homogenized American cities and American life to a remarkable degree. As the economy changed from rural/farming to industrial/commercial, the role of the market in determining relationships not only between seller and buyer but among friends, family, and neighbors expanded and grew (Bellah, Madsen, Sullivan, Swidler, and Tipton, 1985).

America's major cities have, since the 1960s, suffered from the decline of manufacturing, construction, and industries such as steel, coal, and railroads as major economic sectors. With the rise of the service sector (restaurants and hotels, banking, entertainment, insurance, etc.), and the decline of manufacturing and industry, Daniel Bell says the United States (and other similar nations) have entered the Post-Industrial era (Bell, 1973). Changes since World War II in the labor force from primarily blue collar (working class) to white collar (middle class) have been dramatic and is one factor in the increased participation of women in the paid work world (Braverman, 1974).

Urbanization

Concurrent with the advent and expansion of early capitalism was the migration of people from rural areas and foreign countries into American's newly emerging towns and cities to find work and join in the presumed opportunities and excitement of urban life. Migration to the city decreased the role of the family in the lives of the émigrés, thus diminishing the ability of local communities to control the behavior of members who moved to more densely populated, anonymous, and often distant settings. Urbanization is the concentration of large numbers of people into a restricted land area. It fosters social processes different from those in smaller, rural locales. City life is more complex partly because there are proportionately fewer acquaintances among one's associates. As a result, fewer mutually shared views of appropriate expectations or standards develop and spread (Blau, 1977a, b).

In neighborhoods and small towns of the past, children who stole were punished rather than arrested. Storekeepers scolded them and escorted them home to their parents. This was an informal, local solution based on familiarity and shared standards. In the city, acquaintances are few and the odds of knowing a child's parents are diminished. Children who steal are treated as thieves or delinquents. Formal handling of a city youth who steals leads to involvement with a governmental system that handles delinquents. A child's experiences in this system may lead to a life of deviancy and crime, all starting from an incident that was no more or less of a crime than the small-town child's. Urbanization of the social environment makes a difference.

Modernization

A third influence is modernization. Modernization, often concommitant with industrialization and urbanization, involves secularization (in contrast to sacred) of the organization of social life; reliance on the media for information (television, newspapers, radio); the development and use of mass transit systems (trains, buses, planes, highways); reliance on formal, public education for socialization of children (rather than family, clan, or tribe); emphasis on consumer goods such as washing machines, vacuum cleaners, automobiles, videocassette recorders, and so forth. Emphasis on education and other "objective" indicators of social worth encourages a meritocratic stratification system that replaces family, tradition, and charisma as the grounds for status and success. Reliance on impersonal sources of information (television, newspapers) leads over time to exposure to a greater variety of viewpoints, opinions, and analyses than would occur in face-to-face interaction with only acquaintances and friends. The effects of MTV (the music television station) on today's youth are unknown, but some worry that the violence depicted in music videos (particularly toward women) and implicit endorsement of bizarre behaviors may encourage such actions in viewers' lives (Bart, Freeman, and Kimball, 1985). What is taught to children in school, home, church, Scouting, and so forth is often contradicted by messages in books, magazines, television, and the cinema.

Modernization brings competing viewpoints, interpretations, and explanations regarding good and bad, right and wrong, necessary and optional, true and false. As modernization occurs, a national labor market emerges, and people become less concerned with locale and community and more concerned with individual self-interest. Traditional ways of organizing life (around family, clan, or village) are replaced by formal, bureaucratic means. The diminished influence of traditional and time-honored practices leaves holes in the social fabric, and modern life can become lonely, difficult, and demanding. Through the introduction and use of new ideas, products, and artifacts (e.g., baby formula, alcohol, birth control pills, the automobile, television) traditional ways of resolving life-course dilemmas and personal and social problems disappear.

Individualism

Belief in the rights of individuals over those of the collective or community life is a particularly American characteristic. Guarantees in the Declaration of Independence that "all men are created equal" and that individuals have a right to life, liberty, and the pursuit of happiness undergird this view. Such ideas are themselves modern, concurrent with the emergence of capitalism in the seventeenth century (Stacey, 1981; Thompson, 1977). The idea that the individual is more important than the community (family, group, etc.) has, some believe, become so dominant in America that commitment to the common good is threatened (Bellah et al., 1985). When everyone believes his or her desires are the most important concerns in life, reasons to contribute to, or sacrifice for, community are few. Finding common ground between individuals in the absence of agreed-upon standards or moral precepts is difficult. Americans lack a consensus on what is important, how to get things done, and what deserves priority. Bellah and colleagues (1985) say that overemphasis on individual rights excludes concern with tradition, community, and the social context. Without the larger context to protect them, individual rights are meaningless. A challenge for America is to find common ground, and a language to discuss it, that allows identification of a collective purpose and direction. Issues such as these are addressed in Chapter 9, which examines communities.

Demographic and Social Characteristics

Statistics from the U.S. Bureau of the Census provide perspective on the diversities of life in the United States in the 1980s. The total population of the United States in 1988 is about 245 million. At the time of the 1980 Census, it was 226.5 million (U.S. Bureau of the Census, 1983a). Although Americans are having fewer children, the population continues to grow.

Nation of Immigrants

In 1980, the Census Bureau asked Americans to identify their ancestry (U.S. Bureau of the Census, 1983e). About 83 percent reported at least one category of ancestry other than American. The largest ancestry groups were English (50 million), German (49 million), Irish (40 million), Afro-American (21 million), French (13 million), Italian (12 million), and Scottish (10 million). Other categories reporting six million or more were Polish, Mexican, American Indian, and Dutch. The English, German, and Irish were among the first Europeans to arrive in large numbers, although their influx peaked in the late nineteenth century. African-Americans were forcibly brought to the United States between the seventeenth and nineteenth centuries. Most other immigrants, the Italian and Polish, for example, arrived in large numbers early in this century. Restrictions on immigration after World War I prevented large numbers from coming thereafter. Immigrants during the past two decades have included substantial numbers of West Indians, Latin Americans, and Asians (e.g., Vietnamese, Filipino).

Some Americans seem unaware that we have all kinds of names, skin colors, national origins, religions, and ancestral loyalties. Forging a national identity and purpose is therefore a challenge. Ethnic heterogeneity and an emphasis on individualism foster rejection of community and of tradition itself (Bellah et al., 1985).

Prejudices persist against many nationalities who have come to our shores. When John Kennedy ran for president less than three decades ago, he was opposed because he was Catholic. America had never had a Catholic president. Geraldine Ferraro's nomination for vice-president on the Democratic ticket in 1984 was talked about almost as much for her Italian ancestry as for her gender. Mexican immigrants are despised in California and Texas, the Vietnamese are disliked in Louisiana, and prejudice against Jews exists in various parts of the nation. Southerners are called hicks and insincere; Italians are seen as loud and corrupt; the Irish are stereotyped as heavy drinkers; the Polish are called dumb. With so much diversity and minimal appreciation of differences, the development of a common heritage, identity, and purpose becomes problematic. Moreover, the claim that the United States is a melting pot and that different ethnic and racial groups will blend into a homogeneous mass has proved to be inaccurate and, some would claim, undesirable.

Positive identification with national, cultural, and racial origins is on the rise. Italian-Americans, Greek-Americans, Armenian-Americans, Russian-Americans, Polish-Americans, (among others) form organizations and clubs, hold meetings, and work to advance their social, political, and economic interests while affirming their American identity.

Gender, Age, Race, and Marital Status

Figures 1.1, 1.2, and 1.3 show, respectively, the age distribution by gender of the United States in 1970 and 1980, percent change by age group between 1970 and 1980, and the racial composition of the population in 1980 (U.S. Bureau of the Census, 1983a). Figure 1.1 shows more young people than old people in 1980. Males equalled or outnumbered females until age 25, after which women begin to outnumber men. This imbalance increases with age, and the majority of American elderly are women. In 1980 there were 68 men for every 100 women 65 years and over; at age 75 and over, there were only 55 men for every 100 women (U.S. Bureau of the Census, 1984c, p. 19). If current trends persist, the difference will double by the year 2000. The life expectancy in 1983 was 78.3 years for women and 71.0 years for men (U.S. Bureau of the Census, 1985a, p. 1).

Figure 1.2 shows that between 1970 and 1980, the age groups that increased most (by percentage) were the 20 to 39-year-olds and the 65-and-over group. Some categories decreased, including those 14 and under and those 40 to 49. The latter is a result of low fertility during World War II, whereas the former reflects a decline in birth rates among today's young adults. Those aged 20 to 39 are the so-called baby boomers who were born after World War II and are moving through the population distribution as a demographic bulge. When they reach retirement age, with relatively few young people to pay for their retirement and Social Security, social policy conflicts may develop between old and young. The dramatic increase in those aged 85 and older is noteworthy. Advances in medicine and knowledge about diet and exercise help more people live to an advanced age. Problems of the frail elderly (those over 85) are already occurring in some states (for example, Florida) and are expected to increase (Streib, 1988). The median age of the population in 1980 was 30, meaning that one-half of the population was older than this and one-half was younger. If trends in Figure 1.2 continue throughout the 1980s and beyond, the median age will rise. Figure 1.3 shows that 83.1 percent of the United States' population is classified as racially white, with 11.7 percent black, and 6.4 percent (of whatever race) of Spanish origins. American Indians, Asians, and other races make up an additional 5 percent.

Table 1.1 shows the marital status of people 15 years of age and older by sex, race, and Spanish origin in 1980. Considerable differences exist among race, ethnic, and gender groups. Proportionately more whites were married

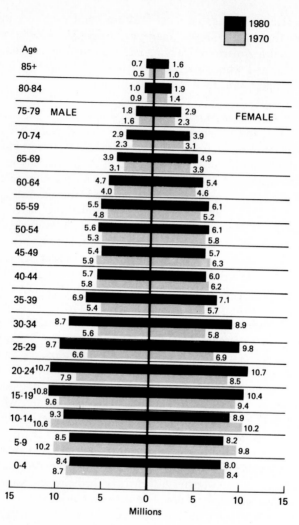

Figure 1.1 Persons by Age and Sex: 1980 and 1970

in 1980 than were Spanish-origin or black citizens and more Spanish-origin than black. Also, a higher percentage of men than women were married. Women were less likely than men to be single and more likely to be divorced, separated, or widowed. This suggests, as later evidence supports, that most single-parent households are headed by women. One reason for lower marriage rates among black women is a dearth of eligible black men. In 1981, the sex ratio of men to women was 89.7 among blacks (for every 100 black

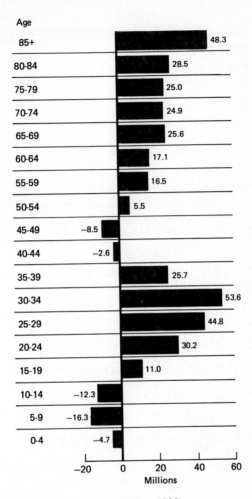

Figure 1.2 Percent Change by Age: 1970 to 1980

women, there were 89.7 black men) compared to 95.2 for whites. Between the ages of 25 and 64, furthermore, the ages at which marriage rates are highest, the sex ratio for blacks is in the low 80s as compared to the mid-90s for whites (U.S. Bureau of the Census, 1982, Table 29). Stated differently, white women outnumber white men after age 34, but black women outnumber black men after age 19 (U.S. Bureau of the Census, 1982, Table 31). Compared to white women, black women's marriage chances are much less.

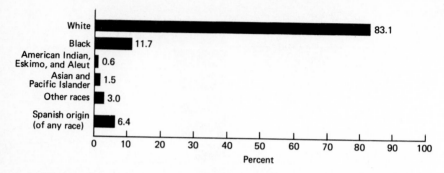

Figure 1.3 Percent Distribution of the Population by Race and Spanish Origin: 1980. *Source:* U.S. Bureau of the Census, *General Population Characteristics, United States Summary* (PC80-1-B1), *1980* Washington, D.C., 1983a.

TABLE 1.1. MARITAL STATUS OF PERSONS 15 YEARS AND OVER BY SEX AND RACE OR SPANISH ORIGIN: 1980 (AS A PERCENTAGE)

	White		Black		Spanish Origin	
Marital Status	*Male*	*Female*	*Male*	*Female*	*Male*	*Female*
Single	28.2	21.2	41.1	34.4	35.6	27.5
Now married	62.5	57.4	42.6	35.1	55.2	52.8
Divorced and separated	6.8	8.8	12.6	17.8	7.5	12.5
Widowed	2.5	12.6	3.8	12.8	1.7	7.2

Source: Adapted from U.S. Bureau of the Census (1983a, Figure 16, p. 15).

Religious Diversity

Ever since the Pilgrims' escape from religious persecution in England, religion has been important in the United States. A sixty-nation survey by Gallup International Research Institutes in the mid-1970s (The Gallup Report, 1985) shows that religious beliefs remain high in the United States but have decreased in Western Europe. When asked if religious beliefs were very important, 56 percent of Americans said "yes" in contrast to 27 percent of Western Europeans. The only major nation in which religion is more important is India, where 81 percent said religious beliefs were very important. A majority of people in all nations surveyed say they identify with a faith or church and believe in the existence of God or a universal spirit, and a majority in the non-Communist world say they believe in life after death.

In a recent Gallup poll, 68 percent of Americans said they belong to a church or synagogue, 40 percent said they attend church or synagogue in a typical week, and 65 percent expressed confidence in the church or organized religion. Half the sample said they were more interested in religious and spiritual matters than they were five years ago (The Gallup Report, 1985, p. 13). In regards to faith, 57 percent ($N = 29, 216$) of Americans are Protestant, 28 percent are Catholic, 2 percent Jewish, 4 percent other, and 9 percent none. Preference for Catholicism is more prevalent in the East (44 percent) whereas preference for Protestantism prevails in the South (74 percent) and Midwest (63 percent). Westerners are most likely to report "other" (10 percent) or "none" (14 percent) as a preference. From 1973 to 1983, growth in Protestant church membership was greatest in fundamentalist or evangelical churches such as Assemblies of God (up 71 percent), Mormons (up 40 percent), Seventh-Day Adventists (up 34 percent), Church of the Nazarene (up 22 percent), and Southern Baptist (up 15 percent). Mainline churches lost membership: Presbyterian Church USA (down 15 percent), Christian (Disciples of Christ; down 13 percent), United Methodist (down 8 percent), Episcopal (down 4 percent), and Lutheran (down 3 percent) (The Gallup Report, 1985, p. 11). The 1980 and 1984 presidential elections spotlighted The Moral Majority, a fundamentalist political movement directed by Jerry Falwell. Some political observers believe this organization was instrumental in defeating a number of congressional candidates in 1980. In a 1980 survey, however, only 40 percent of Americans had heard of The Moral Majority, and although by 1981 this figure had increased to 55 percent, unfavorable outweighed favorable perceptions by a 2:1 ratio.

The church–state relationship pervades America's history. Recent Gallup respondents "believed it was wrong for religious groups to work actively for the defeat of candidates who did not agree with their position on issues but . . . felt it was important for religious organizations to speak out on the moral implications of political issues" (The Gallup Report, 1985, p. 11). Evangelicals and nonevangelicals differ most on three issues: the rights of homosexuals to teach in public schools, the banning of abortion, and prayer in school. Since the 1960s, when mainline churches entered the civil rights movement on the side of blacks, church involvement in the political arena has been extensive. In the 1980s, however, fundamentalist churches are most active in support of so-called traditional values that they believe are under siege by liberals who value nonreligious principles. The diversity of religious faiths and organizations and the intensity of beliefs on all sides suggest that religion will remain a vital aspect of American society for decades to come.

Urban/Rural Patterns

Americans in 1980 were urban dwellers. As shown in Table 1.2, almost three-fourths of the population in 1980 (and 1970) lived in urban areas, one-fourth in rural areas). This pattern varies by race. As shown in Table 1.2,

TABLE 1.2. URBAN AND RURAL U.S. POPULATION, BY RACE: 1970 AND 1980 (IN THOUSANDS, EXCEPT WHERE PERCENT)

			Black and Other	
	Total	*White*	*Total*	*Black*
1970, total population	203,212	177,749	25,463	22,580
Urban	73.5	72.4	80.7	81.3
Inside urbanized areas	58.3	56.8	68.7	69.5
Central cities	31.5	27.9	56.5	58.2
Urban fringe	26.8	28.9	12.3	11.3
Outside urban areas	15.2	15.7	12.0	11.8
Rural	26.5	27.6	19.3	18.7
1980, total population	226,546	188,372	38,174	26,495
Urban	73.7	71.3	85.7	85.3
Inside urbanized areas	61.4	58.5	76.0	75.9
Central cities	29.6	24.6	54.0	57.2
Urban fringe	31.8	33.8	22.0	18.7
Outside urban areas	12.3	12.8	9.7	9.4
Rural	26.3	28.7	14.3	14.7

Source: Adapted from U.S. Bureau of the Census (1983b, Table 27, p. 27).

black Americans are much more likely than whites to live in central cities (57.2 percent to 24.6 percent, respectively) whereas whites are more likely to live on the urban fringe and in rural areas. This pattern has developed since the 1950s when black Americans migrated to cities in search of jobs and a better life. Central-city living is crowded, as figures on population density reveal. In 1980, 3,551 people lived in each square mile of central cities with comparable figures of 2,177 for the urban fringe, 17 for rural America, and 67 for the nation as a whole (U.S. Bureau of the Census, 1983b; Table 24). In understanding problems that affect blacks and whites differentially, residential patterns are important. Research on population density indicates that social problems increase geometrically in crowded urban settings. Reasons for this include isolation and alienation associated with large numbers, opportunities for crime and fewer checks on it because of anonymity of most people encountered, and so forth.

Six U.S. cities had populations of a million or more in 1980 (New York, Chicago, Los Angeles, Philadelphia, Detroit, and Houston); 16 had between 500,000 and 1,000,000 inhabitants; 33 had between 250,000 and 500,000 residents; and 114 had between 100,000 and 150,000 inhabitants. Fifty-one percent of urban dwellers lived in cities of 100,000 or more, but 49 percent lived in communities with 100,000 inhabitants or less. Medium-sized cities and towns, in addition to large cities and rural areas, are home to many Americans. While cities and city life dominate the news, film, and entertainment industries, many Americans live small-town rather than big-city lives. American life is less urban than Western Europe's where, for example, 55,000,000 British live on an island with a land area about the size of Alabama. America's higher crime rates cannot, therefore, be accounted for solely by its urbanization (see below).

Government and Politics

Because of a tradition of state and local autonomy, government in the United States is complex. Besides the federal government, there are fifty state governments, 3,041 county governments, 19,000 municipal governments, 17,000 townships and towns, and 15,000 school districts (U.S. Bureau of the Census, 1984d, Table 433, p. 261). (The number of school districts decreased from 108,000 in 1942 to less than 22,000 in 1967 and to 15,000 in 1982 as a result of a consolidation trend that eliminated smaller schools around the nation.) Governments are a major employer in the American economy, and government employees are referred to as *public-sector* workers. (*Private sector* refers to nongovernment.)

Government employed 16,034,000 workers in 1983, the majority (13 million) in state and local governments (U.S. Bureau of the Census, 1984d, Table 472, p. 292). The payroll for all government employees in October 1983 was $24.5 billion, with one-fourth coming from federal revenues and three-fourths from state and local revenues (U.S. Bureau of the Census, 1984d, Table 473, p. 292). More government employees work in education (almost 7 million; over one-half are teachers) than in any other field. The second largest field of government employment is health and hospitals (1,668,000) and the third is national defense (1,042,000, including international relations). Only 409,000 governmental employees are in the public-welfare sector. (The U.S. Postal Service has 669,000 employees, highways employ 532,000 people, 735,000 work in law enforcement, and natural resources employs 440,000). State and county governments are the major employers of social workers (see Table 1.7 in this chapter). Not-for-profit (and for-profit) social-welfare organizations frequently obtain funding from government. Whereas a federalized system of funding for education, social-welfare services, and so forth would undoubtedly be simpler (as it is in England), the decentralized U.S. system produces variety across states and cities. For this reason, among others, social work's task of mapping the environment is complex (see Chapter 4).

Political participation is a topic of current debate. More Americans vote in presidential elections than at other times and the turnout in the past two presidential elections was about 59 percent, a rate that has not varied dramatically during this century (U.S. Bureau of the Census, 1975b). Women vote at about the same rate as men but have recently begun to vote differently from men. Older people of both sexes are more likely to vote than younger ones; the highest voting age group is 45 and over. Education predicts voting behavior: 80 percent of college graduates vote compared to 43 percent of those who completed elementary school. Employed people vote more frequently than the unemployed. If people register to vote, the overwhelming majority will cast ballots. In both 1976 and 1980, 89 percent of registered voters participated in the presidential election. The increase in black registration and voting in the South between 1964 and 1980 has been greater than in other regions (U.S. Bureau of the Census, 1984a, pp. 1, 2), probably because 50 percent of all blacks in the United States reside in the South and almost 25 percent of the South's population is black, compared to 6 percent in the West and about 11 percent in the Midwest and Northeast (Martin, Wilson, and Dillman, 1988).

Since the mid-1970s, more blacks and women have have been elected to political office, particularly at the local level. In January 1984, 5,654 blacks held elective office in 45 states (no blacks held elective office in Idaho, Montana, New Hampshire, North Dakota, or South Dakota) with 7 percent of these holding federal or state legislative posts. Black candidates have been most successful winning election to city and county offices, and women have succeeded primarily with city and town councils. Fully three-fourths of the 16,881 elected women officials in 1982 held office in a town or city council, with only 5 percent in state legislatures. Blacks comprised 3 percent of all elected officials in 1984, and women comprised 9 percent in 1982. Blacks are 11 percent of the U.S. population, and women are over 50 percent; thus both are underrepresented in elective political office.

A political development since the 1970s has been the rise of special-interest groups that organize around one or a few issues (Etzioni, 1984). Examples are Mothers Against Drunk Drivers (MADD), Right to Life (antiabortion groups), antinuclear-energy groups, pro-nuclear-disarmament groups, environmental protection groups, the American Rifle Association, National Association of Manufacturers, National Farmers Union, pro- and anti-ERA, the John Birch Society, Phyllis Schlafley's Eagle Forum, Amnesty International, American Civil Liberties Union, and so forth. Single-issue groups make it difficult to reach consensus on the *common good*.

If American life is diverse and complex, simple solutions to complex problems threaten the public interest. Political action committees—private, not-for-profit organizations whose sole purpose is to raise and disburse political contributions to candidates of their persuasion—have proliferated. The use of computers to defeat candidates over a single issue (abortion, affirmative action, etc.) contributes to divisiveness, development of opposing camps, and an adversarial approach to politics. In a representative democracy, active involvement of the masses is required. As Thomas Jefferson stated, "Government left to its own devices gains ground." Many Americans see politics as distasteful, and characterize government as "them versus us." The American experiment will succeed only if ordinary citizens participate actively in government (Bellah et al., 1985).

Household Composition/Living Arrangements

Information on families is reported in Chapter 6; thus, we review only select data here. A dramatic change from 1970 to 1980 was the increase in non-family households. In a *nonfamily household*, the householder (renter or owner) lives alone or has no relatives living in the dwelling. Widows who live alone, unmarried couples who cohabit, and unrelated people who share a house are nonfamily households. *Family households*, in contrast, require a householder and at least one other person related to the householder by birth, marriage, or adoption. Between 1970 and 1980, the number of family households increased by 19 percent but nonfamilies increased by 88 percent. Other changes in household and family composition in the 10 years between the two censuses included: (1) the number of married-couple households with children declined but the number of one-parent households more than doubled; (2) most of the increase in the number of family households since 1980 are households headed by women with no spouse present; (3) compared with 1970, women maintaining families in 1980 were younger, more likely to be never married or divorced, and more likely to be black or Spanish-origin; and (4) the size of the average household in 1982 was 2.72 persons, the smallest yet recorded, continuing the decline that has been underway since 1965. Americans are having fewer children than before (U.S. Bureau of the Census, 1983c, p. 1).

Family Circumstances Differ by Race

Figure 1.4 shows that black and white children under age 18 live in different circumstances (U.S. Bureau of the Census, 1983d, p. 5). Eighty-one percent of white children, as compared with 42 percent of black children, under age 18 in 1982 lived in households with both parents present. Reasons for this, as suggested earlier, are related to the lower proportion of black men to black women in the population and the high divorce and widow rates among black women. That 15 percent of white children and 47 percent of black children are in single-parent, female-headed households is important to remember. Family income differs by race. As shown in Figure 1.5 (U.S. Bureau of the Census, 1983f, Figure 27, p. 30), the median income for black families is much lower than for whites. In 1981, median income for white families was $23,500, whereas for black families it was $13,300. (The median is a midpoint on either side of which are 50 percent of the cases.) Black families with both partners present are much better off than female-headed families of either race. The lowest median income is $7,500 per year for black female-

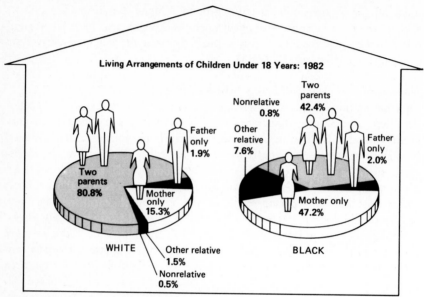

Figure 1.4 Living Arrangements of Children Under 18 Years Old: 1982 and 1970. *Source:* U.S. Bureau of the Census, *Current Population Reports* (Series P–20, No. 380. Washington, D.C., 1983d).

headed families. Figure 1.5 shows that female-headed families had a lower median income in 1981 than in 1971. This means their economic condition worsened. In contrast, income for two-parent families was slightly higher in 1981 for both blacks and whites (the middle segment of Figure 1.5).

The Institutionalized and the Homeless

Over two and a half million Americans lived in institutions in 1980 (U.S. Bureau of the Census, 1984b, Table 3). Nearly 500,000 were in correctional institutions: 41,000 in federal prisons, 261,000 in state prisons, and 164,000 in local jails. The United States has one of the highest incarceration rates in the world and is highest among developed nations. Mental hospitals housed another 256,000 people, and homes for the aged had 1.4 million residents. Many more Americans were in mental hospitals until the deinstitutional-ization movement that began in the 1960s. Community treatment came to be viewed as less debilitating and the state was prohibited from institutional-izing people against their will unless they were dangerous to themselves or to others (Jones and Poletti, 1987). Many released mental patients were *dumped* onto communities that had few resources and little political will to care for

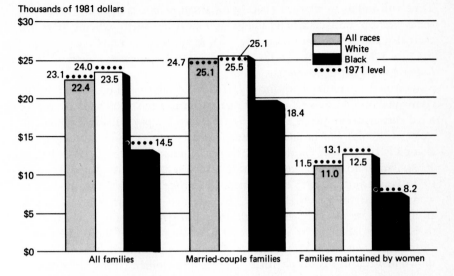

Figure 1.5 Median Family Income in 1971 and 1981, by Type of Family and Race of Householder. *Source:* U.S. Bureau of the Census, *Current Population Reports* (Series P–23, No. 130, Population Profile of the United States: 1982. Washington, D.C., 1983f).

them. As a result, many of these people populate America's streets and are referred to as "homeless."

The plight of Americans with no place to call home is also a problem for American cities (Main, 1983; Sexton, 1983). Estimates of the number of homeless range from 300,000 to millions. Counting them is difficult because of their transiency, mental and emotional problems (Main, 1983), and reluctance to use shelters and missions (from fear of assault, robbery, etc.). Main (1983) identified three major categories of the homeless in a New York City shelter: those with mental or psychiatric problems; those with alcohol and drug problems; and those with economic problems. Many have other problems as well (physical disability, illness, etc.). As reported by Main, the homeless are young, with a mean age of 33 for the shelter's psychiatric admissions, a mean age of 41 for alcoholics, and a mean age of 32 for those with economic problems only. While their numbers may have increased in the years since Ronald Reagan was elected president in 1980 (as many claim), it is also true that America has always had "street people." Some things have changed though. More mentally ill and more women are on the streets. Elderly street women are sometimes referred to as "bag ladies" (Rousseau, 1981). Sexton (1983) argues for a social policy for the homeless that resists judging them as deserving versus undeserving, worthy versus unworthy.

Time will tell as to whether concern for street people is a lasting weight on the American conscience or a passing fad that, like other problems, have had their day and passed into obscurity with few solutions found.

Labor Force Participation

Most American adults work for pay. Table 1.3 shows the proportion in the civilian labor force by sex, age, and marital status from 1960 to 1980. (Labor force participation means a person is employed for pay outside the home or seeks paid employment and is at least 16 years of age.) The most dramatic change is the greater employment rate of married women in 1980 than in 1960. This holds for all age categories but is greatest for the 20 to 24 and 25 to 44 year groups. Men's employment rates over time vary the opposite to women's relative to marital status. Married men in all time periods (and at all ages) are more likely than single men and slightly more so than others to be in the labor force. Single women, in contrast, are more likely than married women to be employed in all age groups and time periods. Not shown in Table 1.3 is the fact that 52 percent of women 16 and older were in the labor force in 1981 compared to 27 percent in 1940, 32 percent in 1950, 35 percent in 1960, and 43 percent in 1970 (U.S. Bureau of the Census, 1982, Table 639, p. 383). The increased labor force participation of women in the last 50 years has been called a "Subtle Revolution" (Smith, 1979) that has permanently changed America's social landscape. Data in Table 1.3 show much less change in men's labor force participation than in women's between 1960 and 1981.

Poverty, Welfare, and Government Benefits

In 1983, 35.3 million Americans, or 15.2 percent of the population, had incomes below the poverty level. Not only did this population increase by 6 million people since 1980, but the percentage rate also increased over the 1970s rates, which ranged between 11.1 and 12.6 percent. The federal government's definition of poverty (in 1983) is a family of four with less than $10,178 income. Nearly one-half of Americans below the poverty line in 1984 received no means-tested benefits (cash or noncash) from the government ". . . either because of reluctance to apply, lack of knowledge about available programs or the application process, or failure to qualify because of ownership of assets such as a house" (U.S. Bureau of the Census, 1985a, p. 34). The poverty rate in 1983 by race/national origins was 12.1 percent for whites, 35.7 percent for blacks, and 28.4 percent for persons of Spanish origin. Among those aged 60 and over, poverty rates in 1981 were higher for blacks than for whites, higher for women than for men, and higher for persons living alone than for those in families. Poverty rates ranged from 6 percent to 7 percent for white men and women living in families to 61 percent for black women living alone (U.S. Bureau of the Census, 1983f, p. 37).

TABLE 1.3. CIVILIAN LABOR FORCE PARTICIPATION RATES BY MARITAL STATUS, SEX, AND AGE: 1960 TO 1980

Year and Marital Status	Male Participation Rates					Female Participation Rates				
	16–19 years	20–24 years	25–44 years	45–64 years	65+ over	16–19 years	20–24 years	25–44 years	45–64 years	65+ over
1960										
Married, spouse present	91.5[a]	97.1	98.7	93.7	36.6	27.2	31.7	33.1	36.0	6.7
Single	42.6[a]	80.3	90.5	80.1	31.2	30.2	77.2	83.2	79.8	24.3
Other[b]	68.8[a]	96.9	94.7	83.2	22.7	43.8	58.0	67.2	60.0	11.4
1970										
Married, spouse present	92.3	94.7	98.0	91.2	29.9	37.8	47.9	42.7	44.0	7.3
Single	54.6	73.8	87.4	75.7	25.2	44.7	73.0	80.5	73.0	19.7
Other[b]	68.8	90.4	92.3	78.5	18.3	48.5	60.3	67.2	61.9	10.0
1980										
Married, spouse present	91.3	96.9	97.3	84.3	20.5	49.3	61.4	60.1	46.9	7.3
Single	59.9	81.3	87.9	66.9	16.8	53.6	75.2	82.0	65.6	13.3
Other[b]	75.0	92.6	93.1	73.3	13.7	50.0	68.4	76.8	60.2	8.2

[a] 14 to 19 years old.
[b] Widowed, divorced, and married (spouse absent).

Source: Adapted from U.S. Bureau of the Census (1982, Table 636, p. 382). Participation rate defined as at work or actively seeking work for pay.

About one in three people below the poverty line in 1983 was in a family headed by a woman with no husband present. Two-fifths of the overall increase in poor families in 1980 is due to families maintained by women. Such families represented 47 percent of all poor families in 1983 (U.S. Bureau of the Census, 1985a, p. 35). It is tragic that a wealthy nation like ours allows nearly one in six of its citizens to live in poverty. While some would argue that freedom includes the right to be poor (Gilder, 1981), others argue that a just nation takes care of its most vulnerable and unfortunate citizens (Piven and Cloward, 1982).

American society is not unmindful of its poor. In 1983, 29.6 percent of the nonfarm population received benefits from one or more government programs. The majority were Social Security recipients, 14.1 percent of the population, who accounted for 48 percent of all government benefit recipients. Medicare, or hospital and physician services for the aged and disabled, was the second largest benefit program in 1983 and was utilized by 26.7 million people, or 40 percent of those receiving benefits of any kind (U.S. Bureau of the Census, 1985a, p. 32). Citizens can qualify for Social Security and Medicare regardless of need (neither requires that income or assets be at or below certain levels to qualify) but qualifying for Food Stamps or Medicaid, as well as Aid to Families with Dependent Children and similar assistance programs, is means-tested. To qualify, an individual or family must meet a criterion of financial or economic *need*. The major means-tested programs in 1983 were Food Stamps and Medicaid, the former serving 8.3 percent of the population, and the latter serving 7.8 percent. Aid to Families with Dependent Children was third, supporting 4.2 percent of the population. Female-headed households with no spouse present and children in the home under 18 were more likely than other types to receive government aid (about one in three of all households received aid). This suggests an inability of female householders to earn enough income to support a family. It may also reflect an assumption that husbands/fathers will be the main wage earner and wives/mothers, the primary rearer of children in families. When divorce, separation, widowhood, or unwed motherhood occurs, the female-headed household needs government subsidy to survive.

The proportion of the gross national product (GNP) and of government outlays going to social welfare has increased dramatically in recent years. In 1965, the year the "War On Poverty" began, total expenditures on all social-welfare programs (including Social Security, public aid, education, veterans' programs, health, housing, and other welfare programs) were $77.2 billion, representing 12.2 percent of the GNP and 43.4 percent of all government expenditures (U.S. Bureau of the Census, 1975a, p. 340). By 1970, this had risen to $145.9 billion, or 15.3 percent of the GNP, and 47.8 percent of all government expenditures, and by 1982 these figures had risen to $592.6 billion or 19.3 percent of the GNP and 55.5 percent of all government outlays. Table 1.4 shows that over one-half (50.8 percent) of such outlays went for Social Security and related insurance programs in 1982. Federal dollars support only 68.6 percent of public aid, 46 percent of health and medical care, and 8.9 percent of education, with the remainder coming from state and local governments. Defense outlays in 1982 accounted for 25.4 percent of all federal outlays, an amount exceeded only by Social Security insurance that is self-supported through its own tax. Those who lament the deteriorating state of our public schools may be surprised to learn that only 4.4 percent of the GNP is spent on education, and percentage increases for education since the 1960s have been far lower than for other purposes (see Table 1.4; and U.S. Bureau of the Census, 1984d, Table 589, p. 354).

Crime

America has high crime rates, particularly for violent crimes, compared to most other nations. In 1978, the homicide rate in the United States was 9.4 (rates per 100,000 of the population of all ages) compared to 1.2 in England, 1.2 in West Germany, 1.0 in Switzerland, 0.8 in The Netherlands (Holland), and 1.3 in Poland. Closest to the United States was 5.7 in Northern Ireland where a civil war is in progress. Finland with 3.0 and Canada with 2.5 had the next highest rates. With the exception of Northern Ireland, the U.S. had at least three times more murders than any other developed nation and four times more than most. How can this be?

Some criminologists believe that the widespread sale and use of firearms contribute to a high U.S. crime rate. This may be part, but not all, of the answer. Firearms were used in 62.4 percent of all murders in the United States in 1981 but in only 24 percent of assault cases and 40 percent of burglaries (U.S. Bureau of the Census, 1982, Table 299, p, 179).

Homicide victims in the United States are disproportionately male and black. In 1979, the homicide rate (murders per 100,000 of the population in specified groups) for white men was 10.1; for white women, 3.0; for black men, 64.6; and for black women, 8. These rates represent large increases for three of the four groups since 1960: Rates for white men increased over 200 percent; rates for white women jumped over 100 percent, and rates for black men increased almost 100 percent. The increase for black women was smallest, 33 percent (U.S. Bureau of the Census, 1982, Table 295, p. 178). Census data indicate that violent felony crimes against persons are strongly related to city size. In 1981, cities of 250,000 or more inhabitants had far more violent crimes than did smaller cities. Data in Table 1.5 illustrate this for violent crimes and property crimes. The crime index reported is the total number of crimes per 100,000 of the population (or standardized on that base). Table 1.5 shows a linear decrease in crimes of all types with decreasing city size. The rape index, for example, is 73 (per 100,000 of the population) in cities of 250,000 or more but 38 in cities of 50,000 to 99,999, and 16 in

TABLE 1.4. GENERAL SOCIAL WELFARE AND DEPARTMENT OF DEFENSE EXPENDITURES IN 1982 AS PERCENTAGE OF GROSS NATIONAL PRODUCT, TOTAL GOVERNMENT OUTLAYS, AND FEDERAL GOVERNMENT OUTLAYS (IN BILLIONS OF DOLLARS OR PERCENTS)

	Defense Expenditures[a]	Social Insurance[b]	Public Aid[c]	Health and Medical	Veterans' Programs	Education	Housing	Other Social Welfare
1982 Total (in billions of dollars)	185,300	300,741	80,786	32,892	24,708	133,874	7,954	11,596
Federal Only	185,300	249,304	55,402	15,073	24,463	11,917	7,176	6,247
State/Local Only	—	51,437	28,384	17,819	245	121,957	778	5,349
Percent Federal	100.0	82.9	68.6	45.8	99.0	8.9	90.2	53.9
Percent of GNP	6.1	9.8	2.6	1.1	.8	4.4	.3	.4
Percent Total Government Outlays	17.4	28.2	7.6	3.1	2.3	12.5	.7	1.1
Percent Federal Government Outlays	25.4	34.2	7.6	2.1	3.4	1.6	1.0	.8

[a] Excludes veterans' programs (see column 5).
[b] Primarily Social Security, which is largely self-funded with its own tax.
[c] Includes AFDC, Food Stamps, state-supported emergency and general assistance programs, and The Federal Supplementary Security Income (SSI) program.
Source: Adapted from U.S. Bureau of the Census (1984a, Tables 537, 589, and 590).

TABLE 1.5. CRIME RATES BY TYPE AND POPULATION SIZE-GROUP: 1981 (OFFENSES KNOWN TO POLICE PER 100,000 POPULATION AS OF JULY 1)

City-Group Size	Violent Crime					Property Crime			
	Total	Murder	Forcible Rape	Robbery	Aggravated Assault	Total	Burglary, Breaking and Entering	Larceny, Theft	Motor Vehicle Theft
Cities with population of									
250,000 or more	1441	23.5	73	844	501	8030	2650	4313	1068
100,000–249,999	826	13.1	56	350	407	7945	2476	4874	595
50,000– 99,999	584	7.4	38	228	310	6371	1927	3881	562
25,000– 49,999	452	5.7	29	155	263	5858	1625	3810	423
10,000– 24,999	342	4.5	20	92	225	4936	1309	3308	319
Fewer than 10,000	291	4.0	16	54	216	4466	1093	3136	237
Suburbs	373	5.6	26	111	230	4503	1376	2792	335
Rural areas	179	7.0	16	22	135	2119	837	1158	125

Source: Adapted from U.S. Bureau of the Census (1982, Table 290, p. 176).

cities of fewer than 10,000 inhabitants. Similar patterns hold for murder and robbery and somewhat less for aggravated assault and crimes against property. Recall from earlier data that proportionately more blacks than whites live in large urban areas, a fact that may account for their greater vulnerability to crime. In summary, there is *more crime per person* in urban areas than in rural areas.

The increase in violent crimes over the past 15 years is disturbing. Table 1.6 shows that all violent crimes increased by 54 percent (from an index of 401 to 617). The greatest increase was in aggravated assault (83 percent) with forcible rape second (67 percent) and robbery third (24 percent). The murder index decreased slightly over this period, from 9.0 to 8.6. Rape is a special form of assault that reflects hostility toward women (Brownmiller, 1975). There is no way to know if the increase in rape is due to a higher frequency of reporting this crime to law enforcement, to an increase in the incidence of rape, or to both factors. Awareness of the crime of rape may have increased during the 1970s when the women's movement was highly visible and active. In the 1980s the women's movement has taken a back seat to

TABLE 1.6. VIOLENT CRIMES AND CRIME RATES, BY TYPE: 1972–1986. (OFFENSES KNOWN TO THE POLICE PER 100,000 INHABITANTS AS OF JULY 1 EXCEPT FOR 1980, WHICH IS APRIL 1)

Rate Per 100,000 Inhabitants By Year	Total All Crimes	Type of Violent Crime				
		Total	Murder	Forcible Rape	Robbery	Aggravated Assault
1972	3961	401	9.0	22.5	181	189
1973	4154	417	9.4	24.5	183	201
1974	4850	461	9.8	26.2	209	216
1975	5282	482	9.6	26.3	218	227
1976	5266	460	8.8	26.4	196	229
1977	5055	467	8.8	29.1	187	242
1978	5109	487	9.0	30.8	191	256
1979	5521	535	9.7	34.5	212	279
1980	5900	581	10.2	36.4	244	291
1981	5800	577	9.8	35.6	251	281
1982	5553	555	9.1	33.6	232	281
1983	5175	538	8.3	33.7	216	279
1984	5031	539	7.9	35.7	205	290
1985	5207	556	7.9	36.7	208	303
1986	5480	617	8.6	37.5	225	346

Source: Adapted from U.S. Bureau of the Census (1982, Table 287, p. 174); U.S. Department of Justice (1983, Table 3, pp. 44–45); U.S. Department of Justice (1984, Table 3, pp. 44–45); U.S. Department of Justice (1985, Table 4, pp. 44–45); U.S. Department of Justice (1986, Table 4, pp. 44–45); and U.S. Department of Justice (1987, Table 4, pp. 44–45).

other issues and it is unclear if the incidence of rape is affected by this development or if factors unrelated to women's social and political status account for the increases shown in Table 1.6. Whatever the explanation, violent crimes against persons are lamentable and a mark of shame on a society such as ours.

SOCIAL WORKERS IN THE 1980s: WHERE THEY WORK, WHAT THEY DO

The nation's diversity suggests that social work as a profession charged with responding to social problems must also be diverse. Data from a recent survey by the National Association of Social Workers (NASW, 1983) show that social workers are employed in many types of settings and in diverse roles and jobs.

Table 1.7 shows types of work activity by auspice of employing organization for 57,000 social workers who responded to the NASW survey. Almost one-half (46 percent) were employed in public service, primarily at local and state levels (see Table 1.7). Another 42 percent worked in the private, not-for-profit sector and 12 percent in the for-profit sector. The proportion in the for-profit sector increased 370 percent from 1972 to 1982, reflecting an increase in privatization of welfare services (Salas, 1982; Frumkin, Martin, and Page, 1987). Table 1.7 shows that most NASW members, about 64 percent, work directly with clients. About 20 percent are in management/administration and this is more pronounced in the private, not-for-profit sector than in the for-profit realm. Other work activities of social workers are: Supervision, 7.2 percent, and Education/Training, 5.6 percent. Table 1.8 reports field of practice, or substantive area, for 1972 and 1982. The more popular areas are, in descending order, mental health, medical or health care, children and youth, mental retardation, and family services. Changes from 1972 to 1982 included growth in the areas of mental retardation, substance abuse, occupational social work, services to the aged, and mental health. Declines appeared in the areas of public assistance, school social work, community organizing, criminal justice, and other areas (unspecified).

Table 1.9 reports type of work by type of organization. The modal (most frequent) organization is a social-service agency (28 percent), followed by general hospital (19 percent), outpatient facility (16 percent), college and university (8 percent), and elementary and secondary school (7.4 percent). About one-half of those in agencies perform direct service jobs, with the remainder concentrated in management/administrative or other supportive positions (see Table 1.9). In hospitals and outpatient facilities, the second and third most frequent employment settings, nearly three-fourths of social workers hold direct service positions.

Table 1.10 shows the race and gender composition of NASW members.

TABLE 1.7. EMPLOYMENT AUSPICE AND JOB ACTIVITY OF NASW MEMBERS, 1982 (*N* = 57,000; AS A PERCENTAGE)

Employment Auspice	Total for Employment Auspice	Primary Job Activity							
		Direct Service	Supervision	Mgmt./ Administration	Policy Develop. Analysis	Consultant	Research	Planning	Educ./ Training
Public service: federal	3.0	64.8	9.2	19.5	1.5	1.5	1.3	0.4	1.8
Public service: local/state	42.2	59.4	9.1	18.8	0.6	2.2	0.6	0.8	8.3
Public service: military	0.5	63.4	4.6	20.6	1.7	0.8	0.4	0.4	7.9
Private: sectarian (not for profit)	8.8	57.9	7.3	26.2	0.2	1.1	0.2	0.5	6.6
Private: nonsectarian (not for profit)	33.6	62.1	6.6	24.2	0.2	1.4	0.7	0.8	3.8
Private: for profit	12.0	86.8	1.4	6.7	0.2	3.3	0.4	0.2	1.2
Total for activity	100.0	63.7	7.2	19.9	0.4	1.9	0.6	0.7	5.6

Source: Adapted from NASW News (November 1983, Tables A and B, p. 6).

TABLE 1.8. PRIMARY PRACTICE AREAS IN 1972 AND 1982 OF NASW MEMBERS (*N* = 57,000; AS A PERCENTAGE)**

Practice Area	1972	1982	Percent Change
Children and youth	11.8	15.5	31.4
Community organizing	3.1	1.8	−41.9
Family services	10.8	11.2	3.7
Criminal justice	2.4	1.7	−29.2
Group services	NA	0.4	—
Medical or health care	16.5	18.1	9.7
Mental health	16.3	26.6	63.2
Public assistance	8.2	1.0	−87.8
School social work	6.7	3.4	−49.2
Services to aged	2.1	4.5	114.2
Alcohol/drug/substance abuse	0.6	2.9	383.3
Mental retardation	1.7	13.3	682.3
Other disabilities	NA	0.5	—
Occupational	0.1	0.4	300.0
Combined areas	NA	4.8	—
Other	10.0	4.0	−60.0

NA, not available.
Source: Adapted from NASW News (November 1983, Table C, p. 6).

In 1982, the large majority were white (88.5 percent); 5.8 percent were black, 1.8 percent Hispanic, and 1.6 percent Asian. The percentage of male members dropped substantially in the 10 years after 1972: from about 41 percent to 27 percent. Nearly three-fourths of NASW members in 1982 were women. Table 1.11 indicates that despite their numerical predominance, women make less money than do men. The modal (most frequent) category for both sexes is $20,000 to $24,999, but 52.7 percent of men make $25,000 or more compared to 23.4 percent of women.

Modally, social workers in 1982 were employed by government, engaged in direct service provision, and worked for a social-service agency. They are also white women who earn between $20,000 and $24,999 a year. Because membership dues for NASW are high (about $100.00 annually), social workers in this sample are, compared to many others, relatively well-off. Based on NASW data, social work appears to be an attractive career choice for women but less so for men. The claim that social workers are moving into other realms besides direct service is not strongly supported by the data. In the for-profit sector, in fact, social workers appear to have found a niche primarily in the provision of services to clients, not in administration or related activities.

TABLE 1.9. JOB ACTIVITY BY TYPE OF EMPLOYING ORGANIZATION OF NASW MEMBERS, 1982 ($N = 57,000$; AS A PERCENTAGE)

Employment Setting	Total in Setting	Primary Job Activity			
		Direct Service	Supervision	Management/Administration	Other[a]
Social service agency	28.0	51.2	12.3	29.8	6.7
Private practice: self-employed	7.0	93.8	0.3	1.4	4.5
Private practice: partnership	3.0	95.6	0.4	1.9	2.2
Membership organization	0.9	38.1	3.5	42.4	15.9
General hospital	19.0	72.2	7.3	18.4	2.1
Institution	3.0	56.7	11.1	28.0	4.7
Outpatient facility	16.0	74.0	6.5	17.0	2.5
Group home/residence	2.0	63.0	11.2	23.6	2.2
Nursing home/hospice	2.0	69.0	5.0	17.3	8.7
Criminal justice/court	1.4	58.9	9.6	25.3	6.3
College/university	8.0	16.4	1.1	8.5	74.1
Elementary/secondary school	7.4	84.0	2.4	5.6	7.7
Non-social-service firm	1.5	39.2	4.0	27.6	29.2

[a] Includes policy development/analysis, consultation, research, planning, education and training.
Source: Adapted from NASW News (November 1983, Table D, p. 7).

TABLE 1.10. RACE/ETHNICITY AND GENDER DISTRIBUTIONS OF NASW MEMBERS, 1982 (N = 57,000; AS A PERCENTAGE)

| Race/Ethnicity | Gender | | | |
	Female	Male	Total	Total 1972
White	64.6	23.9	88.5	90.0
Black	4.5	1.3	5.8	6.9
Hispanic	1.2	0.6	1.8	0.8
Asian	1.1	0.5	1.6	1.6
Other	1.5	0.7	2.2	1.0
Total 1982	73.0	27.0	100.0	
Total 1972	59.4	40.6		100.0

Source: Adapted from NASW News (November 1983, Table E, p. 7).

TABLE 1.11. ANNUAL SALARIES BY GENDER FOR NASW MEMBERS, 1982 (N = 57,000; AS A PERCENTAGE)

| Annual Salary | Gender | | All NASW Members |
	Female	Male	
Under $10,000	9.6	2.5	7.4
10,000–12,499	5.6	1.5	4.3
12,500–14,999	8.6	3.4	6.9
15,000–17,499	14.2	7.2	11.9
17,500–19,999	15.2	9.6	13.5
20,000–24,999	23.4	23.0	23.4
25,000–29,999	13.5	20.5	15.7
30,000–34,999	5.8	14.7	8.5
35,000–39,999	2.0	7.4	3.7
40,000–50,000	1.4	6.0	2.9
Over 50,000	0.7	4.2	1.8

Source: Adapted from NASW News (November 1983, Table F, p. 7).

CONCLUSIONS AND OVERVIEW OF THE BOOK

Chapter 1 documents that today's world and social work's place and role in it are multifaceted, complex, and changing. To meet this challenge, a general theoretical framework is needed. Open Systems Theory (OST) is, we believe, such a framework. We offer OST as a tool for learning about the social environment. Social workers can apply OST to see and understand better the social contexts they confront, and that confront them, in their personal and professional lives. Application of an OST model can help practitioners avoid simplistic solutions while making manageable a complex and changing world.

Chapter 2, "Basic Concepts and Principles of Open Systems Theory," introduces the major themes of OST. This is done to prepare the reader for the Applications chapters (Chapters 4 through 9) that follow. Definitions of basic concepts such as system, theory, open system, general theory, concepts, conceptual framework, and so forth are reviewed.

Chapter 3, "The Philosophical Foundations of Open Systems Theory" has two goals: It reviews the history of "systems theory" in social science and it analyzes the philosophical foundations of OST. The history of systems theory reveals that ever since the late-1800s, social phenomena have been viewed as similar to nonsocial phenomena—such as machines, living organisms (the human body, for example), and so forth. The *type of analogies* used to depict social systems has evolved from a machine model to an organismic model to a morphogenic model (Buckley, 1967). Factional and catastrophic models have also recently been employed (Burrell and Morgan, 1979). Open Systems Theory builds on past developments of social systems theory and extends them.

In pursuing the second goal, two questions are posed: What is the nature of social reality? and What is the basic orientation of theory used to understand it? The first question deals with assumptions regarding the "concrete reality" versus ideational (in the human consciousness only) character of social phenomena: Are social phenomena such as norms, roles, structures, etc., real, above and beyond the individual's conscious belief in them? Open Systems Theory, and most social work theories-in-use, say they are. The second question concerns the status quo versus social change orientation of OST. Used with an organismic (biological system) analogy, OST is status quo in orientation. Used with a nonorganismic analogy (morphogenic, factional, or catastropic), however, OST is social-change oriented. The implications of the types of analogies used with OST are explained and illustrated in Chapter 3.

Chapter 4, "Social Work and Systems Theory: Historial and Current Applications," reviews social work's use of a systems theory perspective. Additionally, it analyzes the philosophical foundations of several theories-in-use by social workers. Chapter 4 demonstrates that most social work theories-in-use are compatible philosophically with OST.

Chapters 5 through 9 are applications of OST concepts and principles to the social contexts of professional–client dyads, families, small groups, social-welfare organizations, and communities. Each chapter has a common structure. The introduction describes the aims of the chapter and presents the OST terms and themes that are applied in the chapter. Only *some* OST concepts are applied in each chapter. The second section presents the application from an OST perspective: What is a professional–client dyad? a family? a group? How do they function? The final section addresses implications for social work. Insights for understanding, practice principles for intervention, and implications for policy or social organization and change are delineated. Specific implications are noted in the body of Chapters 5 through 9; thus each chapter's end section identifies general implications. The text concludes with the Epilogue, which calls for continued exploration of the utility of OST for social work.

Chapter 2

Basic Concepts and Principles of Open Systems Theory

All theories about social systems have one thing in common: They assume that social phenomena are systemic. Social, we recall from Chapter 1, refers to people in collectivities or groups. *Systemic* refers to organized, or inter-related, actions and relationships that persist over time. Friendship cliques, families, work and treatment groups, social-welfare agencies, and communities when viewed as systems are assumed to be organized and enduring and to have certain features, and dynamics, in common. The defining properties of systems, social and otherwise, are explicated below.

Chapter 2 introduces Open Systems Theory. We do this by first defining system, social system, open system, and theory. Material throughout the book is premised on understanding these basic terms. Next, we define Open Systems Theory and review its major concepts and principles. Chapter 2 shows that Open Systems Theory (OST) is a set of general concepts that can be applied to many types of social systems. Open Systems Theory is also a set of principles about how systems are organized and how they operate that can be used to predict relationships and actions. Chapter 2 introduces the primary concepts and principles of OST, whereas Chapters 5 through 9 apply them to a variety of social systems.

DEFINITIONS OF BASIC TERMS

We begin by defining system, social system, open system, and theory.

36

What Is a System?

A *system* is something with interrelated parts. If the parts are related in an orderly way, the system is said to be highly organized or predictable. If the parts relate to each other in random or unpredictable ways, the system is disorganized (factional, catastrophic). Buckley (1967, p. 41) defines a system as "a complex set of elements or components directly or indirectly related in a causal network" and Berrien (1968, pp. 14, 15) defines it as ". . . a set of components interacting with each other [within a boundary that]. . . possesses the property of filtering both the kinds and rate of flow of inputs and outputs to and from the system."

Any system has five defining properties: (1) organization, (2) mutual causality, (3) constancy, (4) spatiality, and (5) boundary.

1. *Organization* indicates that the component parts or elements (see below) of a system are interrelated, tied together, or linked. Component parts alone do not define a system; the *organization* of component parts defines a system. An aggregate of individuals standing in a bus queue who do not know each other and who do not interact (talk) constitute a minimal social system. They may never have seen each other before and would not recognize each other if they met again. If these same people organize themselves to build a bench or shelter, however, their relationship with each other becomes organized. Systems are distinguished from nonsystems, therefore, by the organization among component parts. If elements are randomly related to each other, we conclude that no system exists.

2. *Mutual causality* refers to interdependence. Events that happen to one part of a system affect all parts, directly or indirectly. A death in the family affects all family members, not just the one who died. Members feel grief, their chances for an inheritance go up or down, their companion or cousin no longer writes to them, and so on. If various elements comprise a system, they will be affected by events that occur not only to them directly but to other elements within the system because they mutually and causally affect each other.

3. *Constancy* concerns time and says that systems endure. To form a system, component parts must be related to each other within a particular time period and this time period must be substantial, that is, more than a few seconds or minutes. People in a bus queue who merely stand together for a few minutes do not, normally, comprise a system. Their association and their relationship with each other is too ephemeral or brief.

4. *Spatiality* concerns space. Systems are concrete phenomena rather than abstractions, they take up physical space, and they can be observed. They are not just an intellectual idea but can be observed

directly (firsthand, with the eyes) or indirectly (secondhand, as in verbal reports). *Concrete* systems are specific, tangible social systems such as particular families, small groups, organizations, and so forth. Family as a category of social system is an abstract (general) concept, but *your* family is a concrete system. Your text uses the term *family* in both ways, but its focus is on concrete, real families.

5. Related to spatiality is the concept of *boundary*. A boundary is located at the edge of a system and sets it off from other systems and from its environment. Boundaries filter information and materials that enter and exit from systems. The primary functions of boundaries are (a) demarcation of limits that include some elements and exclude others and (b) filtering of inputs and outputs (see below).

All systems, whether physical, vegetable, human, or social, have these five qualities. If they do not, then they are not *systems*. Because of our interest in social systems, we focus on their unique qualities.

What Is a Social System?

A *social system* is a system composed of human beings and the products of their interaction over time. These products include cultural values and norms, social roles, individual and collective understandings and goals, patterns of relating and interacting, and so forth. Social systems are phenomena that include at least two people (spatiality) who associate with each other (organization) over time (constancy), who are set off from nonsystem members in some way (boundary), and whose association affects all members (mutual causality). Through association, social system members *create* cultural phenomena such as roles, values, goals, norms, and understandings that become a part of the system. These phenomena may, and normally do, causally influence the form (organization) that subsequent interactions take.

Human systems are individuals who belong to social systems. Individuals are complex bundles of biology, psychology, social self, spiritual self, unconscious self, and so forth. Entire books focus on the individual. The human behavior component of the social-work curriculum concentrates on the individual from biological, developmental, social, psychological, and cultural perspectives. Here, we treat the individual person, the human system, as a component part of social systems. In doing this, we do not suggest the individual is unimportant. On the contrary. One book can do only so much, however, and our focus is on the social environment.

What Is an Open System?

Open systems are systems that exchange continuously with other systems and with their environment(s). This involves the movement of inputs and outputs across a system's boundary. An open system accepts inputs (members, ideas, information, resources) continuously and emits outputs (words, actions, products, reports) continuously. Human beings are open systems: They breathe air, eat food, drink water, watch television, listen to music, express ideas, sing songs, touch loved ones. Even the most severely disturbed psychotic must regularly accept air and nourishment or risk death. Von Bertalanffy (1968) says that all living systems are open systems and, as a result, have much in common.

A *closed system* is state-determined. That is, except to disintegrate, it cannot change. A closed system accepts and emits little across its boundary. For example, a rock is a closed system and will remain a rock over time unless it reverts to its constituent minerals. Open systems, in contrast, can change. They exchange with their environments and can, and often do, become transformed. By accepting new members, goals, ideas, or resources, an open system can change fundamentally. This is particularly true of social systems.

Social systems are open systems. Family members, for example, cross the family boundary often. Family members interact continuously with non-family members, through watching television, working with colleagues, playing with classmates. Ideas and experiences from outside are brought into the family when Mom talks about her work at dinner, when a child asks Dad what the teacher meant, when prayers are said at bedtime. The permeable and dynamic nature of social systems and their extensive linkages with other systems and with their environment are defining properties of open systems. They are also basic principles of Open Systems Theory.

What Is Theory?

In social science, *theory* most often indicates a conceptual framework that accounts for a topic or process in the observable world. Social workers employ many theories—for example, ego psychology, task-centered treatment, the problem-solving approach, social learning theory, cognitive-behavioral theory —that are referred to here as *social work theories-in-use* (see Chapter 4). A *conceptual framework* (also known as a school of thought, a substantive theory, or a conceptual scheme) is defined as a set of interrelated concepts that attempt to account for some topic or process. Conceptual frameworks are less developed than theories but are called theory anyway. Social learning theory is a well-developed conceptual framework that uses concepts like behavior, intermittent versus continuous reinforcement, positive and negative reinforcement, and so on to explain how humans learn in relation to their social environment.

Concepts are general words, terms, or phrases that represent a class of events or phenomena in the observable world. Terms like love, anxiety, friendship, family, social interaction, behavior, attitudes, and interorganizational relations are concepts. Concepts direct our attention, shape our perceptions, and help us make sense of experience. They simplify life by providing ready labels for what we preceive, experience, and feel, and they make it possible to communicate with others without having to describe every incident we saw or event we experienced. Concepts are judged on their utility, not their truth. If they are useful, they are employed by social scientists and practitioners; if not, they are dropped. The concept of "possessed by demons" was used in the nineteenth century to describe the mentally ill, wise women were called witches, and the poor were labeled as undeserving. These terms are no longer viewed as useful by social scientists and social work practitioners.

If concepts in a conceptual framework are systematically related to each other in propositional (If X, then Y) form, and if the assumptions (premises) upon which the systematization rests are specified, this is formal theory. Formal social science theory is rare although many conceptual frameworks are highly developed. Open Systems Theory is a well-developed conceptual framework. Its concepts apply to open systems and, for this book, to open social systems. Open Systems Theory is a conceptual framework that depicts social systems as dynamic, permeable, and active. The remainder of Chapter 2 defines and illustrates the basic concepts of Open Systems Theory.

What Is Open Systems Theory?

Open Systems Theory (OST), like general system theory from which it springs, is a *general conceptual framework about open social systems*. The concepts and principles of OST are broad and inclusive; they can be used to account for many social phenomena and events. Five OST principles are explicated in this text:

1. All social systems are open and interdependent with their environment.
2. Systemic dynamics, or processes, are the key to seeing and understanding structure. Internal system exchanges such as those between system and subsystem or system and component part and external exchanges between systems, subsystems, and component parts and the environment are focused on most.
3. Social systems exercise self-control and self-determination. While the environment shapes and constrains the actions of included elements and systems, it is viewed as variable and subject to change.
4. Social systems experience change and conflict continuously and have the potential for fundamental change. The dynamics of self-determination and change that emanate from within are explored throughout the Applications chapters.
5. Because of common forms and processes, knowledge about one system can be transferred to others. Learning about one social system is useful for understanding all social systems.

The generality of Open Systems Theory reflects Ludwig von Bertalanffy's (1968) dream of a theory of *universal concepts and principles that apply to all systems*—biological, social, physical. He believed that general system theory discourages the isolation of specialized scientific disciplines and encourages the transfer of information and learning. General theory is helpful to those who work with different types of systems, for example, to social workers. This entire book attempts to explain and illustrate Open Systems Theory.

OPEN SYSTEMS CONCEPTS AND THEMES

This section of Chapter 2 introduces the basic concepts and principles of Open Systems Theory. Most appear in one form or another throughout the text. We introduce them early so the assumptions and principles that they reflect can be applied in later chapters.

Component Part

The term *component part* refers to the constituent elements of a system. Social system elements can be individuals, married couples, friendship dyads, families, groups, communities, organizations, nation-states, and cultural values, norms, or roles. Identification of an element depends on the level of analysis and the type of question posed, a point that is elaborated below. The generality of the term component part or *element* is useful for the transfer of learning from one system to another. An element in a family may experience dynamics similar to elements in an organization, work group, or profes-sional–client dyad. Learning about an element in one system teaches some-thing about elements in any system. Social systems can have other systems as component parts. Component, or included, systems are called *subsystems*.

Wholeness

Wholeness is an OST principle that favors viewing a system in its *totality*. Parts of a system are viewed in relationship to each other as reflecting the order or organization of the whole. This sounds simple enough but is con-tradictory to the normal American view. The approach to understanding that has dominated the West ever since the onset of the scientific revolution (Kuhn, 1970) is that of *analysis*. Analysis involves breaking down a complex whole into its elemental parts. It assumes that the form, content, or opera-tion of the elemental parts explain the form, content, or operation of the larger entity. For example, "seeing the world in an atom" reflects an analytic approach.

Open Systems Theory favors synthesis over analysis as a means of understanding. *Synthesis* focuses on the combination of parts or elements into complex wholes. Open Systems Theory argues that understanding of social systems can be gained only through focusing on the whole rather than the parts because parts have meaning and relevance only in relation to the whole. Synthesis, in contrast to analysis, emphasizes the causal interrelatedness of systemic parts and the order and organization among them. Later material suggests that the emergent properties of social systems—phenomena such as goals, norms, and values that are more than the individuals involved—are difficult to see or understand without such an approach.

Von Bertalanffy (1968, p. 5) notes that concern with the whole introduces "a basic reorientation in scientific thinking." This reorientation is particularly important for social work. Social work with families is advised to approach the family in need as a family system rather than as a series of individual members. A family is more than its individual members and their characteristics (e.g., their personalities, ages, gender, etc.). Successful intervention requires understanding the family as a totality in relation to the society in which it is lodged and in relation to the roles, values, norms, goals, and interaction patterns and relationships that the family has. Open Systems Theory summarizes this principle as *the whole is greater than the sum of its parts*.

Interdependence

Open Systems Theory views the parts of systems as mutually and causally interrelated to each other and to the whole. It asserts that systems and their environments are mutually interdependent. Each affects and is affected by the other; each depends on the other. This point was made in defining a system. It suggests that the client-services part of a welfare organization affects and is affected by the administrative part and that one can not be understood without the other. The entire agency is affected by the social, cultural, economic, and political environments in which it is embedded (Meyer and Rowan, 1977; Meyer, 1983b) and the environment is similarly affected by the systems (and elements) it includes.

Dynamics/Process

A good approach to understanding an open system is to watch it in action. Open Systems Theory emphasizes social system dynamics. Continuous, ongoing interactions and exchanges exist (1) among the component parts of a system, (2) between a system and its component parts, (3) among autonomous systems, and (4) between systems and their environments. The pervasively dynamic and changing nature of social reality has important implications for social work. Active systems are fluid and susceptible to change. If much is going on, the potential for change is greater than if little is going on. Their dynamic character suggests that social systems have considerable potential for change—growth, learning, and elaboration.

Purpose and Goal-Direction

Open Systems Theory views social (and human) systems as purposeful and goal-directed. Purpose concerns survival, that is, remaining viable. A shipwrecked person forages for roots and berries to remain alive; an organization looks for new revenue when federal funds dry up. Goal-direction refers to the "self-regulating, self-directing, and self-organizing" character of social systems (Buckley, 1967, p. 58). Social systems are neither state-determined, that is, determined by their initial condition (like the rock discussed earlier), nor determined by their environments. They are, rather, within limits imposed by their circumstances, resources, and organization, in control of themselves. They rarely act in random or in totally unpredictable ways. Even if the logic or meaning of a system's goals is unclear to observers, the system is assumed to act in predictable ways with the intent of achieving certain goals or end states. Goals of (human and) social systems are not necessarily logical, rational, nor based on member consensus. They may be decided by one or a few people who dominate or control a system (for example, parents set "family goals"). A system's goals are discovered by observing it in action, watching what it does: Both purpose and goals are *inferred* from a social system's actions. Social workers who rely on OST will observe, even study, the systems they deal with, to infer from observed actions and behaviors what a system's goals are.

To say a system is self-directed means it operates in terms of its own internal rules. *Internal rules* are a preferential hierarchy of values defined as those states, conditions, and objects that a system strives toward and refers to in the making of choices (Miller, 1965, p. 231). To make a decision on whether an employee can attend a conference, an agency director may ask: What will you learn that helps us serve clients better? What will it cost our agency? Are the benefits worth the cost? The values invoked are the utility of the employee's experience for client service and cost to the agency. The director could have said: You can go anywhere you like as long as you cover your duties. This suggests a different value-hierarchy. Systems constantly receive information (feedback) about the consequences of their actions/operations. This information may indicate that actions are outside the limits of the system's own internal rules. When this occurs, a system can take corrective action to bring operations into line with existing rules, change the rules to accommodate the new activities, or do neither. Decisions are made, on the basis of internal rules, regarding what to do next.

It is easier to see the goals of individuals than of social systems. Research shows that formal organizations have multiple, conflicting, and contradictory goals (Scott, 1977; Martin, 1980a). Dominant coalitions (elite leadership groups) may impose their aims on others and determine organizational goals. Even if a social system is extraordinarily well integrated and its members in close agreement, conflicting goals are common. Pressures on the organization from funders, legislators, regulators, and public opinion force welfare organizations to pursue many goals regardless of members' own values and preferences. This underscores the importance of inferring system goals from observation rather than (only) surveying the ideas, beliefs, or views of individuals in the organization (community, family). Identifying the goals of a system by observing action provides insights about the system's circumstances and dynamics and can be useful for identifying levers for intervention and change.

The Social Environment

A system's environment lies beyond its boundary. For the individual, the social contexts of family, school, community, and work organization are environments. A family's environments may include neighborhood, church, children's schools, adults' workplaces, social and civic clubs, political community (city, county, state, and national governments), and so forth. Institutional contexts such as the educational system, economy, political system(s), religion, welfare, military, and marriage and family forms are important environments for concrete social systems. The cultural beliefs, values, norms, mores, and assumptions that accompany these forms, including their ideological justifications, are in the environment. Historical and cultural influences shape the environment, and the environment, in turn, influences the form that concrete systems take.

To understand a concrete social system, such as a family, the family's relationship to its environment must be understood. Meyer (1983a) argues that legitimation for structuring and running organizations such as schools, hospitals, and welfare agencies in particular ways rests in the environment. The boundaries of concrete social systems are highly permeable to influences from the environment, thus the environment has many opportunities to affect internal structures and events.

Open Systems Theory views the system-versus-environment distinction as somewhat arbitrary. The delineation of "system" or "environment" depends partly on the task at hand, including the observer's goals. If it is useful to view a family as the *focal system*, or system of reference, everything beyond the family boundary is the environment. If it is useful to view a community as the focal system, the environment may be the state, region, or nation. Identification of some aspect of social reality as environment is dependent on the identification of some aspect of it as focal system. Open Systems Theory, properly employed, can be used to assess a situation, identify its relevant issues and components, and decide what is system and what is environment for the task at hand.

Hierarchy of Organization: Emergent Properties and Hierarchical Constraints

Hierarchical organization means that systemic phenomena are arranged in order of inclusiveness (or ranks) of organization. Higher levels include and are more complex than lower levels. Figure 2.1 illustrates two subprinciples of hierarchical organization: (1) the principle of emergent characteristics and (2) the principle of hierarchical constraints. From bottom to top, the higher levels of organization of Figure 2.1 are more inclusive and complex. Each higher level includes all that the lower level(s) includes plus qualities unique to its own level. If the upside-down staircase were collapsed, groups would include individuals, organizations would include groups and individuals, communities would include organizations, groups, and individuals, and so forth. The successive cumulation of component parts makes higher levels more complex than lower ones.

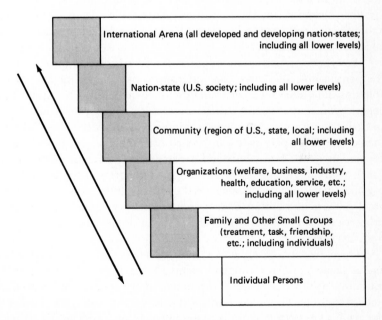

Figure 2.1 Levels of Social Organization illustrating Principles of Emergent Characteristics (ascending) and Hierarchical Constraints (descending). *Source:* Adapted from O'Neall (1972).

With the exception of the most minute or inclusive of systems, social systems tend to be both included in and inclusive of other human or social systems. Most social systems face two directions at once: toward the system that includes them and toward their own component parts (which may include subsystems). Koestler (1969, p. 197) notes that ". . . the face turned toward the lower levels is that of autonomous whole; the one turned outward is that of dependent part." A nation-state may be viewed as an autonomous whole when studying small-town America but a dependent part of the United Nations, North Atlantic Treaty Organization, or multinational corporate network. The concept of hierarchical arrangements is basic to Open Systems Theory. Simon (1962) calls it the architecture of complexity. Nature herself is assumed to be hierarchically organized relative to the evolution of biological systems.

1. The Principle of Emergent Characteristics

The shaded areas in the top five levels of Figure 2.1 are a social system's *emergent properties*. Emergent properties are cultural and social phenomena that emerge from the interactions and exchanges of the members of a social system. Examples of the emergent properties of a group are roles, norms, values, goals, understandings, shared experiences (or episodes; see Chapter 7 on Groups), shared vocabularies and viewpoints, collective memory, dominance and influence patterns, and so forth. These phenomena have historical origins and shape members' behavior.

Emergent properties are important to social systems because they affect the perceptions, behaviors, and interaction patterns of members. A group contains individual members, along with their personal histories, qualities, experiences, and so forth, *and* it contains emergent properties. An organization that employs people is composed of individual employees (their memories, ages, personalities); groups of individuals who are workmates, friends, or in the same units and departments; emergent properties of each group in the organization; and emergent properties of the organization *qua* organization (division of labor; authority structure; rules and regulations; fiscal policies and arrangements; and so forth). Emphasis on the emergent properties of inclusive systems reflects the antireductionistic stance of Open Systems Theory.

Open Systems Theory views emergent phenomena as having *real existence* and as shapers of perception and events. To understand a social system, one must indentify the emergent phenomena that orient members' actions and understandings. This is sometimes difficult because emergent phenomena are not readily observable and may be unrecognized or denied by group members. As noted in Chapter 1, Americans are inclined to deny the influence of intangible social phenomena on their lives. Denial is risky, however. Family therapists who recognize the influence of emergent phenomena require entire families (sometimes three generations) to attend therapy sessions in addition to ostensibly ill members.

2. The Principle of Hierarchical Constraints

The principle of hierarchical constraints states that more inclusive systems constrain or limit the actions/behaviors of included systems and component parts. As noted earlier, a system is organized and operates in accord with internal rules. Systems included within another system are constrained in their operations and activities in line with the internal rules of the inclusive system. Internal rules of the more inclusive system do not totally determine those of the included one. Opportunities, choices, goals, and procedures are nevertheless influenced by the inclusive system. This suggests that when a voluntary agency accepts funds from the state government, concerns about the strings attached are valid. To receive governmental funds, certain procedures have to be followed (e.g., bookkeeping practices, fire codes, staffing patterns, etc.), the adoption of which may, over time, change the voluntary organization in ways that were unanticipated. Adolescents who wear tank tops and shorts to school may be affected by the school's dress code. They may have to decide whether to conform to school policy, to drop out, to protest, or to change schools. Families intentionally shape and constrain the behaviors of their members, children and adults alike. Spouses say, "If you love me [value our marriage], you will be faithful." This involves a member of the inclusive system, the marital dyad, attempting to constrain the other's behavior in respect to the marital norm of fidelity.

The constraining influence of inclusive systems on the activities of included systems ranges from minimal to extensive; it can be unintentional or deliberate. Open Systems Theory argues that hierarchical organization involves constraining influences. The clients of social-welfare organizations are at once autonomous, self-regulating individuals and dependent parts of inclusive systems such as family and kin networks, neighborhoods, organizations, and so forth. This requires social workers to adopt a bifocal conception of their work. In work with individuals, families, and groups, practitioners should remain alert to influences of organizations, neighborhood, community, labor market, and so forth. They should remember also that individuals, families, and groups are capable of self-direction, change, and autonomy and have the potential to influence, even if minimally, the social contexts in which they are embedded.

Despite the constraining influence of inclusive systems, social systems can also change from within. As illustrated in Chapter 6 (on Families), Dibs, a troubled child in a troubled family, was able to change his family as a result of changes in his own behavior (albeit this took years). Energetic and committed people in a community can bring about changes in laws, policies, and practices (cf. Brager and Holloway, 1978). Each type of system (a family, school, welfare organization, friendship dyad), although influenced by its history, environmental circumstances, and resources, develops relatively predictable ways of doing things over time. All families have much in common (by definition) but because families are dynamic and changing, they are also unique. The hierarchical arrangement of systemic phenomena should be viewed more as a predominant than deterministic pattern of social organization. A change-oriented profession such as social work can find this useful.

Conflict, Disruption, and Discontinuity

Conflict, disruption, discontinuity, and stress are normal and routine aspects of social systems. Open systems are exposed routinely to incompatible influences. Although they filter and select inputs (and reject others), most inputs are complex and multifaceted and their effects may not be anticipated. Also, the filtering process is imperfect, as when a new agency director is hired after a nationwide search but proceeds to sexually harrass secretaries, be unsuccessful at fund-raising, and be an embezzler. Such eventualities are not rare; they occur in many settings each day. Conflict is therefore normal, typical, and pervasive rather than rare and exceptional. Conflict can have positive effects leading to a clarification of roles, understandings, and relationships and is not an indication of abnormality or dysfunction (although it can be). Absence of open conflict, as in families where unhealthy interaction sequences have developed, can be far more destructive than open conflict per se (Haley, 1976).

A mechanical system, such as a thermostatically controlled air-conditioning unit, can respond to disjuncture only by seeking a state of *equilibrium* in which the temperature on the dial and that of the surrounding air are the same. Its range of response alternatives is narrow and fixed. Biological systems, such as the human body, have a greater range of potential responses but less than social systems. Biological systems seek a state of homeostasis (Buckley, 1967), which is "normal good health" enjoyed prior to the disturbance caused by accident, surgery, or virus. Social systems can make many different responses to conflict, depending on the system's condition, resources, interaction patterns, goals, internal integration, and so forth. (Buckley [1967] describes a balanced condition of open social systems as a *steady state*.) Social systems can respond to conflict by changing to incorporate new inputs, rejecting new inputs and returning to the status quo, doing nothing and remaining in a state of conflict, and so on. A family can change to accommodate a teenage daughter's demand that she be allowed to stay out later. Parents may allow her to set her own hours as long as she maintains her grades and comes home as promised. This is an example of system elaboration where conflict led to a change in family structure and process. The family can also refuse to change until the daughter becomes angry and moves out of the house or tries to burn the house in spite. Social systems make choices about how to handle conflict, and this can include a decision to do nothing.

Factionalized systems are not highly integrated. Factions are groups or parties that are contentious and self-seeking. Most American communities and cities are factionalized. Factionalized systems may become more divided and turbulent when conflicts erupt (Burrell and Morgan, 1979, p. 67). If a local industry is bought by a large corporation and the corporation decides to close it as a tax write-off, hostile employees may turn against not only the corporation but also local officials. A previously peaceful if not highly consensual community may become openly divided into hostile and opposing camps.

Catastrophic systems are more conflictual than factionalized systems. They have deep internal divisions with subsystem fighting subsystem in an effort to gain control of the inclusive system. El Salvador in the 1980s, with civil war and wholesale destruction of property and people, is a catastrophic system. Catastrophic systems may respond to conflict with more conflict and the destruction of order, property, and life.

If conflict, discontinuity, and disruption are usual conditions, they must not be viewed as destructive only. The consequences of discontinuity may be system disharmony or perpetual crisis but it may also be fundamental change and new ways of coping. The results of conflict depend on many factors including the state of the system when the conflict occurs, the nature of the conflict (e.g., its intensity, what it is about, the number of system elements it affects, its importance to the system), and so forth. Conflict may or may not be resolved. Some systems persist for decades with ongoing frictions unresolved.

Antireductionism

Open Systems Theory is antireductionistic. *Reductionism* is the explanation of complex phenomena by reducing them to their component parts or to lower levels of social organization. A recent example of reductionism can be found in sociobiology, a conceptual framework that says that complex social systems can be understood by studying ants. Sociobiology reduces the social, cultural, economic, political, and religious superstructure of social life to genetically inherited propensities to behave in certain ways as reflected in the behavior of subhuman species, even insects. Open Systems Theory opposes this perspective and argues that social systems should be conceptualized on their *own level of organization* (see Fig. 2.1). To understand a social-welfare agency, the agency as an organization and its relationship to its environment should be studied before focusing on the personalities of individuals.

As an antireductionistic theory, OST promotes a hierarchical perspective as follows: (1) Attend first to the environments in which a system is embedded, (2) study the system as an entity in its own right (at its own level of social organization), and (3) study the component parts of a system. Throughout, pay attention to the dynamics of relationships between (and within) these realms. Antireductionism is an admonishment to conceptualize and study a phenomenon on its own level of organization rather than on the level of its component parts. Similar to the concept of wholeness, antireductionism runs counter to a traditional analytic approach that breaks down wholes into elemental parts. Reductionism distorts reality, diverts attention from the appropriate levels of concern, and fosters faulty diagnosis and intervention. Reductionism is tempting in a society that denies the power of emergent properties and supra-individual phenomena such as roles, status, norms, mores, social class, and so forth.

Reification

Reification is the treatment of social systems as having greater real existence than they actually have. As argued all along, social phenomena—norms, values, roles, ideology—have reality but they are less concrete than are physical phenomena such as cliffs, lakes, and trees. Compared to a mountain, the ocean, or the climate, social phenomena are less tangible, more varied, and more susceptible to deliberate transformation or change by human actors. People who reify view human behavior as overly determined. Such a conception portrays human beings as shaped by external forces and as relatively incapable of self-determination and self-initiated change.

Sociologists are prone to reify whereas psychologists are prone to reduce. Open Systems Theory strikes a balance between the two. It agrees that social/cultural phenomena have real existence and it discourages explanation of complex phenomena by reducing them to their elemental parts. It also contends that social/cultural phenomena, although real, are susceptible to deliberate change. Family members locked into unhealthy interaction sequences *can* change; organizations that emphasize bureaucracy over client service *can* change. And the decision to change can come from *inside* the system.

Isomorphism

The principle of isomorphism is that all living systems share similarities of form or structure with all other living systems. Although differences exist between categories of systems (e.g., individuals and communities) and between concrete systems within a category (my family and your family), a similar form characterizes all. Because of similar form, similar processes occur as well. Learning about one system teaches about all. The principle of isomorphism was alluded to in Chapter 1 and pervades this book. Because of isomorphism, the same set of general concepts can be applied to social systems as varied as families, treatment groups, professional–client dyads, communities, and social-welfare agencies.

Entitivity

Open Systems Theory encourages observers to ask: Does a social system exist? What are the systemic aspects of a situation or problem? By reference to the defining characteristics of a system—organization, mutual causality (interdependence), constancy, spatiality, and boundary—Open Systems Theory encourages the identification of social systems by whether they qualify. It discourages the assumption that a label such as family, organization, or community fits a concrete case a priori. If essential factors are present, a system may exist even though it violates normative definitions or views. If two women or two men establish a home together, this may be a familial system even though it contradicts normative definitions of family. Friends who meet to talk and offer support may constitute a group even if they don't think of themselves this way. Open Systems Theory fosters a nonjudgmental perspective for social work by relying on definitional rather than normative grounds for observing and dealing with the social world.

Entropy/Negative Entropy (Negentropy)

Open Systems Theory is premised on the Second Law of Thermodynamics which, paraphrased, is that "hot things get colder and cold things get hotter." The Second Law of Thermodynamics says that all matter tends toward entropy. Closed systems, according to this principle, change in one way only: They disintegrate or decompose into their most elemental forms. They are unable to become more complex in form or structure because they cannot import new inputs. Only open systems are able to counteract entropy, and even they succumb eventually to entropy. Families and organizations with more inputs are better able to resist entropic forces (disintegration, falling apart) than those with fewer inputs.

Negative entropy or *negentropy* is the ability of an open system to resist entropy. Because living systems are open and can import new and different inputs, they can use these inputs to become more complex. This helps them survive. They use inputs to acquire new knowledge and skills, to develop more elaborate structures that help them survive in complex environments, and to develop new and different goals as opportunities occur. Although all open systems are, by definition, negentropic, some have more negentropy than others. The ability to resist entropic forces is related both to the manner in which inputs are utilized and their availability.

Matter tends toward disorder and disintegration, not order and integration as some theories suggest. To counteract this impetus, social systems are proactive; they expend effort. If a nonprofit, welfare organization fails to establish good relations with resource providers, it may fold. Without the importation and use of new and varied inputs, social systems succumb to entropy. Poor families that have no employed adults and few ties to neighbors and friends are susceptible to break-up. Unsupervised youths get into trouble and are sent to reform school; bored adults take drugs to escape. With no one to buy food or pay for utilities, children become hungry and cold. To have a friend, one must be a friend. To be a friend takes time, energy, thought, commitment, and work. Unless work is done, a friendship disintegrates. Good memories of "what friends we were" may remain, but the friendship, as a concrete relationship, will perish.

Open Systems Theory views social systems as having inherent potential for change but realization of that potential requires energy, time, and commitment. Social systems do not *naturally* tend toward integration, order, unity, harmony, and consensus. Rather, members of concrete systems must cooperate, invest, and commit to create—and enjoy—these qualities in their social contexts. Marriage is not failing in America today. But some partners are unwilling to work at sustaining a particular marriage. When marriage becomes demanding, partners seek a divorce and search for another relationship that demands less or is more satisfying relative to its demands. Making a house a home, an organization that puts client-service first, a community that cares for its homeless, a society committed to the public good: All these require work.

CONCLUSIONS

Chapter 2 has introduced the OST concepts and principles that are applied in Chapters 5 through 9. In these later chapters, we show the relevance of OST principles for understanding, and intervening in, a number of social contexts. The material in Chapter 2 is difficult, and readers may want to return to it as they progress through the Applications chapters. Chapter 3, which follows, examines the philosophical foundations of OST. It argues that OST used in conjuction with an organismic (biological) analogy is somewhat closed-system in nature. Chapters 3 and 4 argue that many theories-in-use by social workers rely on quasi-closed system assumptions. The benefits of OST can be realized only if its concepts and principles are applied in conjunction with a fully open-systems analogy. Chapter 3 begins with a discussion of system analogies.

Chapter 3

The Philosophical Foundations of Open Systems Theory

This chapter explores the philosophical foundations of Open Systems Theory. In selecting a theory to explain or intervene, social workers make decisions about what is true or false, worthwhile or futile, possible or impossible. The better they understand the theoretical models that they employ, the better their chances of making informed choices. Open Systems Theory (and its philosophical parent, general system theory) makes many assumptions about social science, human society, and social science theory. This chapter attempts to lay these bare.

We will examine in this chapter two issues that any social science theory addresses: (1) philosophy of science assumptions and (2) assumptions regarding the nature of human society (Burrell and Morgan, 1979).[1] The *philosophy of science issue* concerns a theory's stance on questions about the nature of social science, knowledge of social reality, human beings, and research methodology. Answers to questions about these determine a theory's view of the world and influence users' observations and interpretations of what they observe (Kuhn, 1970). The *nature of human society issue* concerns assumptions about the patterned associations of humans over time. Are these associations assumed to be orderly and based on consensus or conflictual and based on domination? Is there a status quo or radical change orientation toward the future?

---

[1] The philosophy of science and paradigm typology materials in Chapter 3 draw heavily on Burrell and Morgan (1979).

Before addressing these issues, we review the types of analogies that social scientists have adopted to conceptualize social systems. Open Systems Theory can be used with any of these analogies but, as discussed below, its use in conjunction with morphogenic, factional, and/or catastrophic analogies is most consistent with the assumption that social systems are highly open. Unfortunately, OST has been used often with an organismic analogy and, as a result, is believed to have limitations that it does not have.

TYPES OF ANALOGIES

Although all systems theories assume that social phenomena are systemic, they differ on *the kind of system* social systems are. Five analogies have been used by social scientists to characterize social systems. These are: mechanical, organismic, morphogenic, factional, and catastrophic (Burrell and Morgan, 1979, chapter 4).

Some theorists say that social systems "act like," or are analogous to, machines. As described in Table 3.1, a *mechanical analogy* views social systems as similar to physical machines such as electrical motors or thermostats that control air-conditioning units. In this view, the parts are assumed to be closely associated, finely integrated, and highly coordinated. A change in any component part away from *equilibrium* is counteracted by efforts to reestablish equilibrium (Buckley, 1967, p. 9). Vilfredo Pareto (1934) was among the earliest social scientists to view society as a mechanical system of interrelated parts. The machine analogy of social systems derives from physics, and considerable social science research in the first half of the twentieth century reflected this view (C. Bernard, 1938; Homans, 1950; Mayo, 1933; Roethlisberger and Dickson, 1947).

This analogy encourages a focus on internal integration, maintenance of the status quo, and equilibrium-seeking processes. It is unable to deal with basic conflict, structural elaboration, and fundamental change. Critics say the machine analogy depicts society as a static, closed system. This analogy fails to take into account the complexity and uniqueness of social reality, its differences from physical reality, and the interdependence of social systems and their environments. Critics claim that social reality consists of information, shared meanings, and subjective interpretations, and that conflict and change are normal rather than unusual.

An *organismic analogy* of social systems derives from biology and emerged in reaction to the machine analogy. Society is viewed as analogous to a living organism such as the human body with different organs that are functionally related to each other and to the whole. This analogy assumes that the parts of social systems are functionally unified and work together for the good of the whole (Malinowski, 1922; Radcliffe-Brown, 1952). Talcott Parsons'

TABLE 3.1. ANALOGIES USED BY SOCIAL SCIENTISTS TO DEPICT SOCIAL SYSTEMS

Analogy	Description and Principal Tendency
Mechanical	Assumes perfect coordination and integration of parts; assumes that departures from equilibrium result in corrective actions to return to equilibrium; assumes social systems are like machines; emphasizes order and stability over conflict and change.
Organismic	Assumes high coordination and integration of parts; assumes that departures from homeostasis result in corrective actions to return to homeostasis; assumes society is like a living organism with different organs that cooperate closely to contribute to the survival of the whole; assumes social systems are cohesive because of consensus of citizens, families, communities, etc.; emphasizes order and stability over conflict and change.
Morphogenic	Assumes that social systems change constantly through interaction and exchange with their environment(s); that social systems are highly open; that social systems may be orderly and predictable but may also be disorderly and unpredictable; that social systems have an inherent tendency toward structural elabortion; assumes that order may rest on coercion and domination as well as cooperation and consensus; places about equal emphasis on conflict and change as on order and stability.
Factional	Assumes that social systems are divided into contentious factions that conflict over goals, priorities, resources, and strategies; assumes that conflict is basic and pervasive; assumes that the turbulent division of the system into factions is the principal tendency of the system; emphasizes conflict and change over order and stability.
Catastrophic	Assumes that social systems are severely segmented and warring, that little order or predictability exists, and that conflict may destroy some component parts; complete reorganization of the system is required if the system is to become less chaotic or conflictual; emphasizes conflict and change over order and stability.

Source: Adapted from Burrell and Morgan (1979, Table 4.1, p. 67).

structure-functional social systems theory is based on an organismic analogy. Analogous to living organisms, social systems are viewed as having to perform four types of functions to survive: adaptation, goal attainment, integration, and pattern maintenance. Organismic systems are assumed to seek *homeostasis* or a balanced state where the parts are functioning as they should and are integrated with all others and the whole (Cannon, 1939, pp. 20–24; Buckley, 1967; Burrell and Morgan, 1979). Order is assumed to be based on consensus and the willing cooperation of individuals and subsystems.

Critics reject the organismic analogy's assumptions that the parts of social systems work cooperatively for the benefit of the whole and that common purpose and integration are inherent. Like its machine analogy counterpart, organismic analogies are unable to account for fundamental social change. Organismic analogies also fail to address domination, divisive conflict, coercion, and constraint. In general, this analogy focuses attention on the status quo and incremental change rather than on human potential and radical change (Burrell and Morgan, 1979). Organismic analogies contend that social systems respond to conflict by engaging in adjustments that *return* them to a prior state of harmony, integration, or consensus. Critics say that this is simply not so. Many social scientists have used Open Systems Theory with an organismic analogy. This has led to a neglect of the dynamic qualities and potential for change that concrete social systems have.

A *morphogenic analogy* (see Table 3.1) views social systems as highly open and dynamic and as structure-changing (*morpho* means structure and *genesis* means change) rather than only structure-maintaining (morphostasis). It views social systems as qualitatively different from machines and biological organisms. Conflict can lead to structural elaboration rather than adjustment or correction, thus social systems have the potential to change in fundamental ways. As Burrell and Morgan state, "While a closed system must eventually obtain an equilibrium state, an open system will not. A steady state is not a necessary condition of open systems" (Burrell and Morgan, 1979, p. 59). Social systems under a morphogenic analogy are viewed as both capable of change and as constantly changing. While pigs do not become hippopotami (Radcliffe-Brown, 1952, p. 181), individuals do change their attitudes, families reconstitute themselves after a death, organizations change their tactics, and societies transform their policies, values, and goals (cf. Bellah et al., 1985). Sociocultural systems respond in many ways to conflict and to new information or experiences, and only one of these is a return to a prior state of stability.

Table 3.2 lists nine premises of a morphogenic analogy. The first eight concern processes, indicating that a morphogenic analogy emphasizes change, including how it occurs and what it can lead to. Walter Buckley's (1967) conception of morphogenic social systems focuses on interactions of individuals and groups among themselves and with their environments and is highly compatible with Open Systems Theory. The Open Systems Theory applications in Chapters 5 through 9 of this text employ primarily a morphogenic analogy.

A *factional analogy* (Table 3.1) assumes that systems are composed of various segments, or groups, that contend rather than cooperate with each other. A factional analogy depicts a social system as divided into factions and as characterized by turbulent conflict rather than harmonious integration. Competition, domination, and coercion predominate rather than cooperation, equality, and coordination. A factional analogy may apply to a given system at one time but not at another. Factionalized families embroiled in conflict can change, in which case another analogy, depending on the change, would apply. Open Systems Theory can be used with a factional analogy

TABLE 3.2. BASIC PREMISES OF A MORPHOGENIC ANALOGY

1. New and different systems and organisms arise out of old ones through a complex process that amplifies deviation through reciprocal (mutual) causality (positive feedback and feedforward) and through interactions with the surrounding environment.
2. Fluctuations in a system or organism are not merely random errors or deviations from the significant average; rather, such fluctuations can be the source of a new order.
3. Fluctuations in a system or organism interact, affecting each other and mutually causing whole new systems to arise.
4. Differences produce changes.
5. More highly ordered systems and organisms are produced from less highly ordered, simple systems and organisms; order can arise even from disorder.
6. Very complex systems and organisms can arise through very dense and complex interactions rather than through the summing (assembly, aggregation) of information bits or elements.
7. Change is not only continuous and quantitative but also discontinuous and qualitative.
8. Component parts constrain but do not determine emergent form in morphogenic change.
9. There may be sharp discontinuities between scientific "truths."

Source: Adapted from Lincoln and Guba (1985, Table 2.8, p. 61).

because this analogy, like the morphogenic analogy, assumes that social systems are open and dynamic, that they are in constant interaction with their environments, and that change is normal. A factional analogy employs concepts such as conflict, domination, disorder, competition, and co-optation in place of consensus-oriented terms such as cooperation, integration, and consensus.

The fifth analogy, a *catastrophic analogy*, depicts a system as extremely variable and in a state of flux. A catastrophic system changes so radically and totally that chaos rather than order predominates. Events are random, one event contradicts another, and parts of the system border on collapse. To stabilize, a catastrophic system has to reorganize totally to gain a degree of predictability and routine (Burrell and Morgan, 1979, chapter 4). Once reorganized, a catastrophic analogy may no longer apply, in which case another analogy is selected to represent the system's new condition. As with morphogenic and factional analogies, OST is compatible with a catastrophic analogy because of its emphasis on process and changeability.

Selecting an Appropriate Analogy

With concrete social systems, an analogy should be selected only after the system's condition and situation have been determined. The analogy employed determines the kinds of phenomena and processes attended to. If exchanges with the environment are minimal and if the system is highly cooperative and integrated, an organismic analogy may apply. If a system is closely linked to its environment with minor internal conflicts, a morphogenic analogy may apply. If a system is divided into contending camps, a factional analogy may apply. For best results, an analogy is selected on the basis of facts in the case and not on a priori or ideological grounds. Open Systems Theory's utility is greatest when an analogy that fits a system's concrete conditions and circumstances is employed.

Summary

Subsequent analysis of Open Systems Theory's philosophical foundations reveals that it is highly compatible with a morphogenic analogy. Many social scientists, including social workers, have employed OST with an organismic analogy, leading to an unfortunate emphasis on internal structure and primary concern with consensus, integration, and cooperation. Change, dissent, conflict, segmentation, and domination/control have been ignored. Morphogenic, factional, and catastrophic analogies are compatible with Open Systems Theory because they emphasize process and the elaboration and change of structure that results from process. Least compatible is a mechanical analogy. Its assumptions that systems are relatively closed, highly coordinated, and seek and behave to attain a state of equilibrium are rejected by most social scientists as unwarranted for concrete social systems. A major goal of this text is the application of a morphogenic analogy to the understanding of social contexts with which social workers deal.

PHILOSOPHY OF SCIENCE AND NATURE OF SOCIETY ASSUMPTIONS

The Nature of Social Science

Four philosophy of science questions relevant to social science are as follows: (1) what is human/social reality like? (2) how can, or do, we know this and how is knowledge about it transmitted? (3) what is human nature basically like? and (4) what methodology do we employ to study or observe human/social reality? Burrell and Morgan (1979, p. 3) suggest that most social science theories are either subjectivist or objectivist, depending on their stance relative to the above four questions.

Table 3.3 depicts the two overarching perspectives that predominate in social science and gives subjectivist and objectivist answers to the four questions noted above. *Subjectivist theories* claim that social reality exists primarily in the human consciousness or mind and that free human beings participate actively in the creation and constitution of social reality. *Objectivist theories*

TABLE 3.3. THE SUBJECTIVE-OBJECTIVE DIMENSION: RESPONSES TO FOUR QUESTIONS ABOUT THE NATURE OF SOCIAL SCIENCE

The subjectivist approach to social science	*Issue and question(s) posed*	*The objectivist approach to social science*
Nominalism (in the mind)	*Ontology:* Is social reality external to the individual ("out there" in the world) or the product of individual consciousness (the product of one's mind)?	Realism (external)
Antipositivism (soft, subjective, must be experienced)	*Epistemology:* What are the grounds of knowledge? How can one understand the world and communicate this as knowledge to others? Is knowledge hard, real, tangible, and something that can be acquired or soft, subjective, spiritual, and something that must be experienced?	Positivism (hard, real, tangible)
Voluntarism (people create their environments)	*Human Nature:* What is the relationship between human beings and their environment? Are human beings and their experiences products of their environment or are people the creators of their own environments, controllers rather than controlled?	Determinism (people are products of their environments)
Ideographic (analyze subjective accounts which one generates by "getting inside" situations of everyday life)	*Methodology:* Should the study of social reality be concerned with concepts, their measurement, and the relationships between them (the search for universal laws that explain and govern the reality that is being observed)? Or should the principal concern be an understanding of the way in which individuals create, modify, and interpret the world in which they find themselves?	Nomothetic (use methods of natural science to test hypotheses in accord with scientific rigor)

Source: Adapted from Burrell and Morgan (1979, Chapter 1).

claim that social reality has real, concrete existence above and beyond individuals, that this reality shapes people's actions and perceptions, and that natural science methods can be applied to the study of social reality. We turn now to the answers of each perspective to the four questions posed.

Question 1, on ontology, asks: *What is human reality like?* What is its fundamental character? The objectivist answer is *realism*: Social phenomena have real existence (Table 3.3). Social phenomena exist above and beyond the individual person's consciousness or cognition of them. The subjectivist answer is *nominalism*: The only social reality that exists is in the individual person's consciousness. Outside that consciousness, a phenomenon has no reality. A realist views a role or a norm as a real phenomenon that exists independently of an individual knowing about it. A nominalist claims that a role or norm is real only if a person believes in it. Overall, Open Systems Theory is compatible with the realist perspective. Used in conjunction with interpretivist assumptions (see below), it can be employed within a subjectivist framework, however.

Question 2, on epistemology, asks: *What are the grounds for knowing, understanding, and communicating about social phenomena?* This question concerns how humans are able to know about social phenomena and how knowledge, once known, can be communicated. The objectivist response to this question is *positivism:* Knowledge about social phenomena is "hard, real, and capable of being transmitted in tangible form" (Burrell and Morgan, 1979, p. 1). The subjectivist response, *antipositivism*, claims that knowledge of social reality is soft, subjective, spiritual, even transcendental and cannot be acquired or transmitted but must rather be experienced (Burrell and Morgan, 1979, pp. 1, 2). Consistent with the objectivist or positivist view, Open Systems Theory and most social work theories assume that social facts can be described, written about, and communicated through, for example, didactic instruction, as in this course. This view is changing, however, as social workers increasingly recognize the proactive role of humans in creating, not only reacting to, their social environments (cf. Heineman, 1981; Witkin and Gottschalk, 1987).

Question 3, regarding human nature, asks: *What is the relationship between human beings and their environment?* Are people products or shapers of their environment? The objectivist answer is *determinism*, which indicates that people are viewed primarily as products of their environment and circumstances. The subjectivist answer, *voluntarism*, is that people are free and play a proactive, controlling role in the creation of their own realities. Most theories of human nature fall toward the middle, rather than the extremes, on this issue although behaviorist psychology is fairly deterministic in its conception of human development.

Many Open Systems Theory applications reflect a deterministic view of human nature although Buckley (1967) develops a voluntaristic version.

Buckley emphasizes the potential for humans to create their own realities. Open Systems Theory affirms the importance of the environment but, along with Buckley, affirms also the potential of individual and social systems to be self-directed, to self-correct, and to change.

Question 4, on methodology for investigating social phenomena, asks: *Should the study of social reality be concerned with concepts, their measurement, and the relationships between them or with understanding the ways that individuals create, modify, and interpret the world in which they live?* The objectivist stance is *nomothetic*: Research methodologies from the natural sciences should be employed to search for regularities and laws among social phenomena. The subjectivist stance is *ideographic* or that concern should not be with universal laws or regularities but with the ways individuals actively create, modify, and interpret the world in which they live (Burrell and Morgan, 1979, p. 3). The subjectivist stance denies that an external reality worthy of study exists and rejects methodologies that assume this to be the case. It emphasizes what is unique and particular to the individual as opposed to what is general and universal and claims that reality is relativistic rather than real. This perspective is regarded as "antiscientific" relative to the ground rules of natural science (Burrell and Morgan, 1979, p. 3) and is referred to by Lincoln and Guba (1985) as a post-positivist view.

Open Systems Theory is objectivist on question 4. It favors a nomothetic view and is indeed highly objectivist here since its fundamental concern is with general theory, which holds for all types and forms of open systems. Most research methods used by social workers are nomothetic, taking the form of surveys, attitude measures, and experiments predicated upon assumptions that reality is hard, external to the individual, and capable of being known through the application of objective research methods or tools.

The Nature of Human Society

The second dimension for assessing Open Systems Theory's philosophical foundations concerns the nature of human society, that is, the nature of the patterned associations between people over time. Two views of society have dominated the social science literature: (1) That which views society as characterized by social order and equilibrium versus (2) that which views society as characterized by conflict, domination, coercion, and change (cf. Dahrendorf, 1959; Burrell and Morgan, 1979). As shown in Table 3.4, these two conceptions are labeled as (1) regulation and (2) radical change (Burrell and Morgan, 1979, p. 18). The *regulation concept* emphasizes the underlying cohesiveness and unity of human society. "It attempts to explain why society tends to hold together rather than to fall apart" (Burrell and Morgan, 1979, p. 17). The *radical change concept* seeks explanations for "radical change, deep-seated structural conflict, modes of domination and structural contradiction

TABLE 3.4. THE REGULATION–RADICAL CHANGE DIMENSION AND THE CONCERNS OF EACH DIMENSION

Regulation *is concerned with:*	Radical change *is concerned with:*
(a) the status quo	(a) radical change
(b) social order	(b) structural conflict
(c) consensus	(c) modes of domination
(d) social integration and cohesion	(d) contradiction
(e) solidarity	(e) emancipation
(f) need satisfaction	(f) deprivation
(g) actuality	(g) potentiality

Source: Adapted from Burrell and Morgan (1979, Table 22, p. 18).

which its theorists see as characterizing modern society" (Burrell and Morgan, 1979, p. 17). The radical change perspective focuses on deprivations and false consciousness caused by societal arrangements and is concerned with the possible rather than with what is, "with alternatives rather than with acceptance of the *status quo*" (Burrell and Morgan, 1979, p. 17).

Regulation models of society (see Table 3.4) are concerned with (a) the status quo, (b) social order, (c) consensus (defined as voluntary and spontaneous agreement), (d) social integration and cohesion, (e) solidarity, (f) need satisfaction (which refers to a focus upon satisfaction of individual or system "needs"), and (g) actuality (Burrell and Morgan, 1979, p. 18). Regulation models assume that society has these characteristics, and social scientists, in the process of conducting research, analyze relationships between concepts such as these in order to understand social reality.

Radical change models of society conceptualize society as conflict-ridden. Their concepts include (a) radical change, (b) structural conflict, (c) modes of domination, (d) contradiction, (e) emancipation, (f) deprivation, and (g) potentiality. In models of this type, attention centers on forces and processes that suggest the desirability of change and that, in time, are believed to produce it. Models of this type are concerned with society's potential to *become* rather than with what it *is* (Burrell and Morgan, 1979, p. 17).

Depending on the type of analogy employed, Open Systems Theory can be used within a regulation or radical change perspective. Used with an organismic analogy, OST is regulation-oriented. Used with morphogenic, factional, or catastrophic analogies, OST is change-oriented. Social work views itself as change-oriented yet has traditionally endorsed, and continues to rely on, models of society that are status quo-oriented. Social work is, in many respects, a social engineering profession, concerned with altering the status quo in incremental ways rather than overhauling existing social relations or structures in fundamental ways. Although exceptions to this generalization exist, among them social workers who call for radical structural change (e.g., Piven and Cloward, 1972), the majority of social work theories are regulatory in orientation, and most applications by social workers of social systems theory are regulation-oriented (see Chapter 4).

FOUR SOCIAL SCIENCE PARADIGMS

The above-noted dimensions can be combined into a four-cell typology of social science paradigms (Burrell and Morgan, 1979). With philosophy of science assumptions along a continuum from subjectivist to objectivist and assumptions about society along a continuum from regulatory to radical social change, Figure 3.1 shows four paradigms: (1) Functionalist, (2) Interpretive, (3) Radical Humanist, and (4) Radical Structuralist. These paradigms demarcate four mutually exclusive perspectives of social life. "One cannot operate in more than one paradigm at any given point in time" (Burrell and Morgan, 1979, p. 25).

Most social science theories can be placed in one of the four quadrants of Figure 3.1. We review the primary characteristics of each paradigm with two aims in mind: (1) To examine in detail the assumptions of Open Systems Theory, and (2) to identify assumptions of the theories-in-use by social workers relative to the four paradigms and to Open Systems Theory. The former is done in Chapter 3 and the latter in Chapter 4. Results of the Chapter 4 exercise show that Open Systems Theory is highly compatible with the majority of social work theories-in-use. This may account for social workers' ready acceptance of OST and social system theory over the past two decades.

Functionalist Paradigm

The Functionalist Paradigm is objectivist in its conception of social science/ reality and regulation-oriented in its view of human society. Theories (or conceptual frameworks) in this paradigm, as shown in Figure 3.1, assume that social phenomena have *real* existence and are external to the individual; that knowledge of social reality is hard and factual; that human beings are shaped by their social environments; and that universal laws and relationships between social phenomena can be studied by application of natural science research methods. Many varieties of theory fall into this paradigm, some of which lean more to the subjectivist end of the continuum and some of which incorporate elements from the Radical Humanist and Radical Structuralist Paradigms. Overall, however, functionalist theories share an underlying view of social phenomena's objective reality and are concerned with explaining social order in terms of integration, consensus, and solidarity.

Many theories in the Functionalist Paradigm recognize change and con-

Radical Change Model of Society

Subjectivist View (of social science/ reality)		Objectivist View (of social science/ reality)

Radical Humanist Paradigm	*Radical Structuralist Paradigm*
Conception of social science/ reality:	Conception of social science/ reality:
nominalist	realist
antipositivist	positivist
voluntarist	determinist
ideographic	nomothetic
Conception of human society:	Conception of human society:
radical change	radical change
modes of domination	emancipation
emancipation	potentiality
deprivation	structural conflict
potentiality	modes of domination
	contradiction
	deprivation
Interpretive Paradigm	*Functionalist Paradigm*
Conception of social science/ reality:	Conception of social science/ reality:
nominalist	realist
antipositivist	positivist
voluntarist	determinist
ideographic	nomothetic
Conception of human society:	Conception of human society:
status quo	status quo
social order	social order
consensus	consensus
social integration and cohesion	social integration and cohesion
solidarity	solidarity
actuality	need satisfaction
	actuality

Regulation Model of Society

Figure 3.1 Typology of Social Science Theory

flict but do so within a framework that underscores the contributions of each part of society, for example, the family, religion, the economy, and so on, to societal well-being or integration. Conflict and turbulence are viewed as inevitable, but they, like social change, are viewed as occurring within fairly narrow limits and in accord with systemic rules that call into play stabilizing and equilibrium-producing processes. Coser's (1956) analysis of the "social functions of conflict" is a classic example of Functionalist Paradigm theory.

When Open Systems Theory is used with an *organismic analogy*, it falls into the Functionalist Paradigm. If a social system is assumed to be highly integrated, orderly, and consensual, an organismic analogy may be appropriate. If it is assumed to be changeable or in flux, another analogy is more appropriate. This suggests, as noted earlier, that assessment is necessary to determine the type of analogy that best fits a social problem or client situation. Most applications of Open Systems Theory, according to Burrell and Morgan (1979), have employed an organismic analogy and thus make quasi-closed rather than fully open system assumptions. Though many claim to use an open systems view, an organismic analogy prevents full exploration of the implications of an open systems perspective.

Interpretive Paradigm

The Interpretive Paradigm combines a subjectivist view of social science/reality with a regulation orientation to society. Theories in this paradigm attempt to "understand the world as it is, to understand the fundamental nature of the social world at the level of subjective experience" (Burrell and Morgan, 1979, p. 28). Individual consciousness and subjectivity are basic concepts. Social reality is viewed as having tenuous existence beyond the level of individual consciousness and as consisting of a network of assumptions and meanings that are *intersubjectively* shared. Understanding of social reality is gained by getting inside the perspective of individual actors. People are seen as active creators of their own reality rather than as responders to external influences and stimuli. Universal laws are rejected in favor of highly individual and unique occurrences and events. Social reality is viewed as an emergent process, as an extension of human consciousness and subjective experience. "Everyday life is accorded the status of a miraculous achievement" (Burrell and Morgan, 1979, p. 31).

The Interpretive Paradigm falls toward the regulation end of the radical change/regulation continuum and, because of this, its theories share some characteristics with Functionalist Paradigm theories. The world of human affairs is assumed to be cohesive, ordered, and integrated rather than torn by conflict, domination, contradiction, and change. The orientation of theories in this paradigm is with *social reality as it is* rather than with its potential.

With its emphasis on human consciousness, subjective experience, and the emergent nature of human reality, Interpretive Paradigm theories share some commonalities with Open Systems Theory. Interpretive Paradigm insights and concepts can be used by social workers to explore the role of human consciousness in human affairs. Meaning is particular to concrete contexts, and the meanings people attach to their own and others' behaviors can be explored. If social reality is composed of shared meanings, it can be altered by changed meanings. This perspective is extended in the more activist Radical Humanist Paradigm.

Radical Humanist Paradigm

The Radical Humanist Paradigm reflects a subjectivist view of social science/ reality and a radical change orientation to human society. Like theories in the Interpretive Paradigm, radical humanist models focus on human consciousness. Unlike the interpretive group, however, they stress the importance of transcending or overthrowing social arrangements that limit realization of *full human potential*. Human consciousness is viewed as dominated by the ideological superstructures of modern society, and the major concern is "with *release* from the constraints which existing social arrangments place upon human development. It is a brand of theorizing designed to provide a critique of the status quo" (Burrell and Morgan, 1979, pp. 32, 33).

Four concepts are central to the radical humanist paradigm: totality, consciousness, alienation, and critique. The concept of *totality* is similar to that of wholeness in Open Systems Theory and claims that human society can be understood only by taking into account both objective and subjective aspects of any situation or epoch. Understanding of the totality precedes understanding of component parts because the "whole dominates the parts in an all-embracing sense" (Burrell and Morgan, 1979, p. 298). *Consciousness* is the "force which creates and sustains the social world" (p. 298). Consciousness stems ultimately from each human being's internal processes; however, it is influenced by social reality as it becomes *objectified* and by the continual dialectic between the subjective experience of the world and its objectified manifestations. *Objectification* refers to processes and products of human interaction that result in understandings or practices that treat social phenomena as having greater objective reality than they actually have (that is, reification). Such objectifications of subjective social reality can (and do) influence the subjective experiences of human beings, usually for the worse.

Alienation produces misperceptions about the true nature of social reality. Instead of seeing the social world as their creation (a result of their own conscious experience), alienated people perceive it as a "hard, dominating, external reality" (Burrell and Morgan, 1979, p. 298). A *cognitive wedge* exists between an alienated person's consciousness and the true nature of the social world. This wedge of alienation prevents realization of the true self and of full human potential.

The fourth concept, *critique*, is the attempt of radical humanists to expose the forms and sources of alienation that inhibit the realization of human potential. Different theorists focus on different concepts in providing this critique. Lukacs (1971) for example, focuses on the concept of reification (defined in Chapter 2 of this text); Marcuse (1964) emphasizes the alienating roles of modern technology, science, and logic; Habermas (1976) stresses the alienating effects of language that lead, often, to communication distortions; and Gramsci (1971) concentrates on ideological hegemony or the effects of a belief system propagated by those in control of society to foster beliefs among the *controlled* that present social arrangements are valid and justified (Burrell and Morgan, 1979).

Theories in the Radical Humanist Paradigm agree that *reality is socially created and socially sustained* (Burrell and Morgan, 1979, p. 306). As such, they stand in bold contrast to approaches in the Functionalist Paradigm (and the Radical Structuralist Paradigm) that view social reality as having an independent existence. In almost every respect, the Radical Humanist Paradigm is an inversion of the Functionalist Paradigm. Theories in the latter group emphasize the objective nature of social reality and attend to *what is* whereas radical humanists focus on the subjective nature of social reality with emphasis on *what can be*. Theorists in these two camps seldom communicate except to condemn each other for asking the wrong questions, making wrong assumptions, and pursuing inappropriate interests and goals (Burrell and Morgan, 1979, p. 307).

The Radical Humanist Paradigm contains several concepts for both the Open Systems theorist and social work practitioner. Emphasis on totality is compatible with OST's emphasis on wholeness. The concepts of consciousness, alienation, and critique can be employed to assess the situation of conflicted systems. Recognition of the role of human consciousness in the creation of social systems can increase understanding of human behavior in the social environment and contribute to positive social change.

Radical Structuralist Paradigm

The fourth paradigm combines an objectivist view of social science/reality with a radical change orientation to society. While sharing an objectivist view of social science with the Functionalist Paradigm, radical structuralist theories have different goals. Radical Structuralism is concerned with radical change, emancipation, and potentiality, and it emphasizes structural conflict, modes of domination, contradiction, and deprivation (Burrell and Morgan, 1979, p. 34). Radical Structuralists are concerned with structural relationships in a realist social world. Some focus on the "deep-seated internal contradictions" of social systems, whereas others concentrate on the structure and analysis of power relationships (Burrell and Morgan, 1979, p. 34).

In contrast to Radical Humanists, with whom they share a radical change orientation, Radical Structuralists concern themselves with structural conflict and contradiction. These concepts are absent from the Radical Humanist Paradigm because of its subjectivist stance. Consistent with the humanists, however, Radical Structuralists are concerned about providing a critique of society. *Critique* is aimed at fostering the revolutionary transformation of structural arrangements that prevent people from realizing their full potential. Radical Structuralists disagree that a bloodless revolution can be achieved through a change of consciousness. Believing that societies (or social arrangements) have real existence and are ontologically prior to individual human beings, Radical Structuralists argue that the structural relations of society almost never change of their own accord. "Structures are seen as being changed, first and foremost, through economic or political crises, which generate conflicts of such intensity that the status quo is necessarily disrupted or torn apart and replaced by radically different social forms" (Burrell and Morgan, 1979, p. 358).

Four concepts typify the Radical Structuralist Paradigm: totality, structure, contradiction, and crisis. *Totality* entails concern with "total social formations" as opposed to pieces or parts of reality. *Structure* focuses attention on the patterns and form of social relationships that characterize various totalities and that exist independently of people's conscious awareness of them.

> Structures are treated as hard and concrete facticities, which are relatively persistent and enduring. Social reality for the radical structuralist is not necessarily created and recreated in everyday interaction, as, for example, many interpretive theorists would claim. Reality exists independently of any reaffirmation which takes place in everyday life. (Burrell and Morgan, 1979, p. 358)

The concept of *contradiction* reflects the assumption that social structural arrangements, while enduring, are also characterized by contradictory and antagonistic relationships. The contradictions in social structural arrangements carry within them the seeds for political change and transformation. The fourth concept is *crisis*. In all theories in this paradigm, social change is viewed as involving *"structural dislocation of an extreme form"* (Burrell and Morgan, 1979). When the contradictions of a given totality reach a point at which they can no longer be contained, some type of crisis ensues. The crisis may be economic, political, or whatever, but as a result of it, the totality is transformed and one set of structures (or structural arrangements) is replaced by those of a fundamentally different kind.

Radical Structuralism and Functionalism share an objectivist (realist) conception of social reality, but the former views social change as characterized by contradiction, crisis, and catastrophe, whereas the latter views it as evolutionary. Even the most change-oriented conceptual frameworks in the Functionalist Paradigm are status quo-oriented compared to those in the Radical Structuralist group.

OPEN SYSTEMS THEORY
AND THE FOUR PARADIGMS

Open Systems Theory falls toward the objectivist end of the objectivist-subjectivist continuum on three of the four philosophy of science questions posed in Table 3.3. Open Systems Theory assumes (1) that social reality has real existence and is external to the individual, (2) that knowledge about social reality can be readily learned and communicated, and (3) that social processes follow general laws and can be studied (researched) with the methods of natural science. On the fourth question, about human nature, OST is more subjectivist. It assumes that individuals are not only affected by their environments but also create them. In emphasizing process and free will (or voluntarism), or the ability of individuals to shape their realities and to change, OST affirms the proactive role of human consciousness in creating and interpreting social phenomena. Although OST is positivist in its orientation to knowledge and knowing, its positivism is nontraditional. It is non-reductionist and emphasizes, as noted in Chapter 2, the notion of wholeness. If the full implications of an open systems model were explored, analyses of human/social systems would pay more attention to human and systemic potential and to structural elaboration and change (Burrell and Morgan, 1979).

On the human society issue, OST can be employed for status quo or radical social change purposes. This is determined by the goals of the theorist and by the type of analogy employed. Used with a mechanical or organismic analogy, OST is status quo-oriented. With a morphogenic analogy, it can be status quo- or social change-oriented, and with a factional or catastrophic analogy, it can be radical social change-oriented. The choice of analogy affects the results of an OST application. Because of its variable uses, determined by choice of analogy, we are unable to fix OST in any one of the Burrell and Morgan paradigms.

Ever since von Bertalanffy's statement of Open Systems Theory, most social scientists claim to have abandoned a closed system model, yet they have not fully succeeded. Two factors have hampered realization of this goal: (1) Even when claiming to employ an open systems model, social scientists have continued to utilize closed-system methodologies in their research, that is, experiments, personal interviews, and questionnaire surveys of attitudes, all of which assume the environment to be relatively unimportant. The use of such methodological approaches redirects attention and concern to closed-system assumptions and concepts; (2) the employment of an organismic analogy has limited the utility of Open Systems Theory. When such an analogy is used, attention is directed to integration, functional interdependence, consensus, and stability, and the full implications of openness go undeveloped.

An open system may or may not achieve a steady state whereas a closed system will by its very nature achieve equilibrium (von Bertalanffy, 1968; Burrell and Morgan, 1979; Buckley, 1967).

> An open system can take a wide variety of forms. There are no general laws which dictate that it must achieve a steady state, be goal directed, evolve, regress, or disintegrate. In theory, anything can happen. One of the purposes of open systems theory is to study the pattern of relationships which characterize a system and its relationship to its environment in order to understand the way in which it operates. The open systems approach does not carry with it the implication that any one particular kind of analogy is appropriate for studying all systems, since it is possible to discern different types of open system in practice. (Burrell and Morgan, 1979, p. 59)

We endorse Buckley's (1967) morphogenic view of social systems that depicts social structure as emergent, arising from social interaction. Open Systems Theory views social systems as *structure elaborating* with the consequence that systems can change. Focusing on processes that open systems employ to self-direct and to receive feedback allows us to view them *as if they have goals* and to avoid the assumption that they indeed do (Buckley, 1967).

Open Systems Theory has some distinctive qualities that the Burrell and Morgan typology helps to clarify. First, it attempts to explore the implications of full openness. Relative to Table 3.1, we explicate concepts that are useful for understanding morphogenic systems primarily but also factional and catastrophic systems as well. Additionally, under the proper conditions, OST concepts can be applied to organismic systems. Second, we focus on the problematic nature of control in social systems. In the past, control has been treated in neutral terms such as decision making, leadership, and integration. These concepts deflect attention away from conflict, domination, exploitation, and imply that social systems are characterized by consensus and harmony. This text treats harmony, integration, and consensus as problematic and the results of effort or work not as inherent tendencies of social systems. It also views control as possibly exploitative and as often beneficial to the interests of elites rather than the system as a whole.

Third, we focus attention on system change. We explore the ongoing dialectic between social structure and human process and the ways process produces change over time. Fourth, we identify ways of applying Open Systems Theory within both a subjectivist and objectivist orientation. Social workers who endorse the Interpretive or Radical Humanist Paradigms can, in our opinion, benefit from knowledge and use of open systems concepts and principles. Recognizing that objectivist and subjectivist views are fundamentally irreconcilable, a subjectivist can nevertheless use certain OST concepts when this helps to see or deal with certain *objectified* aspects of social reality. Similarly, objectivists can apply subjectivist concepts to understand emergent social phenomena and the proactive role of human actors in creating social reality.

GUIDELINES FOR CHOOSING AN ANALOGY AND PERSPECTIVE

Selection of an analogy and theoretical perspective should be based on three criteria: (1) the state of the system under study, (2) the goals of the intervention, and (3) the level of the system.

The State of the System

The *state of the system* refers to the status and condition of the focal system (or system of reference). Depending on whether a system is integrated or factionalized, characterized by consensus or dissent, stable or volatile, a practitioner should select an analogy that best reflects it. Most systems that social workers deal with are likely to change dynamically or experience conflict, thus morphogenic and factional analogies may be applied. Parents in troubled families often believe an organismic analogy applies to their family (that is, consensus, absence of conflict, and compliance) whereas conflict, resistance, dissent, and a morphogenic or factionalized analogy, actually fit (Haley, 1976).

The Goals of Intervention

Intervention goals concern the end-state the practitioner seeks to promote. Is the social worker trying to help someone adjust to a situation (e.g., a death in the family), to incrementally change a relationship, or to fundamentally reorganize and change? If the intervention concerns an individual's unreasonable fears or insecurities, a subjectivist type of theory (for example, controlled imaging or relaxation techniques) combined with certain structural concepts may be most useful. A subjectivist/interpretive approach may enable clients to reinterpret their situation and to create a more positive view of the world. Subjectivists can use objectivist concepts to help clients *see* the world as many believe it to be (falsely in the views of the radical humanists). This may help them make better choices and change ineffectual behaviors.

If the task is to assist a state welfare agency characterized by conflict, public disfavor, and low productivity of work (or services being delivered), a structural model in the Functionalist or Radical Structuralist Paradigms may be useful. Open Systems Theory with its orientation to process and its utility for identifying activities and linkages should be particularly useful. If the practitioner's aim is to assist the actors in the system to see what is going on and what is required to stop it, a structural theory with a process component should be appropriate. The goals of intervention should determine the type of framework used. Open systems concepts and principles can be applied, if used properly, to most interventions.

The Level of the System

The *level of the system* refers to whether the target system is small or large. The smaller a system, the more likely subjectivist concepts, in addition to objectivist ones, will be useful. In larger systems, objectivist concepts may be most useful. Entire nation-states have microelements, however, such as heads of states who like or dislike each other. Relations between spouses or between parent and child have both subjectivist and objectivist aspects. Subjectivist approaches may help family members reinterpret behaviors of a parent or child that they misunderstand or find offensive. Objectivist theories can be useful for understanding pressures and pulls from outside the family on various members, the socioeconomic context in which the family exists, and so forth. Selection of an interventive theory that matches the level of the system is important. To eliminate poverty, social policies should avoid reductionist views that blame the poor for their condition. High unemployment, substandard housing, crime, family disorganization, and mental illness are correlates of poverty. To eliminate poverty, entire labor markets, occupational systems, housing and residential patterns, and educational and welfare systems may have to be restructured (Piven and Cloward, 1972).

CONCLUSIONS

Open Systems Theory is compatible philosophically with most theories-in-use by social workers. It extends many of them through its emphasis on full openness and the range of human and social phenomena (from individual to nation-state). Chapter 4 reviews theories-in-use by social work relative to the Burrell and Morgan typology and to OST. It also provides an historical overview of social work's association with various forms of systems theory.

Chapter 4

Social Work and Systems Theory: Historical and Current Applications

Social work, for most of its history, has endorsed a holistic perspective, but it was not until the late 1960s that formal applications of systems theory became prominent in its literature. Emphasis on the person-in-situation or person-environment relationship has dominated social work practice for decades (Bartlett, 1970, 1971). Schwartz's (1976) mediating model characterized mainstream social work thought in the 1950s as assuming a symbiotic-reciprocal relationship between individual and society. Society was viewed as needing capable individuals and individuals as needing a supportive society. The task of social work was to mediate the interests of individual and society to mutual benefit.

Passage of the Social Security Act of 1935 led to an increase in the number of social workers employed by public social welfare organizations. These workers encountered a different clientele from that in private and voluntary agencies and were introduced to new problems and clients. World War II and the postwar era saw an increase in the types and complexity of social welfare activities and work. The economic and social prosperity of the 1950s collapsed in the 1960s with the Vietnam War, national recognition that poverty, racism, and injustice were with us still, and so on. With a focus on poverty and social unrest associated with the civil rights' movement, the Vietnam War, and the student movement, federal support for social welfare benefits and services mushroomed. Social workers found jobs in the "War On Poverty" programs and became increasingly identified with the disadvantaged and disenfranchised. During the 1960s, in accord with the times, social workers favored a macroinstitutional perspective that called for fundamental societal change. Many became activists against the establishment, which was viewed as racist, capitalist, sexist, and status quo-oriented.

Turmoil in society and in social work's institutional environment led to change. The knowledge and technological base of the profession expanded from the practice trilogy of casework, groupwork, and community organization to include social welfare administration, program evaluation, policy analysis, and planning. Casework, the dominant social work method, was modified from a one-on-one focus to a generalist approach that incorporated linking and coordination along with counseling (Siporin, 1975). Social work's knowledge-base expanded to include social and behavioral literature on psychology, economics, biology, human development, organizations, and social change. Social workers increasingly specialized as social work expanded to encompass new arenas and domains (medical social work, industrial social work, and so on; O'Connor and Waring, 1981). Graduate students were allowed to choose among casework/clinical social work, generalist practice, community organization, program evaluation, and social welfare administration. Segments of the profession interested in different specialities founded their own journals (*Journal of Clinical Social Work, Administration in Social Work, Social Work With Groups*) and organizations (Society of Clinical Social Workers; Community Organization and Social Administration Colloquium). The trend toward specialization seems unlikely to abate in the foreseeable future.

Because of its integrative and unifying potential, systems theory was, and is, attractive to social workers. Proponents saw it as helping practitioners to integrate and conceptualize social work's diverse and complex domain. They viewed it as helpful for organizing practice in a complex world. Systems theory has undergone several transformations since social workers first adopted it.

THE EVOLUTION OF SOCIAL WORK'S USE OF SYSTEMS THEORY

As a profession, social work's principal mission is to intervene and change human and social phenomena rather than solely to describe or explain them. Disagreements over whether systems principles and concepts should be used to explain or intervene have shaped the course of development of systems theory in social work (Briar and Miller, 1971; Fischer, 1978).

Six sources or references can be used to trace the evolution of social work's adoption of systems theory concepts. The works chosen are well recognized, have been adopted widely by social work educators, and reflect milestones in social work's relationship with a systems theory perspective.

Hearn

Hearn (1969) was among the early social workers to suggest that General System Theory could serve as an underlying/integrative framework for social work: "[W]e may eventually develop a substantially inclusive, internally consistent and organized conception of social work practice and its approach to social science" (Hearn, 1969, p. 3). Hearn challenged social workers to use General System Theory (GST) and provided examples of applications of GST themes and concepts to social work practice and its domain. Numerous articles that argued for GST and its application in social work appeared in social work journals in response to Hearn's writings (Janchill, 1969; Hartman, 1970; Vickery, 1974; Meyer, 1976; Nelson, 1972; Germain, 1973).

Pincus and Minahan

A social work practice text by Pincus and Minahan (1973) used systems theory as its underlying framework for social work intervention. Their scheme of client system, worker system, target system, and action system offered practitioners a model for organizing practice. Their framework emphasized the importance of schools, social agencies, hospitals, and workplaces in the lives of clients and encouraged practitioners to take these into account. Pincus and Minahan explicated only selected systems theory concepts, but their endorsement signaled that systems theory was accepted as a legitimate perspective for social work practice.

Siporin

Siporin, like Pincus and Minahan, applied systems theory to social work practice (1975). He used Parsonian social systems or structure-functional theory to explicate the helping process. Building on the four functional prerequisites of a healthy social system (adaptation, integration, pattern maintenance, and goal attainment), Siporin explicated the stages of the helping process. Siporin distinguished between social systems theory and ecological theory (see below), arguing that ecological theory "adds a needed dynamic to General Systems Theory" (Siporin, 1975, p. 107). Social workers are advised to focus on the *interaction* between a person's environment and to apply ecological theory to this dynamic. Siporin's belief that GST places too little emphasis on process is a result of the historical use of many social systems' applications of an organismic analogy.

Anderson and Carter

Anderson and Carter (1978), in a social work text on human behavior and the social environment, used systems theory as their theoretical base. Their work reflects the use of systems theory for purposes of explanation rather than intervention. Like Siporin, Anderson and Carter draw heavily on Parsonian social systems theory rather than General System Theory. Similar to this book, their framework is applied to a variety of systems including the individual person, families, groups, organizations, and the community.

Germain and Gitterman

Germain and Gitterman's (1980) ecological perspective is true to social work's traditional person–environment theme. It emphasizes the reciprocal interaction between an organism and the environment and the organism's adaptation to the environment. The ecological model focuses on the reciprocity and symbiosis of organism and environment and the adaptive processes that occur throughout an individual's life. No systems concepts per se are, however, explicated.

Germain and Gitterman's ecological model appeared at a time when enthusiasm for systems theory was waning. The brand of systems theory employed by most social workers is *status quo-oriented* and has been criticized on those grounds (Leighninger, 1978). Others claim that systems theory fails to provide guidance for practice, as early enthusiasts promised. Germain and Gitterman's work endorses a holistic perspective but abandons the particulars of systems theory. Also, it relies basically on an organismic anology of social system dynamics.

Meyer

Carol Meyer's (1983) eco-systems perspective is a recent development. Meyer updates Siporin and responds to Germain. Similar to Siporin, Meyer distinguishes between systems theory and ecological theory and proposes their combination in a single conceptual framework. An *ecosystems view* reinstates systems theory concepts as useful for social work practice. Even more interesting, Meyer invokes concepts from General System Theory not Parsonian social systems theory. Change, process, and the dynamics of systems are emphasized along with individual–environment transactions.

Germain and Gitterman's and Meyer's works attempt to integrate the intervention–explanation dichotomy. Systems theory is employed as a theoretical orientation and an organizing framework. It is presented as helpful to social workers for thinking about people and their situations, for describing and understanding, and for identifying and organizing interventions.

SOCIAL WORK THEORIES-IN-USE AND THE FOUR THEORETICAL PARADIGMS

No surveys document the theories that practicing social workers employ. When asked, many social workers say their approach is eclectic. This means they rely on a number of theories, or conceptual frameworks, rather than only one. They may employ different theories for different purposes, types of targets, and so on. Philosophical or ideological purity is not the norm among social workers. In the 1940s and 1950s, Freudian psychology and psycho-analysis were the dominant paradigms, and vestiges of these perspectives, while less dominant, still persist today. Systems theory, which became popular in the 1970s, remains popular still.

Open Systems Theory helps practitioners deal with macro- as well as microsystems and allows them to generalize learning from one type of system to another. Its popularity among social workers rests on its ability to deal with different sizes and types of systems and, though seldom remarked, its philosophical compatibility with most theories-in-use by practitioners. We turn now to a review of social work theories-in-use to examine their philosophical assumptions in light of the Burrell and Morgan typology from Chapter 3. Fifteen theoretical models are reviewed under four categories of intervention: social work with individuals, family treatment, groupwork practice, community practice. (See Fig. 4.1.)

Social Work with Individuals

Psychosocial Casework

Psychosocial casework (Turner, 1979a; 1979b) is an approach to social work with individuals that employs the person-in-situation theme as its major metaphor. Psychosocial casework rests on Freudian psychology and psycho-analytic theory as its primary theoretical base but diverges from them by emphasizing transactions between individuals and their environments. Concepts from ego psychology (Wasserman, 1979) are used to direct attention to personal consciousness, adaptive mental functions, the development and autonomous functioning of an individual's ego, and the importance of inter-personal relations for understanding individual reality. Role theory (Elkin, 1978) is employed to link individuals with social reality, and concepts from social systems theory (Hollis, 1972) are used to depict the complex variety of structures and processes that social reality can assume. This model of inter-vention with individuals is widely used by social workers.

Psychosocial casework is a Functionalist Paradigm theory (see Fig. 4.1). It entails a basically objectivist as opposed to subjectivist view of human reality. Individual characteristics are assumed to be largely determined by biology and experience, and role/societal phenomena are assumed to have *objective* existence outside the individual's consciousness of them. The primary goal of intervention with individuals is to assist them to reach a more harmonious balance with themselves, their interpersonal relationships, and their environment. No suggestion of a radical alteration of either the individual or his or her social environment is called for, required, or viewed as possible. Attention is given to the creation of improved social relationships, but this takes the form of adjustments aimed at greater consensus, harmony,

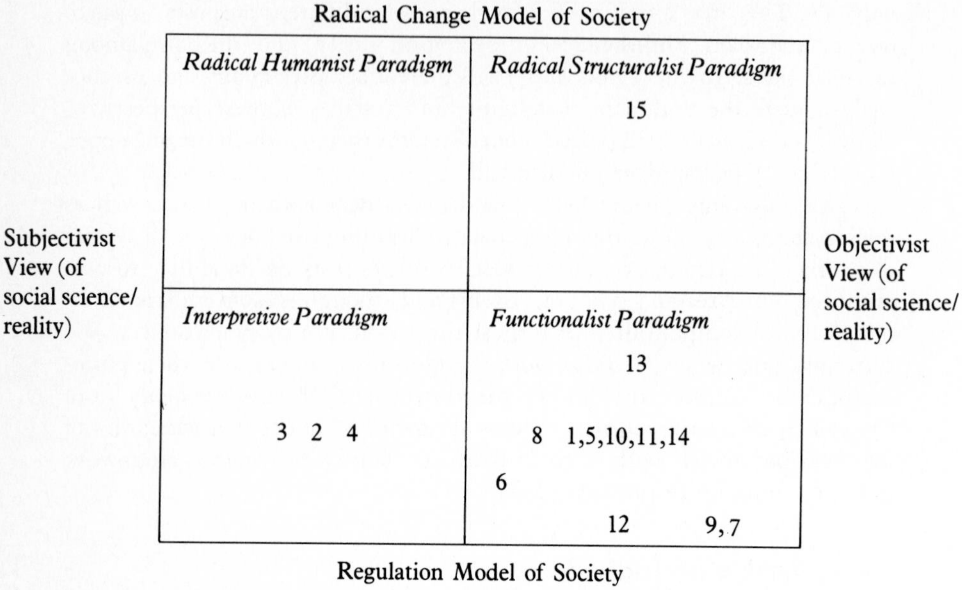

Radical Change Model of Society

Radical Humanist Paradigm	*Radical Structuralist Paradigm* 15
Interpretive Paradigm 3 2 4	*Functionalist Paradigm* 13 8 1,5,10,11,14 6 12 9,7

Subjectivist View (of social science/ reality) — (left side)

Objectivist View (of social science/ reality) — (right side)

Regulation Model of Society

Key:

Social Work with Individuals

1. Psychosocial Casework
2. Problem-Solving Casework
3. Client-Centered Therapy
4. Gestalt Therapy
5. Transactional Analysis
6. Cognitive-Behavioral Approaches
7. Behavior Modification Family Treatment Approaches
8. Conjoint Family Therapy

9. Problem-Solving Therapy
10. Family Systems Therapy
11. Structural Family Therapy Groupwork Practice
12. Remedial Groupwork Model
13. Reciprocal Groupwork Model Community Practice
14. Social Planning Model of Community Practice
15. Social Action Model of Social Change

Figure 4.1 Social Work Theories in Relation to the Two-Dimensional Typology and Four Paradigms.

and integration and does not assume that normal human relationships are characterized by conflict, domination, and dissent. Given these characteristics, psychosocial casework is clearly compatible with Open Systems Theory used with an organismic analogy. Whether it could also be used in conjunction with morphogenic, factional, or catastrophic analogies is less certain.

Problem-Solving Casework

The problem-solving casework approach, first developed by Perlman (1957), is based on the assumption that individuals have the capacity to resolve difficult situations, to interact effectively with their environments, and to direct their own lives. Problem solving is a rational, conscious process and focuses on tangible and discrete problems experienced by clients. Attention is given to the ego functions of perception, judgment, cognition, memory, and choice as aspects of a person's coping skills.

To begin the problem-solving process, a practitioner helps a client to break down the problem into manageable parts. This is followed by priority setting and establishment of goals. As the client implements goals, the practitioner participates actively by focusing, clarifying, encouraging, and providing emotional support. As needed, practitioners assist clients to extract necessary resources in the form of opportunities, social services, and material resources that are available.

The problem-solving approach has two goals. The immediate goal is to address the problems currently experienced by the client, and the second is to strengthen the client's problem-solving capacities. To accomplish these the client must participate actively, consciously focus on problem resolution, and exercise problem-solving tasks by doing.

Reid's (1978) task-centered approach, a type of problem solving, reflects the influence of cognitive and learning theories and is designed for short-term intervention. In a relationship viewed as a task structure, practitioner and client define specific tasks aimed at resolving problems that occur outside of treatment. The *treatment interview* consists of overseeing and reviewing of task implementation. Monitoring allows practitioner and client to identify obstacles to problem resolution and to design tasks for overcoming them.

Because of its objectivist focus, the problem-solving approach falls in the Functionalist Paradigm of Figure 4.1. Compared to Reid, Perlman's perspective is more subjective. Perlman emphasizes the development and strengthening of client's internal problem-solving mechanisms and the role of the therapeutic relationship. Reid's orientation is more objectivist and concentrates on the task structure for designing and implementing of behaviorally specific, concrete, delimited tasks.

Problem solving is environmentally and action oriented. It is used to promote individual adjustment rather than to radically alter society. Problem-solving techniques applied by a social reform-oriented practitioner could, however, be used to induce social change. Problem solving is generic to social work and inherent in almost all forms of direct and indirect practice. Most social work practice texts reflect a generic problem-solving orientation with a sequential ordering of intervention tasks and activities (see Brager and Holloway, 1978; Brager, Specht, and Torczyner, 1987; Compton and Gallaway, 1984; Garvin and Seabury, 1984; Hepworth and Larsen, 1982; Pincus and Minahan, 1973; Siporin, 1975; Toseland and Rivas, 1984). As noted by Lippitt, Watson, and Westley (1958) three decades ago, a generic problem-solving process is evident in the intervention of any practitioner who attempts to induce change regardless of that practitioner's professional orientation, the size of the target system, or the specific content of change efforts.

Phenomenological–Existential Approaches

Phenomenological–existential approaches include an array of helping approaches, all of which have a phenomenological–existential perspective as their philosophical base. These include Existential Social Work (Krill, 1979), Client-Centered Therapy (Rogers, 1951), Gestalt Therapy (Perls, 1969), Meditation Therapy (Keefe, 1979), and Transactional Analysis (Berne, 1970). The common thread in these models is an emphasis on the present, the here and now, rather than the past. There is a concern for individual uniqueness and subjective experience. Individual spontaneity, creativity, and personal responsibility are central, and the orientation is toward health and well-being rather than dysfunction and illness. Phenomenological–existential models "assume that human beings are rational, good and capable of assuming responsibility for themselves and making their own choices that can lead to independent actualization and autonomy" (Okun, 1976, p. 96). Actualization, enrichment, and the fullest expression of individual uniqueness are the goals of intervention.

Because of their popularity among social work practitioners, three phenomenological–existential models are discussed: Client-Centered Therapy, Gestalt Therapy, and Transactional Analysis.

Client-Centered Therapy

Carl Rogers (1951) focuses on an individual's self-image with a goal to promote congruence between that image and one's social relations. The counselor provides a warm and empathetic relationship while extending unconditional positive regard to the client. Using a reflective and nondirective style, a counselor's "responses are targeted consistently on the internal frame of reference and experience of the client" to stimulate self-actualization and fulfillment (Barrett-Lennard, 1979, p. 182). A number of communication techniques are employed to facilitate this including reflection, clarification, summarization, and confrontation.

Gestalt Therapy

Gestalt means "whole" and the founder of this approach, Fritz Perls (1969), viewed the individual as an organic whole. Mind and body are an integrated entity responding to the environment as a unit. Problems arise when individuals experience inconsistencies between themselves and their environment and resort to denial and withdrawal to escape tension.

Gestalt therapy views the human self as consisting of multiple opposing yet complementary parts. Individuals are assertive and passive, loving and hurtful, trusting and suspicious, independent and dependent. In a directive (confronting and frustrating) style, the counselor uses structured exercises and games that focus on these inconsistencies, insisting that the client take responsibility for her or his existence. The counselor's task is to work with these polarities for "it is important that the poles be experienced and teased apart so that each aspect can be seen for what it is and integrated into the personality" to help the individual achieve an organic balance or a wholeness (Blugerman, 1979, p. 275).

Transactional Analysis

Transactional Analysis was created by Eric Berne, a psychoanalyst, and is similar to Gestalt therapy. It is, however, more cognitive and intellectual. Berne viewed life as a grand railway station where people await trains that often never arrive and are forced to decide how to pass their time (Berne, personal communication, 1962).

Berne views the human personality as having three ego states: the Child (feeling and emotions), the Parent (internalized parental and social mores), and the Adult (logical problem-solver). A healthy person is aware of these different states and is able to behave appropriately in each ego state. Berne proposed four possible life style positions: I'm not OK, You're OK; I'm OK; You're not OK; I'm not OK, You're not OK; and I'm OK, You're OK (Okun, 1976). The first three of these positions are problematic and inhibit chances for actualization and intimacy.

Problems arise when individuals engage in *harmful games*, which consist of various combinations of child and parent ego-state transactions that generate tension and conflict and an incapacity of the adult ego-state to mediate (Coburn, 1979). Therapy analyzes these transactions to identify the structure of the games and thus promote greater cognitive awareness. The goal is to help people avoid involvement in harmful games and/or to restructure transactions that promote more desirable pastimes and, ultimately, intimacy.

Phenomenological–existential approaches fall primarily into the Interpretive Paradigm with some extension into the Functionalist Paradigm. Subjective experience, the voluntaristic aspects of human behavior, and the potential to shape one's own reality are emphasized. Social reality beyond the individual is viewed as having real existence, however, and is not totally receptive to change according to individual perceptions or consciousness.

Rogers, Perls, and Berne differ in their emphasis on internal versus external phenomena. Perls is the most internally oriented, focusing almost exclusively on the internal mind-body balance. Berne focuses on transactions and games that, compared to Perls, reflect a behavioral and objectivist orientation. Rogers' concern with self-image as an emergent property of social interaction seems to position him between Perls and Berne on the Subjectivist-Objectivist continuum.

Phenomenological–existential models are regulation-oriented, rather than radical social change-oriented. They are concerned principally with achieving order, balance, and congruence of a person's experiences. Any such change accommodates, or takes place within, the status quo, and the potential for radically changing society is muted.

Cognitive-Behavioral Approaches

Cognitive-behavioral approaches focus on rational thought and problem solving and are based on the assumption that thoughts and beliefs determine emotions and behavior. "The essence of cognitive theory is that it requires the practitioner to discard the concept of the 'unconscious' as the primary force in the psychic life" (Werner, 1979, p. 243). According to this perspective, humans can control their thoughts, beliefs, and values and take responsibility for their lives.

Albert Ellis and William Glasser are two well-known cognitive-behavioral theorists. Ellis' Rational-Emotive-Therapy (or R–E–T; 1962) posits an A–B–C framework. *A* represents a person's acts or experiences that he or she believes, incorrectly, to be a cause of *C*. *B* is the belief or thought system that acutally causes *C*. R–E–T is a directive approach in which "helpers exhort, frustrate, and command the helpees parse out their thoughts and learn to restructure rationally their belief system" (Okun, 1976, p. 104).

Glasser's Reality Therapy (1965) focuses on irrationality and the inconsistencies in individuals' thought and belief systems. By focusing on undesired consequences, Glasser stresses individual responsibility for behavior. Reality Therapy requires that individuals: (1) make value judgments about their own behavior, (2) make plans aimed at desired goals, (3) commit themselves to their plans, and (4) make no excuses if they fail in their commitment. Like Ellis, Glasser's approach is directive, judgmental, and confrontational. Unlike Ellis, however, Glasser suggests a warm and personal involvement of the practitioner (Okun, 1976).

The cognitive-behavioral approach straddles the boundary of the Interpretive and Functional Paradigms. Its exact location depends on the orientation and emphasis of the practitioner. Its objectivist orientation can be learned from the names of the major models, *rational* and *reality*. It is socially oriented and assumes the social world has real existence. Humans are viewed as in continual interaction with their environment, and their thought patterns are influenced by their immediate surroundings. Whereas consciousness is stressed, "awareness must represent a correct consciousness on the part of the patient of his [sic] real nature as a person, as distinguished from what he conceives it to be: of the real nature of his environment, both natural and social, as distinguished from the previously false one; of his real connection with the outside world as differentiated from an illusory one" (Directors of the Robbins Institute, 1955, pp. 91, 92).

This objectivism is, however, tempered by a parallel subjectivist orientation. The combination of objectivist and subjectivist assumptions makes this approach unique. Human *thought* is the mediator, the intervening variable, in the stimulus-response cycle. Thought systems are socially constructed and result from actors' interaction with their environment. A person's unique and personal definition of a situation "guides the selection of stimuli to which one responds and cues expectations and obligations for specific role perform-ances and identity negotiations" (Siporin, 1972, p. 96).

The cognitive-behavioral approach is a theory of regulation. Ellis and Glasser are primarily concerned with helping individuals adjust to and nego-tiate their situations rather than change them radically. This approach is not incompatible, however, with a more radical perspective. Its potential to be radicalized lies with its subjective, rather than objective, side. A practitioner can utilize much of the Radical Humanist perspective when employing this framework.

Behavior Modification

Behavior modification is based on social learning theory. It assumes that behavior is learned, that it is environmentally determined, and that specific reinforcement strategies can be effective in changing it. Behavior is defined as observable actions of persons (or systems) that can be measured in empiri-cal terms. A distinction is made between responsive and operant behavior. *Operant behavior* is construed as voluntary and is controlled by its consequences in the environment whereas *responsive behavior* is involuntary and is controlled by eliciting stimuli that antedate the responses (Stuart, 1971, 1979; Wolpe, 1973).

In intervention situations, social workers as interveners direct and con-trol *schedules of reinforcement.* By not rewarding certain behaviors, therapists can interfere with the stimulus-response bond to eliminate undesired be-havior. Positive reinforcement (reward) is used to strengthen desired behaviors or teach new behaviors. The techniques of behavior modification include modelling, cognitive learning (e.g., contingency contracts), emotional learn-ing (e.g., implosive therapy), and operant conditioning. Behavior modifica-tion deemphasizes the subjective aspects of personality such as traits, values, feelings, and attitudes. Personality or the inner person is conceptualized as a hierarchy of reinforced behaviors. Behavior modification's greatest strength is its success. Its insistence on observable behaviors and attention to measure-ment and controlled experimentation align it with a classical experimental, or natural science, model both ontologically and epistemologically. The burgeoning acceptance and popularity of behavior modification as a social casework method is partly a response to criticisms of the ineffectiveness of social work and partly due to behavior modification's association with the classical experimental method.

Behavior modification falls into the Functionalist Paradigm. It is highly objectivist in orientation: Human behavior is considered to be a product of environmental forces (Burrell and Morgan, 1979). It is highly positivist in regards to the nature of social reality and how one learns about social reality. It is realist in assuming that the social environment has real existence and is the primary determinant of individual behavior. On the regulation/radical social change issue, behavior modification is regulatory in nature. It takes society as it finds it and aims at assisting individuals (or other systems) to accommodate it. B. F. Skinner, the founder of behavior modification, articulated a utopian society in Walden Two (1948) where learning theory principles would reign. Most operant theorists and researchers do not, however, concern themselves with the form that society should ideally take.

Family Treatment Approaches

The models of family treatment used by social workers view the family as a unit rather than a collection of individuals (Briar and Miller, 1971; J. Stein, 1969). Four models in wide use by social workers are discussed: Conjoint Family Therapy (Satir, 1967), Problem-Solving Therapy (Haley, 1976), Family Systems Therapy (Bowen, 1978), and Structural Family Therapy (Minuchin, 1974).

Conjoint Family Therapy

Virginia Satir (1967) views family problems as a consequence of dysfunctional communications. A discrepancy exists between the ostensible message and its metacommunication, or unspoken latent message. Dysfunctional communications are traced to immaturity, generally of the marital couple. Immature persons possess undifferentiated selves, are unclear and uncertain about themselves, and are unable to communicate well. The goal of treatment is to correct dysfunctional communication patterns.

Practitioners using this model are viewed as systems communication therapists (Okun and Rappaport, 1980). Treatment begins with identification of dysfunctional communication patterns. Family members are encouraged and taught to communicate congruently, to unify literal and metacommunications. Family members are taught to appreciate their individuality and uniqueness, to recognize differences as positive, and to differentiate among one another, allowing each member his or her emotional space. The practitioner attends to the affective and subjective experiences of each family member. Autonomy is stressed as family members are encouraged to be candid and self-determining and to take responsibility for their life choices.

Problem-Solving Therapy

Control and power are the central issues and dynamics of Jay Haley's (1976) approach. Relationships in a family are viewed as a power struggle. Family members are engaged in a continual battle for control to define and redefine their relationships. A pattern of governing emerges on two levels. At one

level members attempt to maintain others within certain expected ranges of behavior while on another level they attempt to act as "megagovernors" who establish the rules and limits of the family unit (Okun and Rappaport, 1980). The goal of therapy is to change individual members' behavior (including communications) and, in so doing, to change the governing pattern.

The practitioner assumes the role of *megagovernor*, a directive, powerful, but benevolent implementor of change. This person sets the limits and rules of therapy. The major technique is the giving of directives that are direct and paradoxical. *Direct instructions* are those the counselor wants the member(s) to follow. *Paradoxical instructions* are those the counselor does not want family members to follow but rather expects they will rebel against and in doing so change their behavior. The aim of directives is twofold: to change the sequence of commands and responses that maintain the problem, and to change the hierarchical or megagoverning structure by clarifying the authority and responsibility structure within the family.

Family Systems Therapy

The central issue for Murray Bowen (1978) is that family members are able to differentiate themselves and their interests from the emotional mass of the family. The process of differentiation requires that individuals can distinguish and separate their emotional and intellectual selves. Families in trouble are those whose members are unable to make differentiations and who become ensnarled (fused) into the family emotional relationship system, resulting in an undifferentiated family ego mass.

Triangles are an important concept in Bowen's scheme (Okun and Rappaport, 1980). Triangles occur when tension reaches unmanageable levels in a family subsystem. The subsystem then reaches out to include another member(s) in an effort to defuse the tension. Children are vulnerable to triangulation because they are the least able to differentiate between their emotional and intellectual selves. In troubled families, most members are included in a series of extended and interlocking triangles. The process can extend beyond the immediate family to include extended family, neighbors, public officials, and social-service personnel.

The goal is to differentiate individuals from the family ego mass. Generally one triangle is selected for detriangulation. All triangles in a family are related. Changing one affects the total family. Bowen uses a rational and intellectual approach, generally working with the family member viewed as most capable of differentiating.

Structural Family Therapy

Salvador Minuchin's model of Structural Family Therapy (1974) views the family as a sociocultural system that integrates the demands of the larger society and those of the family system, which, together, shape family mem-

bers. He outlines a family development model to describe transitions in the family life cycle from origins, new coupling, new generation, adult life, decline and death (Okun and Rappaport, 1980). At each stage, family members are faced with new constraints and tasks. To perform stage-related tasks, families must change their structures. This is accomplished by boundary negotiations and modifications. For instance, the birth of a child transforms the married couple into a three-member system while also creating two new subsystems—mother–child and father–child. The relationship of the married couple must be modified to accommodate these emergent structures.

Families are confronted with stress inherent in developmental processes as well as that generated by external forces and from relations within the family. The goal of therapy is to help families rearrange and restructure the boundaries of subsystems in response to stress. Boundaries are seen as problematic when they are enmeshed (too close), disengaged (too distant), and ambiguous. The practitioner joins the family as a supportive force and guides and educates it in clarifying subsystem boundaries as well as changing the family power hierarchy.

All four family treatment models are regulation-oriented. For the most part they address only intrafamily dynamics to the "exclusion of the interaction between the nuclear family and its environment" (Briar and Miller, 1971, p. 192). Families are expected to adjust to society, and thus efforts to change social structure significantly are not part of these approaches. The models are intended to change a family's internal structure; but the goal is to assist families to accommodate the societal status quo.

Groupwork Practice

Remedial Groupwork Model

A remedial groupwork model as developed by Robert Vinter (1967) and his associates (Glasser, Sarri and Vinter, 1974; Sundel, Glasser, Sarri, and Vinter, 1985) is a method for treating individuals through group processes. The group is employed as an instrument and context for inducing individual change. The group is conceived as a social entity consisting of a structure of differentiated and integrated statuses, roles, relationships, and norms. Two levels of phenomena are identified: individual characteristics and interactions, and group properties. Group leaders must attend to both levels. They should use *indirect measures* to influence group structure, process, and development, and use *direct measures* to influence individual characteristics and interactions. The model is sociobehavioral in orientation but is flexible enough to accommodate a variety of clinical procedures and techniques.

The remedial groupwork model falls into the Functionalist Paradigm. A realist orientation is reflected in the view that behavior and interactions are the consequences of the interplay of social structural and psychobiological

factors. Its advocates are positivists and advocate behavioral control, specificity, and precise measurement in their research. It employs an organismic analogy and assumes that individuals and groups naturally tend toward cooperation, cohesion, and consensus rather than conflict, division, and dissent. On the regulation/radical social change continuum, remedial social work is regulation-oriented in nature. When attention is directed to the environment, interventions are limited to the immediate environment with the aim of helping individuals adjust. There is no concern about significantly reordering or changing society.

Reciprocal Groupwork Model

A reciprocal model of social groupwork is associated with William Schwartz (1961) who envisioned the group as a mutual aid system intended to serve the individual and society (Pappell and Rothman, 1966). Schwartz assumed a symbiotic interdependence between individuals and society. Relationships within groups and between groups, organizations, and institutions are intended to promote interactions that foster mutual benefit and survival. The practitioner is viewed as a *mediator* skilled in communication techniques that facilitate interaction (Shulman, 1968, 1984).

The reciprocal model of groupwork falls in the Functionalist Paradigm. Its objectivist perspective is exemplified in its assumption of a preexisting social reality within which social interaction transpires. These social structures are the targets of practitioner interventions.

A regulation orientation is implicit in the assumption that relations between individuals and society are symbiotic. This implies an underlying consensus, a similarity of values and interests. The environment may be the target of interventions although differences can be worked out through communication. The needs and interests of all can be satisfied. Interventions are aimed at finding or restoring harmony that is inherent in the total social system.

Community Practice

Social Planning Model of Community Practice

A social planning model of community practice "presupposes that change in a complex industrial environment requires expert planners who, through the exercise of technical abilities, including the ability to manipulate large bureaucratic organizations, can skillfully guide complex change processes" (Rothman and Tropman, 1987, p. 6). Social planning is a strategy that community experts and organizational technicians use to gather and analyze facts, design and implement programs, and attempt to solve social problems. The community, in this model, is viewed as a social system, a complex network of formal and informal groups and structures linked to one another and

to other structures external to the community. The community is viewed as a dynamic *interactional field*, neither static nor fixed but crowded and turbulent (R. Warren, 1970, p. 150). The community planner's task is to get community decision organizations (CDOs) to find a fit between community resources and needs that "satisfice" (not maximize) the interests of all parties involved. Most forms of community practice entail aspects of social planning. This model constitutes major portions of most community organization texts (cf. Brager, Specht, and Torczyner, 1987; Perlman and Gurin, 1972; Ross, 1967; Grosser, 1973; Kettner, Daley, and Nichols, 1985).

A social planning model falls in the Functionalist Paradigm. Its focus on the substantive problems of communities (e.g., transportation, housing, physical/mental health, delinquency, employment, education, drug abuse) and the involvement of formal organizations that deal with these problems reflect a realist conception of social affairs. The planning process is regulation-oriented rather than radical social change-oriented. The concept of "satisficing," the essence of the approach, is equilibrium-oriented. Conflict strategies may be employed but only within prescribed limits (Rothman and Tropman, 1987, p. 12). Maintaining order and stability and minimizing threats to the status quo are its goals.

Social Action Model of Social Change

A social action model of social change is intended to bring about structural change in social institutions primarily in the form of altered power relationships and reallocated economic and social resources. The historical roots of the social action model are found in the social reform heritage of social work. The approach is associated with the work of Saul Alinsky (1946) and is the theoretical and philosophical base of the radical social work perspective (Galper, 1980; Rose, 1972; Piven and Cloward, 1972; Bailey and Brake, 1975). The model envisions a disadvantaged segment of the population as victims of injustice, inequity, and exploitation. Disadvantaged groups and those sympathetic to their cause are organized into constituencies that exert power to extract concessions from dominant societal groups. Societal resources (economic, social, political) are viewed as scarce, thus the interests of those in power and those not in power are in conflict and are irreconcilable. Justification for conflict stimulation derives from appeals to higher moral principles rather than formalized legal codes. The community organizer manipulates mass organizations and political processes and assumes the role of activist, advocate, agitator, broker, and negotiator. In these roles, the organizer is a partner to the disadvantaged in the struggle against oppression.

The social action model falls in the Radical Structuralist Paradigm. Social activists are realists. They believe that economic, political, and social class stratification creates structures and institutions that allow some segments of the population to prosper and others to suffer. Although they share

an objectivist orientation with most other theories-in-use, they part company with the latter, however, over purpose. A social action model opposes the status quo. It advocates the overthrow of current institutional arrangements. A social activist does not envision harmonious solutions to social problems; the interests of the oppressors and oppressed are irreconcilable. Conflict and discord will mark the emergence of a new social order that in turn will have opposing, contesting elements and will be characterized by struggle and conflict. According to this view, dissent and change are ubiquitous. Integration, consensus, and stability are fleeting and problematic.

THE UTILITY OF OPEN SYSTEMS THEORY FOR SOCIAL WORK

The foregoing review of social work theories-in-use reveals that the majority fall into the Functionalist Paradigm (see Fig. 4.1). Exceptions to this are the social action model that falls in the Radical Structuralist Paradigm and the phenomenological–existential approaches that are in the Interpretive Paradigm. For the most part, social work's theoretical base reflects a realist orientation and an accommodative stance relative to the status quo. This may account for the affinity between social work and Open Systems Theory, which shares many philosophical assumptions with the majority of social work theories-in-use.

In addition to its philosophical compatibility, Open Systems Theory is useful to social work for three reasons: (1) It helps social workers perceive and understand the social environment (Aptekar, 1955; Smalley, 1967; Anderson and Carter, 1978; I. Stein, 1974; Polsky, 1969); (2) it can be used to identify practice principles that apply across different contexts (C. Meyer, 1973; Pincus and Minahan, 1973; Nelsen, 1972; Lathrope, 1969; Janchill, 1969; I. Stein, 1974; Siporin, 1975); and (3) it can help integrate social work theories and unify the profession.

Enhance Perception and Understanding of the Social Environment

A primary goal of this text is to promote perception and understanding of the social environment. Open Systems Theory can be used to conceptualize and simplify complex social systems and system–environment relations. It points to ways that systems change, the levers for initiating change, and the interplay between change and stability. The social environment is composed of many varied social systems. Open Systems Theory aids in understanding their commonalities and distinctiveness.

Identify Practice Principles That Apply to Different Contexts

Ever since the Milford Conference of 1929, social workers have attempted to identify practice principles that apply generically. Von Bertalanffy (1968), the founder of General System Theory upon which Open Systems Theory is based, developed *general* theory to account for the behavior of all "living systems" (J. Miller, 1965). Open Systems Theory identifies general principles for social workers to apply to social systems of different types. Open Systems Theory promotes a *general conception of social work practice* in several ways.

When complex social problems and situations arise, OST helps a practitioner to see and identify the appropriate client or change-target system and to differentiate a system from its environment. It can be used to sort out what is happening or needs to be changed to improve the situation.

Open Systems Theory encourages a focus on interdependence rather than independence. It directs attention to linkages among elements of a system and between systems and their environment, thereby preventing inappropriate intervention.

Open Systems Theory principles suggest that behavior change (normally) precedes attitude change. To change behavior(s), one alters the interactional sequences or structure of a system. This principle is well understood, and frequently applied, by family systems therapists (e.g., Haley, 1976) and in America's best-run corporations (Peters and Waterman, 1982).

Open Systems Theory helps practitioners identify appropriate practice modalities. In clarifying problems, system–environment relations, and behaviors or linkages that must be changed for improvement, OST helps practitioners identify fruitful intervention strategies.

Open Systems Theory is both action- and output-oriented. Results are viewed as consequences of behavior, not as isolated or mysterious events. Moreover, OST focuses on behavior, action, and process as clues to system purpose and understanding.

Open Systems Theory is positive in outlook. Appreciation of the link between action and consequences indicates that change is possible. Because social systems (and individuals) can change, there is reason for hope rather than despair.

Integrate Social Work Theory and Unify the Social Work Profession

Social work's need for theory integration is long-standing. Given the many arenas in which social workers practice (see Chapter 1), social work is necessarily eclectic. Mary Richmond's call in 1917 to focus on the *person-in-situation* culminated in a dual concern with individuals/families and the social environment in which they live. Social work theory consists of many conceptual frameworks that apply to a variety of individual and collective phenomena. Social work's diversity makes improbable the development of a single *grand theory* (Briar and Miller, 1971, p. 20).

Open Systems Theory, as a general theory, can facilitate integration of social work theories in two ways. First, the individual practitioner can use OST to *organize* other theories which he or she employs. Theories about phenomena on different levels of social organization such as individuals, families, and communites can be seen as complementary rather than competitive. Figure 2.1 in Chapter 2 illustrates that systems on one level are component parts (or elements) of systems on more inclusive levels. *General principles that hold across all types (and levels) of systems facilitate integration of theories specific to particular types (or levels).* Open Systems Theory highlights the complementarity, rather than competitiveness, of many conceptual frameworks.

Second, Open Systems Theory can unify social work by fostering communication among specialists. The hierarchical organization of social life (see Chapter 2) and the interdependence of individuals and systems highlight the value of a perspective that helps specialists communicate with each other. Similar to society, social work is factionalized. There is no consensus on goals, domains, practice, methodologies, fields of practice, and so on (O'Connor and Waring, 1981). Social work faculty are divided into opposing camps, such as clinical/social treatment versus planning/administration. Factionalism shows in the popularity of specialized journals such as *Clinical Social Work, Social Work with Groups*, and *Administration in Social Work*. Individuals are oriented to different aspects of reality and believe their own to be the more useful or valid view.

Social work operates in more social problem arenas than most other professions. This is both a strength and a weakness. Through contact with many clients and professionals of all types, social work's diversity is a strength. Social workers are in practically every type of human service organization and, increasingly, can be found in for-profit corporations as well. Diversity is also a weakness, however, because it scatters the troops, engenders conflict over goals (aims, methods), complicates efforts to communicate and cooperate within the profession, and prevents a united front to the outside world. Open Systems Theory cannot arrest the centrifugal forces that appear to drive social work into ever-broader domains, but it can provide a framework for communication. By stressing the complementarity of rival theories, if facilitates exchange among professionals with different practice and theoretical orientations.

CONCLUSIONS

The world we live in is complex, and social workers are forced to rely on many different theories to deal with this complexity. Chapter 4 has demonstrated that most social work theories-in-use are compatible with an OST perspective. Open Systems Theory adds to these theories, however, by focusing on process and change and by providing a framework for their integration.

We turn now to Part Two of the book, which presents applications of Open Systems Theory.

PART TWO

Open Systems Theory– Applications

Chapter 5

The Professional–Client Dyad:
A Two-Party System

INTRODUCTION

Dyads are relationships with two parties. Many examples come to mind: mother–child (or father–child), friend–friend, husband–wife, teacher–student, doctor–patient, priest/pastor–parishioner, coach–player, social worker–client, and so forth. An understanding of dyads is important for social workers because of their pervasiveness and because the professional–client relationship is itself dyadic. Chapter 5 presents a framework for understanding dyadic relations. The professional–client relationship is explicated, with special attention to its power and authority aspects (Schon, 1983). Peer dyadic relations that do not entail power differences—such as friendships, neighbor relations, sibling relations, and so on—are also discussed.

In regards to the professional–client relationship, Chapter 5 has three goals: (1) to present a framework for understanding the power and authority aspects of professional–client relations as a special case of dyadic relations; (2) to enhance understanding of the dynamics that characterize professional–client relations in relation to the structure in which they are initiated and played out; and (3) to increase awareness of the potential for harm as well as good that is inherent in professional–client relations. A major goal of explication is to diminish the negative consequences of asymmetric power inherent in professional–client relations and to foster a more active and determinative role for clients in these relations (Freidson, 1986; Gummer, 1983). Chapter 5 concludes with suggestions directed to this end, including a list of strategies for social welfare organizations, service workers, and clients to reduce the undesirable consequences of power in professional–client relations.

HISTORICAL REVIEW OF THE
PROFESSIONAL–CLIENT RELATIONSHIP

A historical review of professional–client relations in social work provides a
context for understanding their current form. Originally, a caseworker was
viewed as an *active agent* who assisted clients to change (Richmond, 1922).
With the ascendance of Freudian psychology's influence on social work, the
concept of the professional's role shifted to one of neutrality, objectivity, and
passivity. More recently, as exemplified in the work of Gummer (1978, 1983),
the professional has come to be viewed as *society's agent* and as a potent, determinative force in the lives of clients and in the definition of social problems
(Schon, 1983). In recent depictions, the professional–client relationship is
viewed as *a power relation* in which the role and impact of the social worker is
pervasive. The power aspects of such relations are mostly unseen by clients
and often denied by social workers; thus the need to view them critically,
with an eye to identifying steps for minimizing their unintended and poten-
tially destructive consequences, is great.

The *casework method* was described in Mary Richmond's classic work
Social Diagnosis (1917). Richmond outlined procedures for the orderly
gathering of social and personal information pertinent to a client and case
and claimed that the entire therapeutic rationale of the casework method
stemmed from the *relationship between the helper and the helped* (Briar and Miller,
1971, p. 120). Richmond failed to explicate the dynamics of the relationship
or the techniques necessary to effect it, however. This gap in her prescription
left social work receptive to the impact of Freudian psychology in the 1920s.
Social workers turned to psychoanalysis for explanations of why people have
problems and for techniques to resolve them.

The psychoanalytic influence shifted the focus of the casework relationship from an outer- to an inner-person perspective (Lubove, 1972). Thus,
attention was directed away from concrete actions for resolving clients' problems to concern with the individual's internal state. The caseworker and
client came to be viewed as "allies against the enemy within" (Briar and
Miller, 1971, p. 13). The aim of the caseworker was to assist clients to overcome resistance to change. From this Freudian influence, the caseworker was
viewed as a passive agent who enabled and stimulated clients but eschewed
opportunities to influence them directly. The ideology of this conception
claimed that the relationship existed, and functioned, solely for the client's
benefit. A high degree of self-awareness enabled the caseworker to maintain
objectivity in helping the client. (To attain greater self-awareness, many
social workers underwent therapy themselves, a tradition still followed by
some.) By a conscious use of self, the caseworker remained objective and
neutral for the benefit of the client.

The assumptions of passivity and neutrality on the caseworker's part focused attention on client qualities. Little research was done on the impact of the caseworker on client success or failure. It was not until the 1950s that assumptions regarding caseworkers' passivity, neutrality, and objectivity were challenged. Research began to focus on caseworker characteristics and behaviors as influential variables in the treatment process, and some documented their impact on client outcomes (e.g., Palmer, 1965; M. Warren, 1965). The assumption that caseworker variables could be treated as unobtrusive constraints in the intervention process was effectively challenged (O'Connor, 1979).

Even more significant was the research that questioned the traditional views of caseworkers as passive responders to people with problems. Helpers are human too and, like others, are influenced by their backgrounds and socialization and by people with whom they interact and the social contexts in which they function. To assume they can be totally nonjudgmental or neutral belies most evidence on human behavior (London, 1964). Neither helpers nor helping programs can be viewed realistically as passive and neutral. Thus, the concept of caseworker changed from neutral/passive to instrumental/active agent who affects both individual clients and the identification of social problems.

Helpers (social workers, physicians, rehabilitation counselors) partially *define the nature of social problems and deviance* (Freidson, 1965, 1970, 1986). After defining them, they identify who fits or fails to fit their definitions. Helpers determine the standards and procedures by which deviants (or people with problems) are recognized. Additionally, they make contact with the identified persons, and through voluntary or involuntary means, they assure that services are matched with people. Finally, helpers specify the course of treatment that persons receive, and they identify the responses to treatment that are expected. In this sense, helping agents—and the organizations that employ them—are anything but passive, neutral, and reactive. They are proactive participants in the processes of identifying, creating, and maintaining social deviance and social problems.

To avoid a reductionistic tendency to attribute ulterior motives to helping agents, the social context in which helping agents operate must be understood. One aim of Chapter 5 is to describe and explain these contexts. Before doing this, however, we review the Open Systems Theory concepts and themes that are employed for this purpose.

OPEN SYSTEMS CONCEPTS AND THEMES

A number of Open Systems Theory concepts and themes facilitate the analysis of professional–client relations. These include: (1) the relationship between structure and process, (2) power and authority, (3) control, domination, and exploitation, (4) inputs, (5) resources, (6) social exchange, and (7) conflicting interests. The following discussion provides a background for the review of professional–client relations that follows.

Structure and Process

The dynamic relationship between social structure and social process is basic to Open Systems Theory (Burrell and Morgan, 1979). It goes as follows. People interact with each other: They talk to each other, write letters to and telephone one another; hold hands, caress, take care of, go for walks, meet for lunch, work together, physically constrain and hit each other, and so forth. The enactment of these exchanges is *social process*. The defining quality of social process is action, activity, or doing that involves two or more people. As people engage in interpersonal interaction over time and when these interactions assume patterns that are repetitive, predictable, and reproducible, these recurrent interaction patterns are called *social structure*. Social structure is a recurrent pattern of social interaction (or process).

Not all social processes result in social structure, and social structure, once established, is somewhat independent of social process. Over time, however, *the two are dynamically and mutually and causally related*. Each is both product and cause of the other (Berger and Luckmann, 1966). People who interact in a more or less patterned way *create* social structure. When structure is created, it affects subsequent interactions. Concern with the manner in which process leads to structure is reflected in the Open Systems Theory (OST) concept of emergent properties. Concern with the manner in which structure shapes process is reflected in the OST concept of hierarchical constraints. (See Chapter 2.)

Relations between social work professionals and their clients are structured by societal beliefs about the authority of experts over the lay public (Freidson, 1986). Before a particular client sees a particular social worker, aspects of their relationship are *predetermined* by societal beliefs and practices about normatively appropriate professional–client relations. Credentialled professionals increasingly dominate the lives of Americans who turn to them for every kind of problem from impotence to loss of hair to divorce mediation (Bellah and others, 1985). Chapter 5 explains how the prearrangement of professional–client relations gives advantages to professionals.

Power and Authority

In most social systems, some component parts—subsystems, coalitions, individuals, etc.—direct or influence other parts regarding what they can (or must) and cannot do. When one part is able to tell another what to do and make it stick, this shows it *has power* over the instructed part. When the instructed part views the instruction as legitimate, this is authority. *Authority*

is power that is viewed by the affected parties, and by society, as legitimate. Many dyadic relations are authority relations, and the professional–client relationship in which most social workers practice is of this type.

Control, Domination, and Exploitation

Questions of control deal with the distribution and exercise of power. Who is in charge? Who makes decisions for whom? In a highly integrated (or closely linked) system, control may be concentrated in the hands of a few. In factional systems (those that are loosely linked with few or weak ties between elements), control is necessarily lodged in different sectors that often compete for control of other sectors or the whole.

People, or subsystems, without power may be dominated by those who have it. People with power may behave benevolently toward those without it, but their ability to decide for them, or instruct them, nevertheless allows for domination. *Exploitation* refers to the use of power by controllers (Clegg and Dunkerley, 1979) to extract benefit from those over whom they hold power and to retain these benefits for themselves. Serfs in the Middle Ages who tilled the farms of feudal lords were exploited because profits from their labor were taken by the lord for himself. Some contend that today's poor are exploited as a reserve army of labor for a changing capitalist labor market that sometimes needs more workers and sometimes needs fewer (Piven and Cloward, 1972, 1982; Galper, 1980).

Professionals are in control of the professional–client relationship. Consequently, they are dominant, often making decisions for clients. Such decisions, though well-intentioned, can be exploitative. The Medicaid recipient sent to a hospital for unnecessary tests may be exploited by the physician, although no harm is intended. Rationalizations such as, "Nothing serious is wrong, but the patient will feel better if she has the tests," may be offered in defense of actions that, in effect, exploit both patient and society (through raising entitlement program costs that are passed on to the public through higher taxes). Although professional associations and welfare organizations try to prevent such occurrences through formal codes of ethics, rules, and procedures, the potential for exploitation stems from the unequal power of professional and client.

Inputs

Inputs are defined in Open Systems Theory as that which is brought into a system for processing and transformation to produce an output for exchange with the environment. Many factors are inputs to the professional–client relationship, including characteristics of: (1) the professional and client, (2) the professional's position and employing organization, and (3) the broader

society's, professional accrediting bodies', and employing organization's ideological assumptions about service provision. In our model of professional–client relations, inputs are the resources that professional and client bring to the relationship.

Resources

Resources are qualities that individuals bring with them to social-exchange relationships. Depending on many factors, participants' resources may or may not become inputs to the relationship. Resources include both personal qualities (such as health status, age, gender, race, etc.) and impersonal materials (such as money, wealth, social position) that people have control over, access to, or possession of. Two categories include: (1) *personal resources* that involve characteristics assigned by society (ascribed characteristics) or earned by individuals (achieved characteristics); and (2) *positional resources* that accompany occupancy of an organizational or professional position. *Ascribed personal resources* include race, ethnicity, age, and gender. It is advantageous in American society to be white, Protestant, Anglo-Saxon, and male. As a group, persons with these attributes enjoy advantages that others lack (Meeker and Weitzel-O'Neill, 1977; Webster and Driskell, 1978; Wagner, Ford, and Ford, 1986). With the exception of religion, these qualities are ascribed at birth and cannot be changed. *Achieved personal resources* include formal education, knowledge, and skills (e.g., to speak a foreign language or operate a computer) that are acquired through actions of the individual.

Positional resources are a result of occupancy of an office or position in a formal work organization, professional association, labor union, and so forth. Like achieved personal resources, positional resources may be *earned* by the person but this is not necessary. The boss's son who becomes company vice-president without appropriate education or experience can enjoy the resources (prestige, income, authority) associated with the position even if he knows little about the job.

Resource differentials are important for understanding the professional–client relationship. Because of education, professional training, and organizational position, helping professionals enjoy more resources than most clients whom they serve, especially if the clients lack education or training, employment, good health, and so forth. Conceptualization of gender and ethnicity/race as resources in interpersonal relations is useful for understanding the dynamics of dyadic social exchange (Martin, 1985).

Social Exchange

The concept of *exchange* is fundamental to Open Systems Theory because of the assumption that open systems are in constant interaction with other systems and with their environment. Exchange refers to boundary-crossing

activities in which give-and-take occurs between two (or more) systems. From a pragmatic perspective, exchange is the process of trading outputs for inputs from the environment or from other systems. Although the concept of exchange applies to all living systems, the type focused on in Chapter 5 is social exchange. Blau's (1964) conception of social exchange as "voluntary actions of individuals" is used to conceptualize power and peer relations.

Conflicting Interests

Conflicting interests are situations in which the objective interests (e.g., material wealth, health status) and/or subjective interests (e.g., sense of well-being, satisfaction, self-esteem) of a person or category of persons (e.g., professionals vs. clients) are inconsistent or contradictory. Objective interests reflect material well-being such as earnings, wealth, tax rates or benefits, health status, and so forth. Subjective interests concern reality as it is personally experienced. Clients who are objectively (materially) well-off may feel subjectively unhappy or dissatisfied. Social workers have conflicting objective and subjective interests. They make modest salaries and hold moderately prestigious positions but are claimed to perceive as a benefit of their work the subjective satisfactions of working with people, helping people, and so forth (Anderson and Martin, 1982).

The concept of conflicting interests is useful for examining the extent to which the goals and aims of professionals are congruent with those of clients. Professionals prefer 9 to 5 office hours whereas clients prefer weekends and evenings. Worker and client benefit if their relationship leads to objective and subjective gains for clients and for workers. The potential for conflict in an asymmetric power/authority relationship is addressed below.

A MODEL OF DYADIC RELATIONS

This section presents a model of dyadic relationships. It begins by defining dyad, power relations, and peer relations. This is followed by a discussion of power and authority and a consideration of power in bureaucracies (see Chapter 8). An exchange model of social behavior is developed with emphasis on implications for professional–client relations. It is followed by Rosenthal's (1974) model of traditional versus participatory professional–client relations. The final segment concerns peer relations.

Definitions

The dyadic (or two-party) relation is the simplest and most fundamental form of social relationship and is pervasive (Blau, 1964). Monogamous marriage and the modal type of professional–client relationship are dyadic. As

shown in Table 5.1, two categories of dyadic relations can be identified based on: (1) the quantity of resources possessed by each party in the relationship, and (2) the motivation of the two parties for entering the relationship. *Peer relations* result if the parties to the relationship have *symmetric (equal or nearly equal) resources* relevant to the relationship, and *power relations* result if the parties have *asymmetric (unequal) resources* relevant to the relationship.

Peer and power relationships can be differentiated as those entered into largely for their intrinsic pleasure versus those entered into for extrinsic ends or goals. *Intrinsic relations* are entered into *for their own sake*, with no particular instrumental result expected; for example, because a person is fun to be with, has similar interests, or makes one feel good. *Extrinsic relations* are entered into for realization of an instrumental result; for example, to complete a tax form, fill a tooth cavity, or learn a language. Table 5.1 shows that peer relations with intrinsically motivated members include best friendships and true-love relationships. Peer relations between parties with extrinsic motivation include the example of a physician choosing as his or her lawyer a person with resources similar to oneself.

Power relations based on intrinsic motivation include relations between parents and children and, to a lesser degree, husbands and wives (Laws, 1979; Thorne, 1982). In parent–child relations, resources are asymmetrical— parents are older, bigger, more educated, and experienced—and the relationship is entered into as an end in itself. The legitimate power of parent over child is called *parental authority*. Although the husband–wife relation is also entered into for its own sake, an asymmetry of resources stems from a societal preference for males over females, thus giving males an advantage. Social problems such as wife-beating and rape are aspects of patriarchal authority that sanctions men's dominance over women (Dobash and Dobash, 1979).

Power relations based on extrinsic motivation include most professional–

TABLE 5.1. PEER AND POWER DYADIC RELATIONSHIPS BASED ON QUANTITY OF RESOURCES AND MOTIVATION FOR ENTERING THE RELATIONSHIP

Motivation for entering the relationship	Quantity of Resources	
	Symmetric	*Asymmetric*
Intrinsic (end in itself)	Peer relations—e.g., "true love," best friends	Power relations—e.g., parent–child relation in families
Extrinsic (as means to an end)	Peer relations—e.g., physician chooses best friend as his/her personal lawyer	Power relations—e.g., typical relationship between social worker and client

Source: Adapted from Blau (1964).

client relations. Encounters with physician, lawyer, accountant, investment counselor, home decorator, or therapist are extrinsic power relations for most clients. The social worker–client relation, where education, professional association, and employer provide workers with resource advantages, is a power relationship entered into for extrinsic reasons such as the need for income, health care, rent subsidies, or family counseling.

Power and Authority in Professional–Client Relations

Power is the ability of Person A (or System A) to make Person B (or System B) follow A's wishes even against B's will (Weber, 1947; Martin, 1981). People with power have the ability to make others do their bidding. Dominant ideology in American society, in the social sciences, and in the profession of social work claims that people do what they do because they want to, not because they have to (Perlmutter and Alexander, 1978; Mayhew, 1980). Yet coercion and constraint are everywhere in social life as studies of work (Edwards, 1979) and family (Rapp, 1978; Vandepol, 1982) show.

When power is viewed as legitimate or appropriate, it is called *authority*; thus, authority is power of a particular type. Examples of legitimate power include parent over child, teacher over student, physician over patient, social worker over client. Social worker–client relations are legitimate power relations or, more palatably, authority relations with the social worker in the advantaged position.

The Sources of Professional Authority

From whence does professional authority spring? Legitimation for the authority of professional service providers comes from three sources: (1) the professional *self* or the education, knowledge, and credentials a professional has; (2) the professional association and its body of knowledge, expertise, and status; and (3) the organization that employs the service provider (e.g., hospital, welfare agency, runaway shelter). Freidson (1970) contends that authority is grounded primarily in the last two, the profession and the organization. Individual professionals have authority by virtue of being certified as members in good standing of a profession or employees of an organization (Epstein and Conrad, 1978). If a person loses his or her license or is fired from an organizational position, that person no longer has authority to see clients. Regardless of objective skills, the practitioner is forbidden to practice. Likewise a person who never had training but is licensed or employed (for example, a physician who fakes a diploma for an M.D. degree) can provide services, even though such services may be inappropriate or low in quality.

Gaining legitimation varies from one profession to another, but it generally includes obtaining the proper credentials, usually in the form of higher-

education degrees. In some professions, postdegree examinations are required; for example, the CPA and bar exams for accountants and lawyers. In social work, a post-Master of Social Work examination is given by the National Association of Social Work, the Academy of Certified Social Work (ACSW) exam, but the decision to take it is optional, and the ability to obtain social work jobs does not depend upon passing it.

Social workers' legitimacy rests on their education, licensure, and employment credentials but particularly on their employing organization. Because their legitimacy stems from social welfare organizations, social workers need to be knowledgeable of organizational structure and dynamics (see Chapter 8). Relations between social worker and client are *structured by the organization prior to the arrival of worker or client.* The patterned, taken-for-granted ways of providing services to clients and of defining, viewing, and treating clients predate worker and client. This example of the concept of structure, defined earlier, illustrates how social contexts orchestrate or prearrange the interaction exchanges of individuals.

Values and Goals: Profession vs. Organization

The professional socialization process involves identification and endorsement of a set of values and goals. Among physicians, there is a commitment to the sustaining of life and alleviation of pain; among lawyers, an obligation to assure the client of fair and impartial representation; among social workers, a commitment to help people as quickly and appropriately as possible. Though the content of professional values and goals varies from profession to profession, each has them.

When a service provider delivers services in a free-standing or associational context, efforts to act in accord with one's values or goals may go unchallenged. Moreover, when the practitioner is self-employed, he or she can make decisions that reflect personal or professional values, goals, and best judgment. If service is provided in an organizational context, however, rules may prevent the service provider from recommending or providing services for clients in line with his or her personal values. In this case, conflict can arise.

Daniels (1969) describes conflicts in the practice of psychiatry in the military, the latter being the classic model of bureaucracy. Psychiatrists are sometimes ordered by superiors to make particular diagnoses or prescribe certain solutions. A base commander may order a psychiatrist to diagnose Joe Doe as psychotic so Joe can be medically discharged from the army. This creates a dilemma for the psychiatrist. If the psychiatrist fails to make the prescribed diagnosis, the commander may retaliate by denying a promotion or seeking a demotion or transfer for the psychiatrist. If the psychiatrist goes along with the commander, professional ethics may be violated. Whether or not the psychiatrist goes along, that person may experience stress. Engaging

in unethical practices can destroy a professional reputation and self-respect, but fighting the hierarchy of authority will take its toll as well.

Daniels asks: Who in the example is the client? the soldier or the military? In bureaucratic organizations with a strict hierarchy of authority, persons near the top have authority, and when they issue directives, they expect subordinates to obey. Professionals are obliged by their profession's code of ethics to base recommendations on professional judgment, not organizational authority. The military superior may explain to the psychiatrist that the decision is needed for the good of the organization. The superior may feel that some decisions in the clients' presumed best interests are against the organization's best interests. When the superior's wishes prevail over the psychiatrist's professional judgment, the organization rather than the soldier becomes the client (Daniels, 1969).

Conflicts between the interests of organization and client are pervasive (Martin, 1980a, 1980b). The complicated process that welfare clients endure to apply for benefits is a case in point (Awad, 1978). If clients' best interests were the primary concern, the process would be simple and quick. Welfare agencies are under pressure to reduce the welfare rolls and to guarantee that "undeserving welfare cheaters" do not slip through the maze. Organizational interests may receive priority over those of clients, and the application process—concerned with weeding out and preventing fraud—is made complex, arduous, and demeaning. Many eligible citizens forego applying for welfare benefits to avoid the application process.

CONTROL OF THE SERVICE-DELIVERY SETTING AND PROCESS

One source of conflict between clients and service providers is the control or staging of service delivery. Services are provided at the convenience of professionals rather than clients.

> Highly placed individuals, by virtue of their greater wealth and power, are able to control or stage their encounters with subordinates in such ways as to impress them. For example, they may display their wealth in their personal appearance and in the very settings in which encounters take place. Also, the subordinate goes to his/her superior, not the reverse. . . . The power [sic] to dictate explicitly where a meeting will be held is a convincing display of power. (Della Fave, 1980, p. 956)

Encounters between social workers and clients occur at places and times dictated by, and convenient to, social workers. Drug and alcohol abusers, as well as the mentally distressed, need services in the evenings and on weekends, yet social workers prefer a 9 to 5 schedule on weekdays. The ability to make someone wait is a display of power (B. Schwartz, 1974). Physicians are known to schedule multiple clients for each appointment time, causing some to wait. Such practices are not unheard of in social welfare organizations. Mental health centers may schedule five clients for every four appointment times on the assumption that one client will fail to show. If all show, the fifth is worked in or another counselor sees him or her. Considerations of clients' waiting time and preference for a particular counselor may be a lower priority than the use of staff time. Such strategies are administratively reasonable but reflect the primacy of the agency's interests over clients' interests.

The Dynamics of Problem Definition

Clients are disadvantaged in negotiation processes with professionals. The professional is aware, though the client is not, that a problem is being negotiated rather than factually identified (Scheff, 1968). Professionals know that problem definition is variable and problematic. Scheff describes a skillful lawyer who guides a client to state a case so that advantageous claims can be made or justified. He also describes a psychiatrist who rejects a woman's explanation of her problem until she says what the psychiatrist wanted to hear. Lack of awareness of problem-definition dynamics makes a client vulnerable and dependent on the professional in the problem-identification process (Scheff, 1968).

Formal control is Scheff's (1968) term for a professional's control over the form of the professional–client relationship. Because of the power differential, professionals decide the nature of clients' problems, recommend alternative solutions, determine, indeed, if a problem exists. Regardless of what clients say or the facts indicate, professionals have the authority to decide whether or not a problem exists. *Agenda control* is the authority to decide what is discussed, at what point topics are discussed, and the manner in which they are discussed. Clients may be unsuccessful in proposing topics they are concerned about or, if they manage to, may find the professional unreceptive. Because the control of professional–client relations is in the hands of professionals, professionals dominate in the relationship. If professionals' actions reflect self-interest (or organizational interests) rather than clients' interests, this domination can lead to exploitation.

Professional–Client Relations as Social Exchange

A social-exchange perspective clarifies the causes and consequence of power differences in professional–client relations. Blau (1964) defines social exchange as "...voluntary actions of individuals that are motivated by the returns they are expected to bring and typically do in fact bring from others" (p. 94). Four assumptions underly the social-exchange perspective.

1. *Unspecified obligations.* The obligations of social exchange, in contrast to those of economic exchange, are unspecified, remaining at an implicit rather than explicit level. Friends rarely say to each other, "You owe me now because I helped you move." Obligations associated with such favors remain at an implicit level.

2. *Trust.* Because obligations are not specified in social exchange, trust between persons who exchange with each other is required. When individuals assist or make supportive statements to one another, this obligates recipient to giver. The nature of this obligation is unspecified, however, and the manner of reciprocation (and its content) is (are) implicit. The giver must *trust* that the recipient will discharge his or her obligation. If trust is absent, people may cease interacting with each other. If they are interacting, we can infer that trust, or authority, is present (Blau, 1964).

3. *Attraction.* The third assumption, attraction, refers to motivations for interacting with others. Persons are attracted to each other for reasons varying along a continuum from intrinsic to extrinsic (Blau, 1964). Although relationships usually have elements of both, they are predominantly toward one end of the continuum. Relationships in families, friendship dyads, peer groups, churches, and neighborhoods are based primarily on intrinsic motivations whereas relations in factories, schools, hospitals, and social welfare organizations are based primarily on extrinsic motivations.

4. *Resources.* The fourth assumption is that individuals enter exchange relations with varying types and amounts of resources, and the symmetry or asymmetry of these resources influences the type of relationship that ensues. As defined earlier, resources are attributes or assets that people bring to their relationships (Rogers, 1974). Some resources stem from the position one occupies in a formal organization (see Chapter 8). An organization's chief executive officer has more resources than a line worker because of the position each occupies. The position of executive entails numerous perquisites, including honor, esteem, high salary, and assumptions on the part of others that the incumbent deserves respect and deference (Della Fave, 1980). An executive in a social welfare organization has more organizational resources than a service worker, and a service worker has more resources than most clients have. Most social welfare clients who seek assistance (and benefits) from social work professionals have few material resources. Clients with few resources, as explained below, are frequently disadvantaged in their dealings with social work professionals.

An Exchange Model of the Relationship

Table 5.2 identifies the range of power and peer relations that result from various combinations of attraction and resource quantity. On the left is attraction or the motivation for entering the relation, shown as intrinsic or extrinsic. Across the table "quantity of professional resources" and "quantity of client resources" are shown in two categories: few and many. All people, including professionals and clients, have many and varied resources, thus the actual exchange process is more complex than depicted here. Table 5.2 allows us, nevertheless, to make several points about power in professional–client relations from a social exchange perspective.

Table 5.2 shows that professionals and clients normally enter into relations with each other for extrinsic reasons (thus cells e, f, g, and h are the focus of our analysis). Most clients seek financial aid for emergency shelter or food in severely cold weather from the Red Cross or Salvation Army eligibility officer because the officer controls valued resources, not because the officer is the clients' sister or friend. This reflects the societal norm that services are provided by strangers who, because of professional and/or organizational qualifications, are granted legitimacy to provide them. Entering a relationship with extrinsic motivation does not prevent professionals and clients from developing warm, courteous relations with each other but the relationship is viewed, typically, by both parties as a means to an end more than an end in itself. Resource quantity is depicted in Table 5.2 as input to the relationship. As noted earlier, resources include material possessions such

TABLE 5.2. ATTRACTION AND RESOURCE QUANTITY AS DETERMINANTS OF THE TYPE OF EXCHANGE RELATIONSHIP EXPERIENCED BY CLIENTS VIS-À-VIS PROFESSIONAL SERVICE PROVIDERS

Primary attraction for the relationship[a]	Quantity of resources of the professional			
	Few		Many	
	Quantity of resources of the client			
	Few	Many	Few	Many
Intrinsic (as an end in itself)	(a)	(b)	(c)	(d)
Extrinsic (as a means to an end)	Peer, toward symmetrical	Power, somewhat asymmetrical	Power, very asymmetrical	Peer, toward symmetrical
	(e)	(f)	(g)	(h)

[a] Arrows indicate the likelihood that intrinsic aspects of the professional–client relation (which begins as an extrinsic relation) will develop between the parties over time.
Source: Adapted from Blau (1964).

as income or wealth and they include personal characteristics such as physical or emotional health, age, race/ethnicity, and gender. Arrows from cells e, f, g, and h to cells a, b, c, and d in Table 5.2 represent the odds that intrinsic attraction will develop between a client and a professional. Intrinsic attraction is more likely to develop in professional–client relations where both parties have approximately equal quantities of resources, that is, in peer rather than power relations. In general, resource symmetry promotes peer relations whereas resource asymmetry promotes power relations.

Cell (g): Very asymmetrical resources, power relations. When clients have few resources and professionals have many resources, the relationship between them is a very asymmetrical, power relation. Many clients in need of social welfare services have few resources. These include people who are disabled, elderly, poor, mentally ill, retarded, sick, very young, unemployed, physically handicapped, undocumented aliens, unskilled, and homeless. As shown by the short arrow (directed at cell c) in Table 5.2, the odds are slim that intrinsic attraction will develop between professional and client in such relations. Even if the client tries to establish a friendship, the professional is likely to view the client as unacceptable. The social distance between professional and client is great in this condition and the professional is obliged to protect low-resource clients from abusive uses of the power that the professional has over the client.

Cell (e): Toward symmetrical resources, peer relations. When both client and professional have few resources, power is diminished and the odds for intrinsic attraction increase. Relations of this type are found in feminist women's health centers where laypersons who are skilled in certain health-care tasks, but who lack formal credentials, provide information and services to clients (Thurston, 1987; Ruzek, 1978). Rather than treatment by experts, service delivery is viewed as empowerment or the sharing of information and skills. The aim is to help clients provide their own care and assume greater responsibility for their own well-being. Lay workers who assist clients are often similar in education and social status to the clients they serve. Peer relations such as this exist also in mental health settings when paraprofessionals conduct intake interviews and in programs for the elderly when aides conduct home visits and provide transportation services for aged citizens. Resource equality fosters the development of mutual, intrinsic attraction and diminishes the potential for abuses attributable to large status differences.

Cell (f): Somewhat asymmetrical resources, power relations. Relations in which the client has more resources than the professional are rife with contradictions. When a client has greater wealth or social status than the professional, the client may have the upper hand in the relationship. Professional qualifications and organizational position nevertheless provide some advantages to the professional. The client's status may be higher in other contexts but the professional's is higher in the relationship per se. The relationship between an upper-class child and his or her teacher provides an example. The teacher has authority over the child but the child's social-class standing reduces the potency of this authority. The child's parents may make it clear that certain things are not to be done to their child. Wealthy families who seek counseling from social workers are another example. Outside the helping relationship, the family has more resources but in the relationship, the professional has authority. In such circumstances, offsetting resources mitigate abuses of professional authority. Professionals are cognizant of the high status of their clients and this encourages them to be careful and courteous. The arrow in Table 5.2 from cell (f) to (b) shows that the odds are slim that mutual friendship will develop between professional and client in these circumstances. Low-resource professionals are unlikely to be perceived by high-resource clients as desirable friends or mates.

Cell (h): Toward symmetrical resources, peer relations. Professional–client relations in which both professional and client have many resources is shown in cell (h). In this case, professional authority is apt to take the form of advice or aid from a friend. Power aspects of the relationship, despite the professional's authority, are minimal. The odds that friendship will develop are high. Professional and client may be friends prior to the beginning of the relationship. Similar resources may lead them to meet each other in social contexts and frequent contact among status equals promotes the development of friendship and mutually respectful relations (Blau, 1977a, b).

Conclusions. Most clients of social welfare organizations have far fewer resources than service providers do, and they feel the stigma of their resource deficit. This may account for the reluctance of the poor, elderly, and infirm to visit physicians and welfare agencies. Persons with very different resources have difficulty interacting in regards to personal issues such as illnesses, dire-need situations, and emergencies (Della Fave, 1980). People with problems cannot be faulted for avoiding relationships that add inferiority feelings to their already disadvantaged financial, health, or other problematic condition.

TWO MODELS OF
PROFESSIONAL–CLIENT RELATIONS

Clients in our society are expected to trust, accept advice from, and be obedient to professionals. Professionals are viewed as experts into whose hands trusting and obedient clients place themselves, expecting that their problems will be accurately diagnosed, responded to, and alleviated (Rosenthal, 1974; Freidson, 1986). This conception rests on some dubious assumptions.

Rosenthal (1974, p. 13) identifies two models of professional–client relations, a traditional model and a participatory model, that contrast the objective interests of professionals and clients. Rosenthal argues that *the objective interests of professionals and clients are in conflict.* Professionals benefit most from clients who require little time, energy, and emotional drain, whereas clients benefit most by obtaining as much of a professional's time, energy, and emotional involvement as they can. As illustrated in Table 5.3, the Participatory Model emphasizes the divergent and conflicting interests of professionals and clients, whereas the Traditional Model emphasizes convergence and consensus.

Six questions appear in the left column of Table 5.3. In response to Question 1, "What is proper client behavior vis-à-vis professional service

TABLE 5.3. TRADITIONAL AND PARTICIPATORY MODELS OF THE PROFESSIONAL–CLIENT RELATIONSHIP

Questions regarding the professional–client relationship	Traditional Answer	Participatory Answer
1. What is proper client behavior?	It consists of little effort at understanding; passive, trusting delegation of responsibility; and following of instructions.	It involves an active, skeptical effort to be informed and to share responsibility by making mutually agreeable choices.
2. What are the chances for receiving effective professional service?	Ineffective professional service is rare.	Ineffective professional service is common.
3. What is the nature of client problems?	They are routine and technical, having a best solution inaccessible to lay understanding.	They involve open, unpredictable individualized choices, understandable to a layperson, for which there is no single best answer.
4. How probable is the client to receive disinterested service from the professional?	Professionals can and do make the client's interest their own.	Disinterested professional service is virtually impossible.
5. How clear-cut and enforceable are professional standards?	High standards are set and maintained by the professions themselves and by the courts.	Standards are neither clearly set nor effectively enforced by the professions or the courts.
6. How accessible is effective professional service to paying clients?	Effective professional service is accessible to all paying clients.	Many paying clients have difficulty finding effective professional service.

Source: Adapted from Douglas Rosenthal, *Lawyer and Client: Who's in Charge?* (New York: Russell Sage Foundation, 1974, p. 13, Table 1.1).

providers?" the traditional model says it consists of little effort at understanding; a passive, trusting delegation of responsibility; and obedience to professionals' instructions. The participatory answer is that client behavior involves an active, skeptical effort to be informed and to share responsibility in making mutually agreeable choices.

In regards to Question 2, "What are the chances for receiving effective professional service?" the traditional model says that ineffective service is rare and effective service is the norm. The participatory response is that ineffective professional service is more common than rare. In response to Question 3 on the nature of clients' problems, the traditional model states that clients' problems: (a) are routine, (b) are technically comprehensible only to a professional, and (c) have a best solution that is inaccessible to lay understanding but routinely known to professionals. The participatory response is that clients' problems involve open, unpredictable, individualized choices that are understandable to a layperson and for which, typically, there is no single best solution. The participatory response is that clients' problems, as well as their solutions, are negotiated, not cut and dried.

Question 4 asks whether the clients can receive disinterested service from professionals. The traditional response is that professionals make the client's interests their own and deliver services disinterestedly. The participatory view is that the chances of receiving disinterested professional services are slim. Rosenthal suggests that the offered solutions to clients' problems are often in the best interests of the professional rather than the client. Clients may be exploited to benefit the professional while receiving assurances that the clients' best interests are being served. An example of this, noted earlier, is a recommendation by physicians for unnecessary tests or surgery. Question 5 asks "How clear-cut and enforceable are professional standards?" The traditional answer is that high standards are set and maintained by professionals through self-policing or by the courts. The participatory answer is that standards are not effectively enforced by either the profession or the courts. Question 6 asks: "How accessible is effective professional service to paying clients?" The traditional answer is that effective professional service is accessible to all paying clients. The participatory answer is that many paying clients have difficulty finding effective professional service.

Rosenthal concludes that relations between professionals and clients are less straightforward than frequently assumed. In a study of 300 legal cases involving personal injury claims, Rosenthal tested the hypothesis that clients who play a participatory role in the legal process receive more favorable judgments than those who behave as a traditional client. Data analysis confirmed his hypothesis. Participatory clients received better rulings. All lawyers surveyed expressed a preference for traditional clients, however, and disapproved of participatory clients. They said participatory clients were too difficult and demanding and they much preferred clients who were passive, unquestioning, and compliant. The disliked participatory clients nevertheless received better results in court.

The views of professional and client are important inputs to the professional–client relationship. Professionals who view clients as proactive participants can encourage their initiative and involvement and guard against tendencies to dislike clients who challenge their perceptions, recommendations, and solutions. Clients who view an active role as legitimate can contribute to the problem definition and resolution process. Whether clients succeed in obtaining the best and most appropriate service is the primary issue, not whether they are liked by professionals. Elimination of the objective conflict of interests between professionals and clients would be difficult, but exploitation can be minimized by professionals who promote clients' awareness, participation, and assumption of responsibility. Rosenthal's Participatory Model seems most likely to foster this end.

INTRINSIC DYADIC RELATIONS

Thus far we have focused on extrinsic dyadic relations or those entered into by clients in search of services from professionals. As noted earlier, most such relations are asymmetrical—with professionals having greater resources, and power, than clients. This section focuses on intrinsic relations: relations entered into for their own sake, for no purpose other than the relationship itself. Intrinsic relations between persons of equal resources are friendship relations. Intrinsic relations between persons of unequal resources may be family relations, including parent–child relations and, as suggested earlier, husband–wife relations. Because Chapter 6 on the family deals with parent–child and husband–wife relations, we focus our attention here on friendship.

Dyadic friendship relations involve two people with equal or near-equal resources that are entered into because the parties enjoy, or benefit subjectively from, the relationship. Having equal resources does not imply the same resources. A quiet, shy person may be attracted to an outgoing, garrulous person. Qualities absent in oneself may be attractive in another. A *smart* woman may be friends with a *pretty* woman (not to imply one cannot be both) because each values the other's qualities. Blau (1964) says that intrinsic, peer relations such as friendships are those in which an individual is most likely to be accepted for herself or himself. Such relations are experienced as freeing, or least constraining, and may explain why teenagers prefer peers over parents as they make the transition to adulthood. The authority of parent–child relations is absent in friendship relations, and the chances of being perceived and accepted "for oneself" are greater among peers.

Friendship relations develop primarily among people with equal or near-equal resources. Close friends often share social class backgrounds, affluence, ethnicity, gender, race, religion, regional origins, life experiences (such as military service in Vietnam; work as summer camp counselor), hobbies, and skills (at tennis, skiing, golf, crossword puzzles, or picking locks). Only rarely are poor and rich, or educated and uneducated, people best friends.

Race and gender are social resources that influence the social exchange process (Toren and Kraus, 1987). Our society values whites over blacks and men are valued over women; thus, best friendships are less likely to form across race and gender lines. Some research supports this. Relatively few best-friend choices involve members of different races, and although men often say women are their best friends, women usually name other women, not men. This may result from sex-role scripts that cause men to perceive of women as relationship experts and women to perceive of men as lacking in interpersonal skills (Laws, 1979). Social movements that combat racism and sexism can be viewed as efforts to eliminate both societal scripts and practices that view some categories of people as of lesser worth than others (Freeman, 1984).

IMPLICATIONS FOR SOCIAL WORK

Professional–client relations are power relations. Wishing otherwise does not make it so. The rhetoric of the social work literature on professional–client relations glosses over power, leading to unawareness and denial (Gummer, 1983). This has unfortunate consequences. Clients know that professional–client relations are asymmetrical. Workers who are unaware of this, or who deny it, undermine client trust. Moreover, denial by workers can lead to abuses committed in the guise of helping.

Our discussion will, it is hoped, enhance social workers' awareness that some aspects of the professional–client relationship are upsetting for clients. This is true regardless of how well-intentioned workers are. Workers need to be aware of this, honest about it, and committed to minimizing authority's negative effects.

Chapter 5 has implications for three levels of social organization: (1) the social welfare organization, (2) service delivery worker, and (3) the client.

1. *At the level of the organization*, social welfare administrators are advised to protect service workers from bureaucratic regulations that pressure them to go against their professional judgment. They should demand that workers provide a high quality of service (Martin, 1987; Martin and Whiddon, 1988). A more radical suggestion is to abandon bureaucratic organizations and to deliver services in a collectivist format (Rothschild-Whitt, 1979). Collectivist organizations

reach decisions on a consensual rather than hierarchical basis (see Chapter 8). Consensus and equality foster mutual respect among members and diminish chances that the organization will become the client, as in Daniels' example of military psychiatry. Making decisions on a consensual basis requires prodigious amounts of time (Blum, 1982), however, and organizational efficiency is hurt. Despite this, organizations that attempt to minimize unnecessary regulations keep clients' interests in the forefront of attention and minimize worker alienation (Weinstein, 1979; Thurston, 1987).

2. *At the level of service delivery*, professionals can acknowledge their power over clients and take steps to minimize its negative consequences. Courtesies such as addressing clients by a title and surname (Ms. Jones) communicate respect. Workers can join with clients to develop informal helping networks. Technology transfer from worker to client can, over time, teach clients to help themselves and remove the need to seek assistance from professionals. Such an approach is exemplified in the self-help feminist health movement in which service providers teach self-examination and health-care skills to clients (Ruzek, 1978; Thurston, 1987). Recent evidence that some diagnostic health-care procedures can be mastered by elementary school children suggests that many activities now controlled by professionals can be delegated to clients themselves.

3. *At the level of the client*, a number of alternatives to power relationships can be identified (Emerson, 1962). These include: (a) muster sufficient (relevant) resources to balance the relationship or to imbalance it in the client's favor; (b) seek the service elsewhere; (c) organize with other clients to coerce professionals to provide service; and (d) do without the service. A fifth alternative (e) is to provide services on a self-help basis (Gottschalk, 1973). Instead of seeking services from clinics, agencies, or programs, clients can join together to provide service informally. The attraction of self-help is obvious from Table 5.2. Self-help involves cooperation among peers, and power aspects of helping relationships can be avoided. Problems concerning expertise and technology may arise, however, when needed services are complex or when access to drugs, equipment, and facilities is restricted by law (Thurston, 1987). Even here, workers can educate clients about the uses and limitations of interventive technologies to help them become discerning consumers rather than passive recipients of expert treatment.

Many people do without services rather than endure the indignities of asymmetrical, power relations. Doing without is, of course, one avenue for avoiding relationships that foster feelings of inferiority and powerlessness.

Such a solution has little to recommend it, however, in a prosperous nation such as America. Responsibility rests with policymakers, welfare administrators, and service providers to develop and implement alternative service delivery modes that maximize client dignity and control. Those who need social services must not be prevented from receiving them because of asymmetrical power and control in the service-delivery arena.

CONCLUSIONS

An Open Systems Theory model of dyads provides insights about the professional–client relationship. It also facilitates understanding of peer relations, such as friendships. It is our hope that the reader employs greater understanding to maximize clients' rights and empowerment and to minimize the negative consequences of professional authority.

Chapter 6

Marriages and Families as Open Systems

The family is the "...basic social unit in society in which relations are culturally and socially defined either by law, tradition, religion, and/or some combination of these" (Goode, 1964, p. 2). People are born into families (*family of orientation*) and chances are great that they will establish families of their own (*family of procreation*). For much of their lives, most people are members of at least two families. Chapter 6 examines marriages and family as open social systems. Distinctions are drawn between families as inclusive versus included systems, and alternative definitions of family are discussed. Historical marriage and family forms are reviewed with particular attention to the nuclear family, the modal family form in the Western world.

The family is described as a type of task group, a small, multi-generational group with a past and a future with many normatively associated tasks and duties. In traditional family groups, the marital pair (or single-parent head) is viewed as the family's leadership or dominant subsystem. Family structure is viewed as emerging from repeated patterns or sequences of interaction that change as family circumstances and situations change. Prior to the concluding section, a case example of a problem family is presented, based on a book by Virginia Axline, *Dibs: In Search of Self* (1964). The example illustrates that, through the mechanism of feedback, a family can set its goals and exercise control over its destiny. It illustrates also that fundamental change in a system component leads, over time, to change in the total system.

OPEN SYSTEMS CONCEPTS AND THEMES

A number of Open Systems Theory concepts and themes are used to characterize marriage and family systems, including: (1) avoidance of reductionism in problem diagnosis and intervention; (2) qualitative system change that occurs from inside the system and emanates from a low resource/low power member; (3) the number of subsystems in relation to system size; (4) system survival and work on the part of system members; (5) conflict in human systems as normal and predictable; (6) indeterminate boundaries in relation to factionalized systems; (7) complex/elaborated systems as more viable than simple/narrow ones; (8) flexible/versatile systems as more viable than rigid systems; and (9) feedback as a self-control mechanism that allows open systems to shape their destinies. Each of these is discussed below.

Antireductionistic Thinking and Attribution

The concept of antireductionism was defined in Chapter 2. It admonishes avoidance of attributing to individual members outputs that are *system outputs*. In the context of families, behavior of family members is viewed as a family output. This is consistent with conceptualizing the actions of component parts as shaped or constrained by the inclusive system. As argued later, a housewife's depression or a teenager's delinquency are family, not individual, problems. Practitioners who recognize this are less likely to blame the victim and more likely to approach problems on an appropriate level of intervention.

Qualitative Change Can Emanate from a Low Resource/Low Power Component

Qualitative change refers to fundamental alterations in the structure of a system that, in turn, lead to a changed process. Altered process can also lead to altered structure. *Quantitative change* is incremental alteration that adds to or subtracts from previous patterns whereas qualitative change results in different interactional sequences or patterns. Because the components of a system are interdependent, a qualitative change in one component part changes the total system.

When a system changes qualitatively, members relate to each other differently from before. Sequences of events that were prevalent are abandoned and new ones emerge. Systems that are hierarchically structured—that is, those in which some elements have authority (or power) over others—are most readily changed if those higher in the hierarchy change their behaviors. Qualitative change can also emanate from the bottom of authority hierarchies, although low resource/low power members normally have less influence. The

Dibs example (at the conclusion of the present chapter) illustrates that change from below, although slow, can foster healthiness in an entire family.

The Number of Subsystems Increases Geometrically with Increases in System Size

Larger social systems are more complex than smaller ones because of the geometric increase in number of potential subsystems accompanying membership size increases. A system with two members has potential for one social system: that between the two members. With the addition of a third member the number increases to four: (1) the original dyad (a and b); (2) and (3) each member of the original dyad with the new member (a and c; b and c); and (4) all three members together (a, b, and c). With four members, the number increases to 11; with five, to 26.

The point is emphasized for two reasons. First, it explains why some family therapists require total family involvement in early treatment sessions. They want to observe how members interact in their most inclusive context (Haley, 1976; Bowen, 1978; Minuchin, 1974; Satir, 1967). Observation of the most inclusive system can provide clues for understanding numerous subsystemic relationships that, if examined first, can bias comprehension of the totality. Second, it highlights the complexity of social systems, even small ones. The addition of members—new baby, grandmother, cousin, or housekeeper—increases the interactional complexity of the family context and requires adjustment by all. Literature dealing with marital happiness reports that marital partners are seldom as happy after the birth of their first child as they were before, and this continues until the last child leaves home as a young adult (Glenn and McLanahan, 1981; Goetting, 1986; White, Booth, and Edwards, 1986). New members lead to changes in internal structure and dynamics. Families that resist or avoid changes that accompany such an event—such as Dibs' family in the case example in this chapter—can develop problems.

Survival Requires Work on the Part of System Members

The maintenance of social systems requires considerable effort, or work, on the part of system members. In families with children, such things as food preparation, clothing and shelter, instruction and teaching, and love must be provided if the children are to thrive. Someone must do this work and do it regularly. If it is not done, children can go hungry, dirty, unclothed, unloved, or worse (Justice, Calvert, and Justice, 1985). Representatives of the state (government) may intervene and remove the children from homes where such work is not done.

Adult relationships also require work. Whereas mutual affection, respect, and liking may make such work pleasurable, one or both partners must nevertheless perform it. Grocery shopping, getting home on time, doing laundry, being affectionate, keeping one's promises, buying gifts, and being thoughtful are typical family tasks. Work as a necessity for system survival is highlighted in the conception of families as task groups.

Conflict in Open Systems Is Normal and Can Be Healthy and Productive

Chapter 2 argued that social systems are characterized by conflicts, tension, discontinuity, and disruption. This is expected and normal rather than unusual or pathological. Humans are proactive, strong-willed, and unpredictable; if everyone were the same, life would be dull. Even systems depicted as harmonious, peaceful, and consensual have underlying conflicts of opinion, interest, and material well-being. Even in monasteries, where the normative philosophy is total submission to God, day-to-day interpersonal dynamics may be peppered with rebellion, rule violations, and disagreements.

Except for physical violence (which is always abhorrent), the consequences of family conflict depend on the way it is handled and whether all parties are allowed to win. Some forms of conflict are destructive, but these are associated generally with *denial* of conflict when it occurs (Haley, 1976). A positive consequence of open conflict is that misunderstandings that were previously unstated can be brought into the open and clarified.

Open Systems with Indistinct Boundaries May Be Factionalized and Unstable

Factionalized open systems are those with internal components that are not highly interdependent. As discussed in Chapter 2, when factionalized systems are confronted with pressures from inside or out, they may split into independent elements or systems. One theme of the present chapter is that social systems with indistinct boundaries become factionalized and unstable. A psychologically absent father can throw a family into a state of indeterminancy and block effective family functioning. If a system is uncertain of its elements, its ability to operate predictably is reduced. This does not imply that rigid boundaries are desirable but rather that system viability is hampered by indistinct boundaries and that certainty is usually superior to uncertainty.

Complex Systems Are More Viable than Simple Systems

Systems that are capable of accepting and processing a wide range and variety of inputs survive and thrive better than other systems. Complex systems have more options. A person with three types of skills (e.g., computer technology, auto mechanics, and television repair) is more likely to find a job than someone with no skills.

Through the processes of growth and learning, living systems tend to become more complex and elaborate over time. The build-up and storage of free and usable information and energy allow open systems to enhance their chances for survival and prosperity (Buckley, 1967). This suggests that families that accept new inputs, continuously learn, and are able to change are the most viable.

Flexible Systems Are More Viable than Rigid Ones

Systems that change as circumstances change are more viable than those that are locked into narrow or rigid ways of doing things. As subsequent material suggests, a family's authority structure must change as children move into adolescence. If a family clings to old ways of reaching decisions or meting out punishments, its adolescents may become disruptive at home, school, or both. Rigid adherence to unproductive interaction sequences is a frequent precipitant of pathology in children.

Feedback Allows an Open System to Exercise Self-control

Although human/social systems are influenced by their environments, they also influence their environments. Their responses to environmental influences are not, furthermore, passive or predetermined. Feedback is the mechanism that allows open systems, such as families, to exercise self-control. Feedback is part of the cyclical exchange process between a system and its environment. To define the concept of feedback, the exchange process is reviewed. The concepts of input, throughput/work, output, and two types of feedback (positive and negative) are defined.

Inputs are (1) information (e.g., ideas, communications, etc.) or (2) matter/energy (e.g., food for the body; employees for an organization) that enters a system by crossing its boundary. Open systems are selective regarding the inputs they accept. Parents in a family may attempt to reject inputs from their children's peer environment by forbidding certain behaviors (e.g., tobacco or birth control pills) in the context of the home. They may fail to insulate children from these entirely but prohibition of their use in the home constitutes input selectivity. Inputs are used by open systems for both maintenance and production purposes. Some inputs are used by the system to produce outputs that are exchanged with the environment for new inputs.

Throughput or work consists of doing something to inputs to give them order, form, or organization so they become useful to a system. Throughputting can be defined as the transforming, combining, analyzing, synthesizing, separating, or organizing of inputs to produce outputs for internal use or for exchange with the environment. If a student must learn examination materials through reading and the student fails to read, he or she may fail the exam. Even if the student reads but fails to study—that is, reviews the material, takes notes on it, organizes and reflects on what has been read, memorizes—the student may score poorly. The activity of studying material that has been read is an example of throughput or work. Work in Open Systems Theory is more than physical activity for which a person receives pay in an occupation or job. It is the processing of inputs to produce outputs. When parents discuss ethics or rules with children with a goal of establishing family standards, this is an example of work in the family.

If children behave well in public, this makes parents proud and is viewed by them (and others) as a family accomplishment or output. *Outputs* are the products of systems. Some outputs cross a system's boundary—for example, a child behaves courteously—whereas others remain inside the system—for example, family members like each other, feel loyal to the family. Some outputs that cross the boundary are exchanged with the environment for new inputs. The acquisition of inputs is a continuous activity because open systems require many and varied inputs for survival and prosperity (families need food, clothing, transportation, ideas, good will, services from schools, hospitals, movie theatres, etc.). Importation of varied inputs that are transformed in the system contributes to the available use, and potential for export, of more and varied outputs. Similar to capital accumulation in industry, more inputs lead to more outputs and more outputs lead to more inputs. The process is cyclical and, to a degree, cumulative.

Feedback is a form of input that is available to a system as a result of its outputs. Many outputs that cross a system's boundary are reacted to in some way by the environment(s). Feedback occurs when a system: (1) *recognizes* the environment's reactions to its outputs, (2) *accepts* this information as new input, and (3) *uses* this new input to: (a) correct the system toward a previous goal or (b) pursue a new goal. The type of feedback that corrects is *negative feedback*; the type that leads to pursuit of new goals is *positive feedback*. A single bit or instance of feedback can be both negative and positive if it both corrects the system and prompts it toward a new goal.

As the Dibs example shows, a teacher's reaction to Dibs' behavior at school entered Dibs' family through the mother and served as both negative and positive feedback. It was negative feedback because it prompted the mother to take corrective action. She sought therapeutic help for Dibs to improve his behavior at home and at school (this assumes that Dibs' mother wanted him to have good behavior prior to this point). However, it was also positive feedback because it prompted Dibs' mother to seek therapy for herself and to change the way she behaved in the family. Over time, Dibs' father developed new goals and began to act differently toward both Dibs and Dibs' mother. Whether a particular bit of feedback is negative or positive is less important than the principle of self-control embodied in this concept. Because of the feedback principle, open systems are capable of self-direction and self-control. Although influenced by their environment, open systems use information from the environment to make decisions about which goals and directions to pursue.

FAMILIES AS SOCIAL SYSTEMS

Families serve their members in two ways. First, they link individuals with the larger society. Upon being born into a family, children have a group of individuals (relatives, friends, neighbors, and associates of their parents) who are interested in them, identify them as "one of us," talk to them, and spend time with them. *Families of orientation* provide members with ties to other families and to individuals who relate to them in predictable and regularized ways. Second, families serve their members by socializing the young into language, skills, knowledge, and roles that they are expected to display, know, or perform. It is in families—natural, adoptive, and foster—that infants learn to be human.

Primary socialization of new societal members takes place in families. Children are taught to speak, to connect words with ideas, to receive and give affection, to master motor and cognitive skills. Because the family gets "first crack" at society's newborns, its impact on the young is profound.

What Is a Family?

Anthropologists define a family as a social system that contains at least two generations, parent and child, although the normative family form in the West also includes a father. Margaret Mead (1949) notes that the social invention of fatherhood is recent historically and that this may explain the ambiguousness of the *fathering role*. By the anthropologists' definition, a married couple does not become a family until it has produced or acquired a child and, furthermore, a woman who is not married can establish a family by producing a child.

The U.S. Bureau of the Census defines a *family household* as two or more individuals related by birth, marriage, or adoption residing in the same household (U.S Bureau of the Census, 1985b, p. 1). The three types of family household are: (1) married-couple families, (2) other families with male householder (no wife present), and (3) other families with female householder (no husband present). Under the federal definition, married couples with no children are a family; unmarried mothers or fathers with their children are a family; a brother and sister sharing a dwelling are a family; and grandparents and their grandchildren are a family. *Nonfamily households* consist of unmarried couples with no children present, unrelated persons in the same household, and people living alone.

Table 6.1 describes American households, family and nonfamily, in the mid-1980s. There were 85,407,000 households in 1984, approximately 73 percent of which were occupied by families and 28.5 percent of which contained children under 18 years of age. Average family size in 1986 was 3.21 people, down from 3.58 in 1970 and 3.76 in 1940 (U.S. Bureau of the Census, 1986a, Table 2, p. 3). (Average *household size* decreased even more with a mean in 1986 of 2.67 people compared to 3.14 in 1970 and 3.67 in 1940.) American families are the smallest ever, reflecting a trend that began in the 1960s.

From Table 6.1, we see that of the approximately 62 million *family* households in 1984, 50 million (about 81 percent) contained married couples, and of married-couple households, 49 percent had children under 18 years of age in the home. Married-couple families with children under 18 constituted only 28.5 percent of all households in 1984, substantially less than the 1970 level of 40.3 percent. One-parent families accounted for roughly 26 percent of all households with children under 18 in 1984, double the rate of about 13 percent in 1970. One-parent households have increased dramatically. Increases in one-parent families and in families without minor children reflect changes in life style and demography of the American population. As noted in Chapter 1, Americans are living longer and the percentage of the population over 65 is increasing. More Americans live alone than ever before. Between 1970 and 1986, the number of Americans living alone increased from 12 million to 25 million. Eighty-five percent of nonfamily households in 1984 contained people who lived alone. Women, as shown in Table 6.1, are more likely to live alone than men (62 percent of all living-alone households are women).

There were 2.2 million households of unmarried couples in 1986, a 400 percent increase over their number in 1970 (U.S. Bureau of the Census, 1986a, p. 2). The large majority of these, 70 percent, contained two adults only, while the remainder had one or more children. The increase is dramatic but is placed in perspective by noting that only 4 of every 100 American (household) couples in 1986 were unmarried. The majority of adults in unmarried couple households in 1986 had never been married (52 percent) and most of the remainder were divorced (34 percent).

From these data, two points are emphasized. First, families should not be equated with the television stereotype of "two parents, two children, and a dog." In 1984, only 29 percent of U.S. households contained two parents with at least one child under 18; 71 percent contained other configurations of related or unrelated individuals. Second, family forms change over time. They have done this historically and will continue to. The family form in which a person lives is less important than the quality and nature of the rela-

TABLE 6.1. HOUSEHOLD COMPOSITION, BY PRESENCE OF OWN CHILDREN UNDER 18: 1984, 1980, AND 1970 (NUMBERS IN THOUSANDS)

Subject	1984		1980		1970		Change, 1980–84		Change, 1970–80	
	Number	Percent	Number	Percent	Number	Percent	Number	Percent	Number	Percent
All households	85,407	100.0	80,776	100.0	63,401	100.0	4,631	100.0	17,375	100.0
Family households	61,997	72.6	59,550	73.7	51,456	81.2	2,447	52.8	8,094	46.6
Married-couple family	50,090	58.6	49,112	60.8	44,728	70.5	978	21.1	4,384	25.3
No own children under 18	25,750	30.1	24,151	29.9	19,196	30.3	1,599	34.5	4,955	28.5
With own children under 18	24,339	28.5	24,961	30.9	25,532	40.3	−622	−13.4	−571	−3.3
One child under 18	9,546	11.2	9,671	12.0	8,163	12.9	−125	−2.7	1,508	8.7
Two children under 18	9,557	11.2	9,448	11.7	8,045	12.7	69	1.5	1,443	8.3
Three or more children under 18	5,236	6.1	5,802	7.2	9,325	14.7	−566	−12.2	−3,523	−20.3
Other family, male householder	2,030	2.4	1,733	2.1	1,228	1.9	297	6.4	505	2.9
No own children under 18	1,231	1.4	1,117	1.4	887	1.4	114	2.5	230	1.3
With own children under 18	799	0.9	616	0.8	341	0.5	183	4.0	275	1.6
One child under 18	506	0.6	374	0.5	179	0.3	132	2.9	195	1.1
Two children under 18	224	0.3	165	0.2	87	0.1	59	1.3	78	0.4
Three or more children under 18	69	0.1	77	0.1	75	0.1	−8	−0.2	2	—
Other family, female householder	9,878	11.6	8,705	10.8	5,500	8.7	1,173	25.3	3,205	18.4
No own children under 18	3,970	4.6	3,261	4.0	2,642	4.2	709	15.3	619	3.6
With own children under 18	5,907	6.9	5,445	6.7	2,858	4.5	462	10.0	2,587	14.9
One child under 18	2,810	3.3	2,398	3.0	1,008	1.6	412	8.9	1,390	8.0
Two children under 18	1,985	2.3	1,817	2.2	810	1.3	168	3.6	1,007	5.8
Three or more children under 18	1,113	1.3	1,230	1.5	1,040	1.6	−117	−2.5	190	1.1
Nonfamily households	23,410	27.4	21,226	26.3	11,945	18.8	2,184	47.2	9,281	53.4
Male householder	9,752	11.4	8,807	10.9	4,063	6.4	945	20.4	4,744	27.3
Living alone	7,529	8.8	6,966	8.6	3,532	5.6	563	12.2	3,434	19.8
Female householder	13,658	16.0	12,419	15.4	7,882	12.4	1,239	26.8	4,537	26.1
Living alone	12,425	14.5	11,330	14.0	7,319	11.5	1,095	23.6	4,011	23.1

Source: U.S. Bureau of the Census (1985b, Table A, p. 2).

tionships among family members. Although the U.S. Bureau of the Census does not count unmarried couples as families, you may someday provide *family counseling* to unmarried couples who share a household. Families take many forms, and you, unlike the federal government or the anthropologists, are free to define them broadly. You can focus on the quality of interpersonal relationships among intensely involved people, regardless of their legal or consanguineal (blood) relations.

Families are intense and long-term. They have a history and a projected future. Even lifelong friendships lose intensity with time, whereas family members stay in contact through weddings, christenings, funerals, and reunions. Because of children, divorced or separated parents stay involved in each other's lives for years (if not a lifetime) after parting. The permanency aspects of families distinguish them from most other forms of social organization. Although some people sever all contacts with their families by disappearing or running away, most maintain family ties throughout their lives.

Families as Inclusive and Included Systems

Two perspectives on the family as a system include: (1) viewing it as *inclusive* or (2) viewing it as *included*. Family counselors and therapists view the family as an *inclusive system* where the focus is on how the family shapes or influences the behavior and perceptions of its members. They pay attention to the form and quality of intrafamily relationships and to the consequences of these relationships for family members. Coleman (1963, p. 63) claims that "[T]he essence of a social system is interdependence and the essence of interdependence is people's investment of themselves in other people and in collectivities that exist within the system. It is these investments that tie the system together and give it strength." Because of the intensity and duration of members' involvement, families are among the most interdependent of social systems.

Many family therapists say the family should be viewed not as individual persons or personalities but as an interpersonal or group phenomenon (Haley, 1976; Satir, 1967; Minuchin, 1974). Interpersonal factors are, they claim, the major concern of family treatment. Haley defines family as "...relationships of influence and patterns of communication."

Conceptions of family as an *included system* focus on its institutional aspects and functions. They are concerned with how a family fits with other social institutions such as the economy, political or governmental structure, educational system, military, religious, and welfare institutions, the health sector, and so forth. By analyzing the family as an included system, concern is directed toward identification of the consequences for the family of its linkages with the environment (Verzaro-Lawrence, 1981). Linkages that are important include:

1. *Kin networks.* What are they? How strong and frequently do relatives visit, call, or write the family?
2. *Social or friendship networks.* Does the family have friends or people unrelated by blood or marriage who are intrinsically involved with one or more of its members?
3. *Occupational or labor market ties.* Do one or more family members work for pay outside the home? What kinds of jobs do they have; at what status levels? What level of income does the family make? If no adult works, how does the family manage? Are there welfare payments? Insurance? Pensions? Social Security?
4. *Educational system ties.* Are one or more school-age children attending school? If so, how are they doing? What reports do their teachers send home?
5. *Memberships/activities of family members in voluntary organizations, etc.* Do family members participate in voluntary organizations outside the home; for example, political parties or campaigns, charitable organizations, special-interest groups such as country music clubs, hunting or garden clubs? Do the children belong to Scouting, sports teams, acting studios, neighborhood clubs?
6. *Religious activities.* Do family members belong to and attend church services or activities?

Questions such as these alert social workers to the family's integration in, or isolation from, the broader society. What are the consequences of family isolation? A predominant characteristic of families that abuse children is their social isolation from neighbors, relatives, and friends (Gil, 1970; Holland, 1973; Justice, Calvert, and Justice, 1985). Isolated families have fewer inputs because their weak ties limit the variety and quantity of inputs available to them. Families with few inputs do less throughputting and, ultimately, have both limited and low rates of outputs. Fewer outputs lead to fewer inputs.

Two points are emphasized here. First, Open Systems Theory prompts social workers to focus on the interrelatedness of the inclusive and included statuses of a family. The nature and form of intrafamily relationships and communication patterns are highly related to the nature and form of a family's external, or across-the-boundary, linkages. Whether intervention is initiated at the relationship level or the level of family linkages depends on the prac-titioner's perspective and options as well as the family's objective situation.

Second, many practitioners define social work with families as having a primary goal of linking them with other institutional sectors (Epstein and Conrad, 1978). This perspective argues that linkages with the environment—for example, school system for children, employment or other relationships for adults—are essential conditions for family health. A second goal may be improvement in intrafamily relations. Open Systems Theory supports this view by stressing the importance of intersystem linkages as a prerequisite for productive internal functioning.

HISTORICAL OVERVIEW OF FAMILY AND MARRIAGE FORMS

Family Forms

In the modern, industrialized Western world, the normative or ideal family form is the *nuclear family*. A nuclear family has two generations of members: parents and their offspring. A nuclear family form focuses on the conjugal or marital relationship, whereas other family forms emphasize consanguineal or blood relationships.

Goode observes that, "No nuclear family *system* exists if by that we mean a system in which most families maintain few or no relations with their more extended kin" (1964, p. 51). Nevertheless, the nuclear family is less dependent than other family forms on the wider kinship network. As a consequence, resources and support from the extended kinship system are lower in societies that emphasize the marital bond over the extended kinship network.

A nuclear family form is taken for granted in the industrialized West but is historically recent and rare as an ideal type (Osmond, 1980). In most cultures historically, emphasis was given either to consanguineal (blood) or affinal (in-law) ties rather than to the marriage bond per se. This results in elaborated family systems where more than one marital pair and their offspring reside under one roof. Family forms that have characterized human society for much of its history (and still do today) include: (1) extended families, (2) stem families, and (3) joint families.

Extended families have at least three generations under one roof. These are: grandmother and grandfather, their offspring, and their offsprings' children. The extended family is *stretched out* over more generations than the nuclear family is. An extended family form has been most characteristic historically of societies in the Far East, particularly China, and in Africa and Arabia.

The *stem family* is a modified version of the extended family. "Under this system only one child, usually the eldest son, inherited the family property; and he had some responsibility for his sisters until they married and for his brothers until they were grown. Thus, the property, family title, and responsibility were in the hands of one person" (Goode, 1964, p. 45). Most typical of feudal and postfeudal Europe (and some parts of Japan as well as some immigrant farm families in the United States), this family form entails three generations under one roof (grandparents, parents, and the parents' offspring) but for only one child, usually the eldest son, of the grandparents.

Joint families are expanded or stretched out horizontally as well as generationally. In joint families, all of the siblings—usually of one sex only—of one set of parents marry and remain inside the parents' household along with their offspring. The household consists of a number of small family groupings (mother, father, and offspring) who remain together in a common living site and who share a joint budget, child care, and homemaking responsibilities. This particular family form has been most characteristic of India and other Hindu societies.

Marriage Forms

Marriage forms have varied both historically and cross-culturally. In the industrialized West, the form associated with the nuclear family form is *monogamy*, or the marriage of one husband and one wife. Having more than one husband or wife is referred to as *polygamy*. The special form of polygamy in which a husband has more than one wife is *polygyny*; the form in which a wife has more than one husband is *polyandry*.

Marriage forms vary with family forms so that combinations across societies are quite complex. Co-varying with these, furthermore, are the issues of (1) lineage reckoning (or descent) and (2) the location of new families. *Lineage (or descent) reckoning* refers to the manner in which surnames, kinship, responsibilities, and wealth are passed from one generation to the next (e.g., this can be patrilineal, matrilineal, or bilineal). In the United States, lineage is patrilineal; thus, children take the surnames of their fathers. *Location of newlyweds* can include living with or near the father's relatives, the mother's relatives, or neither. In the United States, a newly married couple establishes its own residence at a separate site from either set of parents. This is referred to as a *neolocal* (or new location) pattern.

Is the Norm the Mode?

A society's normative (preferred or ideal) marriage and family forms may not be modal—that is, typical of a majority of the population. In fact, it may characterize a numerical minority. In the United States, where the nuclear family with monogamous marriage is the norm, only 45 percent of the population lives in an arrangement of this type (U.S. Bureau of the Census, 1983b). Fifteen percent of American families are headed by women with no adult men present, and the proportion in this category is growing. Additionally, many live in households with no offspring, no spouse, unrelated parties, with parents, in institutions, and so forth. It is inappropriate to equate a society's ideal family and marriage forms with actual conditions. There is evidence that in societies where polygamy is the ideal, it is not atypical for as little as 2 percent of the population to reside in such a situation (Goode, 1964; Murdock, 1949).

The forms of marriage and family that a society has are related to other aspects of societal organization and culture. According to Osmond (1980), major influences on family forms are the economic system (e.g., hunting and gardening, intensive vs. extensive agriculture, industrialization, and so forth), the political system, the stratification system, the kinship system, and the religious/ideological system. Primary emphasis is given, by a majority of cross-cultural researchers, to the role of the economy in determining a society's family form. Osmond (1980), among others, claims that the effects of the economic system are mediated by the type of stratification system that develops. Stratification is the form and distribution of wealth and power in a society. Those who control a society's wealth may establish and maintain an ideology, or belief system, that justifies the status quo (Laws, 1979; Offe, 1976). Thus, a society's family form may be described as morally correct because it supports or complements other societal structures that assure the advantages enjoyed by power elites. Sanday (1981) claims that religious ideology is used to justify the subordinate status of women in Western culture.

Problems with Monogamy and the Nuclear Family

Monogamy and the nuclear family form are not without problems. Primary among these is the isolation—physical, geographical, and social—that results from having the family boundary drawn around a small number of adults and children. Children are limited to one adult of each gender in a two-parent family for close emotional attachments and relationships. The marital partners' intimate world is constrained to one other person, and this person is of the opposite sex. Opportunities to share child care, cooking, cleaning, and other household chores are limited by the absence of other adults (LaRossa and LaRossa, 1981). Data from other cultures that include grandparents or other adults as family members indicate that the ability to share household tasks, particularly child rearing and child care, is viewed positively by adults, particularly women.

If monogamy and the nuclear family fail to meet the needs of people, why are they normative? For one thing, norms are slow to change. Some sociologists argue, furthermore, that the nuclear family is functional for a society that requires frequent geographical moves (Parsons and Bales, 1955). It is easier to move a small family from one city to another as required by the husband's or wife's career. Another argument is that monogamy stems from a religious ideology that proclaims it to be ordained by God (Goode, 1964). Osmond (1980) claims that monogamy is a result of increased stratification in society, that is, greater differences in status and wealth. This position is consistent with Mayhew and Schollaert's (1980) research on the nuclear family. They find that increases in population size lead to increases in wealth, and greater wealth leads to greater inequality. (Greater inequality means that income differences between families are larger.) Greater inequality leads, in turn, to a nuclear family form. Wealth is easier to retain in small, sharply defined families than in extended, joint, or communal family forms.

Regardless of the explanation, many Americans live in familial circumstances that deviate from monogamous and nuclear family forms. Some of these are described below.

EMERGENT FAMILY FORMS: VARIATIONS ON THE NUCLEAR FAMILY NORM

The nuclear family as idealized in mid-twentieth-century sociology consisted of a husband/father who worked to support the family, a wife/mother who raised the children full-time, and their biological, dependent children (Parsons and Bales, 1955). Families formed by married adults have the combined resources of two adult members to support the family and to link it with the environment. The family can use these resources for bearing and rearing children and to maintain and promote work roles. Both marital status and parental responsibilities require the investment of time and resources; thus, intact nuclear families have advantages over some other family forms.

Traditional nuclear families are in the minority in the late twentieth century. As noted earlier, most American women work for pay, less than one-third of all families have children under 18 in the home, unmarried-couple households have increased dramatically, and 15 percent of all families are headed by a single parent. In addition, Americans are marrying later and having fewer children than ever before. A variety of relationship and familial forms have emerged, or spread, in the last half of the twentieth century.

Single-Parent Families

Single-parent families are modified nuclear families. They have two generations, parent and child, but only one parent in the household. No co-parent (live-in friend or relative) is present either. One family in seven, as defined by the Bureau of the Census, is headed by a single parent, the majority of whom are women. Custody is awarded to the mother in eight of ten child-custody settlements (Black, 1979). Single, separated, divorced, or widowed women with dependent children are less likely than men in similar circumstances to remarry, mostly because they are unable to find eligible partners. Men marry younger women; thus, the pool of eligible men for older, particularly black, women is restricted. In 1982, 22 percent of all dependent (under 18) American children lived with only one parent (U.S. Bureau of the Census, 1983d).

It is estimated that by the year 2000, one out of every two American children will have lived at least some of its growing-up years in a one-parent household.

Single-parent families face special challenges. With only one adult in the household, the single parent has no ally with whom to form a parental subsystem. This can be good or bad, depending on the decision-making and control strategies of the parent. If a good relationship is established and maintained, some single parents have better relationships with, and control over, their children than do parents in two-parent families (Crossman and Adams, 1980). Financial worries are a major problem for single-parent families, particularly those headed by women. Over 50 percent live in poverty (Wallerstein and Kelly, 1979), a status they may attain at the point of divorce when the husband's earnings are withdrawn from the family. Women's lower earnings (about 59 percent of men's earnings) contribute to this situation as does the failure of ex-husbands to make child-support payments.

Some people view single-parent families as pathological rather than as a viable alternative to the nuclear family, yet little research supports this view. Single-parent families, like two-parent families, have problems. Whether they are able to overcome these problems depends on many things, including the age, maturity, and work experience of the single parent, the neighborhood the family lives in, the ability of the parent to care for the children and to hold a job, and the resources available to the family.

Cohabiting Couples

As noted earlier, cohabiting adult households increased dramatically in the 1970s and 1980s. When two adults, male and female, who are unrelated by blood or marriage share a household or "live together," this is called *cohabitation*. The U.S. Bureau of the Census defines cohabitation as a heterosexual couple living together for at least five days per week for three or more months who are not legally or religiously married, are sexually intimate, and may or may not have marriage as a goal (U.S. Bureau of the Census, 1983d). In the mid-1980s, there were over two million such couples in the United States, a 400 percent increase from 1970 (U.S. Bureau of the Census, 1986a) and most of this growth occurred among couples with no children present. The prevalence of cohabitation is a change not only from earlier decades but also from the entire history of our nation. As recently as the 1960s, ummarried people who lived together were considered immoral, and most people who did it were very poor or very rich and were assumed to know, but not care, about social convention.

Cohabitation is looked upon by a minority of young people as trial marriage (Kotken, 1985). It is one way to share kitchen, bathroom, dirty laundry, utility and telephone bills, and household chores without the permanency or commitment of marriage. Yet research shows that many cohabiting couples never do marry (R.E.L. Watson, 1983). Perhaps reluctance to marry was an impetus for cohabiting in the first place (DeMaris, 1984). Young people are marrying later, suggesting a wariness among American youth toward marriage. The median age at first marriage in 1986 was 25.7 for men and 23.1 for women. This is the highest ever for women and the highest since 1980 for men (U.S. Bureau of the Census, 1986a, p. 4).

Blended Families

Blended families occur when one or both parents bring children with them from a former marriage (Whiteside and Auerbach, 1978). Blended families are also called step-families, reconstituted families, and a variety of other terms including merged, remarried, sequential, recoupled, and combined (Kent, 1980; Hamner and Turner, 1985). One of the adults in the family is not the biological parent of one (or more) of the dependent children in the household. The phenomenon of blended families is certainly not new, but with the dramatic increase in divorce and remarriage, it has become more pervasive. Blended families face many challenges associated with incorporating a stepparent into the natural parent–child relationship. Children are sometimes resentful and jealous and resist a stepparent's attempts to exercise authority over them. Additionally, the stepparent may come to the marriage with children of one's own who may likewise resent the other adult and the other adult's children.

Visher and Visher (1978; 1979) view blended families as more open, by necessity, than nuclear families because elements of two preexisting families must somehow be blended into one. The parent–child bond between each adult and the adult's children must be expanded to allow for an adult–adult bond of the marital partners and a stepparent–stepchild bond between the nonbiological parent and child. Societal norms for how much parenting of stepchildren a stepparent should do, and how he or she should do it, are not well developed (Jacobson, 1979; Kent, 1980). Successful blending requires a great deal of work, and the years of blended family formation may be difficult. From an Open Systems Theory perspective, the behaviors of family members can be interpreted as efforts to define and maintain boundaries, to exchange affect appropriately, and to negotiate shared purposes (Kent, 1980).

Foster Families

Foster families provide substitute care for children whose own families do not, or cannot, adequately care for them (Hubbell, 1981). About 500,000 American children are in foster care, residing either in foster homes or in institutions (Hampson and Tavormin, 1980). Foster families can be any type of family—nuclear, single-parent, blended, and so on—that is approved, usually by a social welfare agency, to provide foster care. Foster care consists of providing both a home, including food, shelter, and clothing, and emotional support for the foster child. Providing foster care is a challenge because most foster children have spent at least two years in care and some have spent six. Forty-seven percent have resided in more than two foster homes (Hubbell, 1981). Foster children are frequently unwanted or abused by their natural parents. Both their trust of adults and their receptivity to forming close relationships are often low. Furthermore, children who are removed from natural parents and placed with total strangers may feel abandoned and alone and they may be unruly and hostile (Finkelstein, 1980). The trauma associated with being removed can precipitate emotional disorders such as depression, lack of affection, neurosis, and psychosomatic and psychoneurotic disturbances (Finkelstein, 1980). The challenge for foster parents is to reach out to a child who is upset, withdrawn, and fearful and draw it into the family fold. Disequilibrium and conflict that accompany the addition of a new family member are likely to occur.

Gay and Lesbian Families

In the past decade, the gay rights movement has supported homosexual men and women to "come out of the closet" regarding their sexual preferences. This was supported by the American Psychiatric Association and the American Psychological Association, both of which in the 1970s removed homosexuality from their lists of mental illnesses. There are estimates that as much as ten percent of the population is predominantly homosexual and many more have had sexual experiences with members of the same sex. Estimates of the number of lesbian mothers in the population range from 200,000 to 3 million, and related data estimate that one in five male homosexuals has been married (Hoeffer, 1981; Hotvedt and Mandel, 1982). The number of parents who are homosexual is substantial.

Gay and lesbian households take primarily two forms. Two adults of the same gender share a household without children, or two adults, typically lesbians, form a household that includes one of the women's children (Kirkpatrick, Smith, and Roy, 1981). Lesbian mothers have difficulty obtaining custody of their children and may have bitter, and losing, battles with former husbands. Public opinion is typically against granting them custody. Lower earnings from employment, problems in obtaining custody, and the stigma of living openly as lesbians make child rearing and everday family life a special challenge for lesbian mothers. Gay fathers face similar obstacles. Research by Miller (1979) reports that homosexual fathers are equally as likely as other fathers to rear healthy, happy children. Myths and stereotypes that gay men are more likely than straight men to molest children in their care are unfounded (Scallen, 1982). National crime data confirm that over 90 percent of sexual abuse of minors involves an adult male and a female child, a heterosexual rather than homosexual crime.

Estimates of the number of gay and lesbian households are tentative because many living in such arrangements do not acknowledge it. There is little question, however, that the number of such households is on the increase. With the advent and spread of Acquired Immune Deficiency Syndrome (AIDS), more gay men are becoming monogamous in their sexual relations and staying in long-term relationships. Lesbian women are choosing artificial insemination to avoid custody disputes with a male partner. As prejudice against gay and lesbian couples and parents decreases, estimates of the number of such households will become more accurate.

Families in Communes

Communes are collective households where people unrelated by blood or marriage share a common ideology or purpose and, often, economic living arrangements. Communes can be defined as:

> A group of five or more adults (plus possible children) most of whom are unrelated by marriage or blood, who have decided to live together, without compulsion, primarily for the pursuit of some ideological or personal goals for which a collective household is deemed essential (Urban Communes Project, 1976; as cited in Ferrar, 1982, p. 14).

Ferrar (1982) found a minority of communal households to contain families (22 of 57 in her sample). Communes with families incorporate them in a variety of ways. [Families were defined as a married couple or single parent with biological or adopted children (Ferrar, 1982, p. 14).] Communes are not as widespread as they were in earlier times (including the 1960s), but data from the late 1970s estimated that over 45,000 existed, with approximately 800,000 residents (Macklin, 1980). Although few Americans live in communes, they are possibly precursors of social change away from nuclear family and separate dwelling living arrangements (Kanter, 1973; J. Bernard, 1972).

Family problems in communes take two major forms. The first is, *distractions of children for adults without children*. When families are in the minority, adult residents without children often resent the scheduling (of meals, bedtimes, adult supervision, transportation, etc.), orderliness, and caretaking that children typically require (Ferrar, 1982, p. 9). Unless nonfamily adults are highly committed to the inclusion of children, they may encourage adults with children to leave. In communes with religious aims, children's interruptions and demands are particularly resented. The second problem encountered in communes centers around *interfamily conflicts over child rearing and care*. When families are in the majority, problems develop over differences of opinion and practice regading how to discipline, supervise, and care for children (Ferrar, 1982, pp. 18–20). Coordinating multiple-family meals, child care and supervision, and so on requires cooperation and commitment. Ferrar concludes that communes vary greatly one from the other and that some provide a more satisfactory setting for family life than others. The challenge of working out daily living arrangements for many unrelated adults, and children, is clearly great.

Migrant Families

Migrant families move across a state or county line at least once every 12 months (Hamner and Turner, 1985). Migrant families move in order to obtain seasonal employment, typically of an agricultural nature. They load food, clothes, household goods, and children in crowded cars or trucks and follow the growing season as spring and summer arrive each year. Many migrant families are black, Mexican-American, Puerto Rican, or Haitian, and almost all are poor. States with the most migrant families are California, Florida, and Texas.

Migrant families comprise a small proportion of American families but have more than their share of social problems. Some migrant families have many children and substandard housing and nutrition. Their continual moving takes children away from regular schooling (Constable, 1978), and the long hours and hard work associated with agriculture prevent parents from spending much time with their children. Migrant children often begin work in the fields at very young ages (five or six) or are left to care for younger siblings (Hamner and Turner, 1985). Maintaining a family while on the move with little support from other institutions—such as schools, churches, city recreation departments, and so on—makes migrant life especially demanding.

Dual-Career Families

Dual-career families are on the increase. These are families in which both adults are highly invested in a paid work career (Rapoport and Rapoport, 1976). But a career is more than paid employment. It involves a high degree of commitment, continuous work, and a progression toward greater responsibility and advancement (Hall, 1985). A recent survey of college students showed that 81 percent of women expected to combine a career with marriage and children, and 91 percent of men expressed support for wives with careers (Nadelson and Nadelson, 1980). Fully 75 percent of college men felt that they would spend as much time rearing their children as their future wives would.

Many women have worked, and do work, outside the home for pay, but women's commitment to a career on a large scale is a recent development. When both parents are involved in work that demands great time and energy, they may view child bearing and child rearing as not worth their costs (Nadelson and Nadelson, 1980). The implications of this are numerous. Dual-career couples can decide to delay child bearing, to have fewer children, or to have no children.

Hunt and Hunt (1982) worry that dual-career couples will stop having children, viewing them as too demanding in light of career demands. They are concerned that child bearing will be left primarily to an underclass of citizens with less education and less disposable wealth. They question the movement of women into full-fledged careers and see careers as entrapping, rather than freeing, both women and men in an antifamily life style that allows little time for children. They recommend less time and commitment for career and more for family concerns for both women and men.

Two-earner or two-worker families experience similar, if less severe, problems. Kingston and Nock (1987) report that in marriages where both members are employed, the amount of time a couple spends together decreases. Furthermore, the less time a couple spends together, the less satisfied they are with the marriage. Competition between work and family for time and energy is great, and how this dilemma is resolved will affect our nation's future. Day care for employed parents is popular with American citizens, but schools, employers, and the government have so far done little to provide it. Research by Martin, Seymour, Courage, Godbey, and Tate (1988) suggests that as more women rise to positions of leadership in corporations and unions, day care and other policies and benefits to support workers in discharging family responsibilities will increase.

Joint-Custody Families

Joint-custody families occur when judges award custody of children to both parents after a divorce. This indicates that child-rearing responsibilities are shared equally. A child may live one week with one parent, the second week with the other parent, the third week with the first parent, and so on. In such cases, the child literally has two homes. If both parents remarry, the child has four parents (and possibly several siblings and step-siblings) to relate to. Many divorced people refuse to move from the locality of their divorced spouse so they can have time with their child(ren). Joint-custody arrangements underscore the utility of an open systems perspective. A child's common membership in two separate families links the families and requires ongoing adjustments (work) by all concerned. The difficulties of joint custody have probably contributed to the growing incidence of child-snatching, where one parent literally steals the child, and hides it, from the other parent (Elliott, 1982).

Commuter Marriages

Partners in commuter marriages live in different cities and, sometimes, states. Some take turns commuting to the other's residence on alternate weekends, while others spend summers and vacations together but most time apart. One reason for commuter marriages is the difficulty of two career couples in finding acceptable jobs in the same locale. Without dependent children, commuter marriages can be fun and add excitement to a relationship. When children are involved, decisions have to be made about which parent they will live with and which house is home. Research shows that commuter marriages are a rare but growing phenomenon. They are much less common, furthermore, among young adults with dependent children than among the childless, young or old.

PARENTING

Parenting concerns the bearing and rearing of children. Children require a great deal of time and work, and the majority of women respond to parenthood by adjusting their paid work involvement to accommodate the family (Nieva, 1985). Numerous studies show that the number and ages of children influence women's, more than men's, work activities. Because women are normatively responsible for the family, parenthood influences such things as whether they will seek to work, the positions they will seek, the working conditions they will accept, and the satisfactions they will derive (Nieva and Gutek, 1981). Recent labor-force data on married mothers contradict the notion that mothers of preschool-aged children stay home full-time. Over one-half of all married mothers with young children (under six) were in the labor force in 1985 , almost triple the rate in 1960 (53.4 percent in 1985, 18.6 percent in 1960; U.S. Bureau of the Census, 1986b, Table 5).

As noted earlier, some women who face the dual demands of child rearing and work choose to remain childless. Hunt and Hunt (1982) propose that the stigma attached to remaining single and childless has lessened with the acceptance of alternative life styles. Women and men feel less compelled to have children. Furthermore, there is some evidence that women as well as men with demanding jobs or professional careers expect family involvement to be secondary in importance to their lives (Regan and Roland, 1985).

Tasks associated with parenting are dealt with below as aspects of the division of labor in families and in conjunction with our discussion of the family as a task group.

WHAT IS A SUCCESSFUL FAMILY?

Society expects families to meet the basic biological, material, emotional, psychological, intellectual, and spiritual needs of their members. Family success is not the possession of wealth, material possessions, or status, but fulfillment of normative expectations that include the provision of shelter, clothing, food, and nourishment; socialization and instruction of children; love and support, and so on. Members of successful families work together to care for their own and each other's needs. Parents have primary responsibility for family success when children are young, but as parents age, the tables may turn and adult children may become the primary caretakers (Glenn and McLanahan, 1981).

From an Open Systems Theory perspective, successful families work at maintaining linkages with other systems in their environment. Places of employment, schools, churches, voluntary organizations (such as Kiwanis, the Urban League, community action programs, employee unions), neighbors, political parties, recreational and friendship groups provide resources for a family and outlets for family outputs. Internally successful families talk straight and play fair. Grownups act like adults and allow children to be children. Communication patterns are clear, honest, respectful of generational lines, and productive. The role of communication in fostering family success, and failure, is addressed later in the chapter.

THE MARITAL RELATIONSHIP

Marriage links together individual men and women, but it also links families of orientation. Who marries whom is therefore important to marital partners' families. Marriage has been, historically, an *economic alliance of families of orientation* that was arranged by parents rather than by the partners. Romantic love as the basis for marriage is recent and is feasible, according to some sociologists, only in cultures with a nuclear family form (Goode, 1964). When marriage is an economic alliance of families, the choice of a partner is too important to leave to the whims of the young or to the vagaries of emotions such as romantic love.

Who Marries Whom?

Most people marry someone similar to themselves. Although there is normative freedom to marry anyone, marriage patterns reflect a great deal of *homogamy* (marriage between persons with similar class, ethnic, racial, or religious characteristics) in mate selection (Goode, 1964; Adams, 1986). This may result from individual preferences, but social pressures encourage it as well. If children marry partners who are different from themselves in significant ways, ties with parents or siblings may suffer. Working-class parents in England oppose their sons marrying middle-class women because they see it as threatening family ties (Bott, 1957). This reflects both awareness of the social barriers that separate classes and a desire to maintain family cohesion.

Marriage involves a systemic process of *coupling* of two previously independent elements. As a couple establishes a home and permanent relationship, new social phenomena emerge. Among these are the development of family (as opposed to individual only) roles, values, and goals, and ways of doing things. Uncertainty is associated with this process and, as a result, the first years of marriage may be difficult and full of conflict. For similar reasons, the birth of a child, who is dependent and demanding of time, emotion, and energy, is likely to stimulate conflict and change (LaRossa and LaRossa, 1981).

Who Are the Leaders in Families?

Adults are the leaders in successful families. In healthy families, the adults form a leadership subsystem within the more inclusive family system. From an OST perspective, the marital dyad is the dominant or leadership subsystem of the family. Parents are bigger in size, older in age, and physically and mentally advanced relative to their offspring. Parents have more resources, options, and responsibilities. A societal norm gives parents the right to tell their children what to do and when to do it. The norm of parental authority gives parents a right to have power over their children (for a discussion of power and authority, review Chapter 5).

Who Performs Family Work? The Division of Labor in Marriages and Families

As noted earlier, families have many obligations. They are expected to shelter, clothe, feed, socialize, instruct, love, cherish, and value their members. To fulfill these mandates, a great deal of work is required. *Division of labor* refers to how work is divided up among family members. Clegg and Dunkerley (1979) refer to family work as the *domestic division of labor*.

Most household work is planned and executed by women. Oakley's (1974) study of 40 British housewives reports an average of 77 hours a week in housework (10.1 hours a day). Today's women spend more hours on housework than women 50 years ago did, an average of 72 now and 57 then (Laws, 1979, p. 106, Table 2.1). Urban women do more housework than rural women. Oakley's respondents said they enjoyed some tasks more than others. Sixty percent enjoyed cooking and 50 percent enjoyed shopping, whereas they mostly disliked ironing (75 percent), dishwashing (65 percent), and house cleaning (50 percent).

Men typically perform traditionally masculine household chores such as yardwork, car care, household repairs, and garbage removal (Walker and Woods, 1975; Berk, 1985). Walker (1970) and Walker and Woods (1975) found that husbands' contribution to child care averaged 20 minutes a day and entailed chauffeuring children, helping them with school work, and other nonphysical care. Husbands spent 12 minutes a day in food preparation if their wives were employed (six minutes if wives were unemployed) and 24 minutes on shopping and other management activities. Less than six minutes were spent, on average, on clothing care (laundry).

A woman's involvement in household work varies with the number of children she has and whether she works outside the home (Walker and Woods, 1975). More children increases the time spent on home and family work but employment decreases it. For example, wives without children average 34 hours a week on home and family chores, those with one child average 48 hours, and those with four children average 57 hours. Wives not employed outside the home perform 8.1 hours of housework daily, but those who work 30 hours a week or more average 4.8 hours. Home and family work is primarily Mom's regardless of her number of children and employment situation. Walker (1970) and Walker and Woods (1975) found that 1,296 husbands in Syracuse, New York, spent an average of 1.6 hours a day on housework regardless of whether their wives were employed full-time, part-time, or not at all. Children spent about one hour a day on housework, and this did not vary by whether the mother worked or by the children's ages. Laws concludes that children are not a major resource for domestic labor and that housework remains "women's work" not "women's and men's work" nor "women's and children's work" (Laws, 1979, p. 9).

Over one-half of adult women in the United States work outside the home for pay. In 1986, 65 percent of single women, 76 percent of divorced, 62 percent of separated, and 55 percent of married women with husband present were employed for pay (U.S. Bureau of the Census, 1986c, pp. 382, 383). If women work outside the home for pay, why does home and family work fall mostly to them? The social roles of wife/mother and husband/father are normatively defined by society. Girls have been taught that housework and children are their responsibilities, and boys are taught that supporting and protecting the family are theirs. Pressures to conform to *gender-specific* scripts such as these are present throughout life and contribute to sex-role conformity (Laws, 1979). If women or men violate such norms, they may be reminded by in-laws, parents, spouse, children, ministers, and so on to repent and conform.

Times are changing, however. Housework is increasingly defined as family work in some countries. Swedish billboards show family members doing household chores with the slogan, "Don't help Mother!" Because household work in Sweden is viewed as everyone's responsibility, family members are enjoined to do their share because it is *fair*, not to "help mother." Stereotypical gender prescriptions are generally unsatisfying to both men and women (Pleck, 1975). Hesselbart (1980) found people more concerned with men's performance of fathering duties than is generally assumed. Proportionately more men and women agreed that "the most important thing a father can teach his son is to be a good father and family member" (64 percent) than agreed that "the most important thing a mother can teach her daughter is to be a good mother and family member" (45 percent). This suggests that many adults believe too little attention is paid to teaching sons about their family responsibilities and roles (Gasser and Taylor, 1976).

Women dislike sole responsibility for housework partly because it is unsatisfying (Berk, 1985). Oakley's housewives disliked housework for three reasons: (1) It is monotonous; that is, it must be repeated over and over and produces no palpable or lasting effects; (2) it is fragmentary; several tasks must be done at once with little opportunity for completing one before having to start another; and (3) housework never ends! Other negatives are dullness of tasks (such as ironing or folding clothes, washing dishes) and isolation in a separate dwelling away from other family members (except small children), neighbors, and friends.

Housewife Depression as a Family Output

Full-time housewives suffer from depression more than do women who work for pay (Bernard, 1981; Chesler, 1972) and more than other members of their families. How can this be explained? A tenet of OST is that *system stability is a system property, not a property of component parts*. A depressed housewife may signal that a family is in trouble. Open Systems Theory requires that a housewife's depression be viewed as a family output, that the housewife's ties to the environment be focused upon, that the temptation to view the problem as the housewife's alone be resisted, and that attention be paid to the need, and potential, for total system change.

The depressed housewife can take pills or see a psychiatrist to improve her emotional outlook or she can assess her situation and change the way she spends her time. Child care can be arranged for dependent children, and the husband can change his behavior relative to family work. Family arrangements that restrict a housewife/mother to an isolated nuclear family dwelling for most of each day, limit her company to that of small children, and make her responsible for performing tasks that are monotonous, fragmented, neverending, and dull can lead to depression. Many married women seek employment, despite their housework responsibilities, to make extrafamily contacts and friends and to be around others like themselves (Fox and Hesse–Biber, 1984; Martin, 1980c; Brown, 1976). This can prevent depression that stems from isolation and boredom.

Viewing a housewife's depression as a family output prevents attributing (reducing) her problem to herself alone. Family arrangements, internal and external, can contribute to depression—and other problematic behavior—in family members, and changes in arrangements can help resolve problems. This is discussed further in the section on Communication in Families.

THE FAMILY AS A MULTITUDE OF SYSTEMS

A family of five can have 25 subsystems in addition to the total system of five members. Table 6.2 lists the 26-system potential of a family composed of Juan and Maria (father and mother) and their three children, Patti, Frank, and Angela. The permutations shown in Table 6.2 include every combination of family member in groups of two, three, four, and five. Family therapists are concerned with family subsystems because they exist in all families and are often denied or distorted in families with problems (Haley, 1976; Bowen, 1978).

The number of family subsystems increases geometrically with family size. A married couple without children form a single system. When a child arrives, the number of potential subsystems increases to four: mother and father; mother and child; father and child; mother, father, and child. The addition of a second child increases the total to 11. The formula for deter-

TABLE 6.2. POTENTIAL SUBSYSTEMS IN A FAMILY OF FIVE

	Juan *(Father)*	*Maria* *(Mother)*
Patti *(age 14)*	*Frank* *(age 10)*	*Angela* *(age 8)*

Potential subsystems:

(1) Juan, Maria, Patti, Frank & Angela [the totality]	(14) Juan, Maria, & Angela
(2) Juan & Maria	(15) Juan, Patti, & Angela
(3) Juan & Patti	(16) Juan, Frank, & Angela
(4) Juan & Frank	(17) Juan, Patti, & Frank
(5) Juan & Angela	(18) Maria, Patti, & Frank
(6) Maria & Patti	(19) Maria, Patti, & Angela
(7) Maria & Frank	(20) Maria, Frank, & Angela
(8) Maria & Angela	(21) Patti, Frank, & Angela
(9) Patti & Frank	(22) Juan, Maria, Patti, & Frank
(10) Patti & Angela	(23) Juan, Maria, Patti, & Angela
(11) Frank & Angela	(24) Juan, Maria, Frank, & Angela
(12) Juan, Maria, & Patti	(25) Juan, Patti, Frank, & Angela
(13) Juan, Maria, & Frank	(26) Maria, Patti, Frank, & Angela

mining the number of potential subsystems based on family size is shown in Equation 1.

$$\text{Number of potential subsystems} = 2^n - (n + 1) \qquad \textit{(Equation 1)}$$

where n is the number of individuals in the family. With a three-child, two-parent family such as shown in Table 6.2, the formula is:

$$2^5 - (5 + 1) = 32 - 6, \text{ or } 26. \qquad \textit{(Equation 2)}$$

Family therapists concerned about subsystem dynamics often require the total family to attend initial treatment sessions (Haley, 1976; Jackson, 1959; Satir, 1967). Individuals experience their families uniquely. As examination of the subsystems in Table 6.2 suggests, each member belongs to a unique set of family subsystems. A therapist risks co-optation if the perspectives or biases of some individuals are communicated before the totality is understood. If family arrangements are the source of an individual's problems, therapists are more effective if they see the totality first. Some therapists require three generations (parents, children, grandparents) to attend initial sessions in order to observe intra- and intergenerational dynamics firsthand.

THE FAMILY AS A TASK GROUP

One way to view families is as small task groups with the parents as leaders (Tallman, 1970).[1] Task groups are groups that perform work (see Chapter 7). Family tasks take two forms: (1) instrumental and (2) socioemotional (see Table 6.3). *Instrumental tasks* include the performance of routine work necessary to meet the material needs of family members for shelter, clothing, food, transportation, income, and so on. *Socioemotional tasks* are relationship work such as loving, hugging, showing positive regard, correcting children, and so on. Table 6.3 lists some instrumental and socioemotional tasks that society expects families to perform. The two types of tasks are not totally separate. The manner in which instrumental tasks are performed, such as bathing a child or serving meals, has socioemotional aspects, and socioemotional tasks such as teaching family values require concrete work such as explaining and demonstrating through behavior what is important.

Parents' ability to lead children in a family can be viewed in terms of three dimensions: (1) leader–member relations, (2) the task structure, and (3) leader, or parental, power (Coles, Alexander, and Schiavo, 1974).

---

[1] Our discussion of families as task groups draws extensively on the work of Coles, Alexander, and Schiavo (1974).

TABLE 6.3. INSTRUMENTAL AND SOCIOEMOTIONAL TASKS OF FAMILIES

Instrumental Tasks	*Socioemotional Tasks*
Earning money to support the family	Showing affection to each other
Paying bills	Communication of support, regard
Buying food, clothes, furniture	Hugging, caressing, loving
Preparing food, serving meals	Showing sympathy and empathy
Washing, folding, ironing clothes	Building relationships based on mutual trust
Hanging drapes or curtains	and respect
Cleaning up after meals, washing dishes, putting food away	Teaching family values, honesty, character, respect for others
Cleaning house (bathrooms, floors, etc.)	Imparting goals
Changing bed sheets and towels	Playing with children
Cutting grass, bushes, lawn care	Sexual intimacy among adults
Repairing and maintaining house	Buying and giving gifts, having parties
Straightening rooms	Taking children to social events
Changing oil in car, buying gas	Teaching children to be kind
Washing car	Correcting and punishing children
Feeding and care of pets	Resolving conflicts and problems
Setting priorities and goals	Mediating disputes between members
Making plans, saving money, making decisions	Teaching children to give and take, to relate to others
Bathing and dressing children	Attending functions in which family members are involved
Supervising, watching children	
Driving children to school, day care, lessons, recreation	
Teaching children to brush teeth, bathe, put toys away, dress themselves	
Teaching children to sit up, walk, talk	
Taking children for health care: doctor, dentist	
Assigning tasks and supervising their completion	

1. *Leader–member relations.* This concerns the quality of leader–member relations. Similar to the concept of group climate or atmosphere in small-group research (Fiedler, 1967), this refers to the degree to which feelings among family members are positive or negative (also see Chapter 7 on groups). Do children like their parents? Do parents like their children? When leader–member relations are positive, parents are better able to gain compliance from children.

2. *Task structure.* Task structure concerns the extent to which family tasks (see Table 6.3) are specific, concrete, and easy to organize versus diffuse, ambiguous, and difficult to organize. Structured tasks have clear-cut goals and identifiable means of achieving them and include many of the instrumental tasks in Table 6.3. Unstructured tasks, including most socioemotional tasks, are more problematic. When

family tasks are highly structured, the parenting or leadership job is easier. Many tasks with young children such as teaching them to put away their toys, to brush their teeth, to dress themselves, to take out the garbage, and to put away their clothes are structured and thus easy to communicate, organize, and monitor. Socioemotional tasks such as communicating support, building character, and showing trust are, on the other hand, diffuse and more difficult to organize, execute, and monitor. When children enter adolescence, socioemotional tasks often take precedence over instrumental tasks. To remain effective, parents of adolescents have to change their leadership style and focus (Coles, Alexander, and Schiavo, 1974).

3. *Leader position-power*. Leader, or parental, position-power refers to the amount of power parents have over their children. This is greater when children are small than when they grow up. With small children, parents enjoy high position-power because of the advantages of size, age, resources, expertise, and the extreme dependency of children for food, shelter, and care. As children grow up, parents' position-power diminishes. Family dynamics change as children grow from young, small, and dependent into older, bigger, and more independent members.

Families and Adolescence: Changes in Parents' Leadership Style

The three dimensions of parental leadership can be used to understand changes that families as task groups undergo when children reach adolescence (Coles, Alexander, and Schiavo, 1974). This perspective suggests that delinquency is a family output rather than a child-specific problem.

1. *Leader–member relations*. When children reach adolescence, the group climate or quality of parent–child relations often deteriorates (McCord, 1979). Older children are less accepting of their parents and demand more independence, rights, and privileges. Adolescents challenge parental authority and demand to be treated as adults. Relations between parents and child may be hostile and riddled with conflict. Relations of parents with each other may also deteriorate (Burr, 1970). Leadership in such families is difficult because adolescent children are less willing to follow.

2. *Task structure*. Families with adolescents face many ambiguous tasks such as what to do about the adolescent's sexual activities, use of alcohol and drugs, relationships with peers and dates, demands for money and use of the car, study habits and behavior in school, and divergence of attitudes and values toward education, career, sexual relations, and so on. Parental leadership is difficult in such circum-

stances because parents are unsure about what to do and how to go about it. Parents who can adapt in order to deal with the uncertainty and ambiguity associated with these tasks are more effective in dealing with adolescent children (Jacob, 1975).

3. *Leader position-power*. Parents have less position-power over adolescent children. As children grow in size and age, they become more involved with peers, school, and job and less dependent on parents and family for emotional and material needs. As their alternatives increase, they are less susceptible to parents' attempts to reward and punish, the contingencies that parents of young children control almost totally. Parents retain control of many privileges, including financial (allowance) and other resources (use of the family car), but the manner in which they exercise control is important. Influence strategies that adolescents perceive as inappropriate elicit resistance and alienation (Deutsch, 1973). Parents' loss of position-power is gradual during elementary school but accelerates when a child reaches adolescence (Coles, Alexander, and Schiavo, 1974).

In summary, parenting is easier with young children than with adolescents because leadership conditions are more favorable with small children. In families with adolescents, the group atmosphere is poorer, leadership tasks are more ambiguous, and parents have less power. To compensate, the family's leadership and structure must change. A child's opinions, goals, and priorities must be taken into account, and the youngster must be incorporated into the leadership subsystem by including the child in decision-making activities. Additionally, effective parental leadership style changes from an emphasis on instrumental tasks to a focus on socioemotional tasks (Coles, Alexander, and Schiavo, 1974). Whereas a task-oriented leader can ensure the efficient management of the physical, socialization, and learning needs of young children, relationship-oriented leadership is needed to bring adolescents into the problem-solving structure of the family.

> The very skills that are most effective when children are younger, that is, instrumental leadership skills such as assigning tasks, defining goals, [and] monitoring performance work against the family when the children reach adolescence whereas the skills that are most effective when there are adolescents in the family, that is, democratic leadership, warmth, and consideration may not be sufficient to get the job done in families with younger children. The adolescent family is different, as a group leadership situation, from the pre-adolescent family. This change in the family requires a change in family leadership, that is, a different leader or a leader who can change her/his style. (Coles, Alexander, and Schiavo, 1974, p. 7)

A task-group conception of families with the parents as leaders is useful for three reasons. First, it discourages the attribution of family problems to individual members, particularly to children who are young and dependent. Adolescent delinquency can be viewed as a family output associated with certain types of family—and societal—arrangements and processes, not solely a problem of the adolescent per se. Second, it emphasizes the leadership subsystem's role in shaping the family context and behavior of family members. Parents have a great deal of influence over their children's behavior in the family and in relation to the outside world. Families are the context within which children learn to be members of both family and society. Third, it identifies member deviancy as a family output that requires qualitative change if improvement is to occur. In OST terms, families that are successful task groups learn and change as their members change. As children grow older, adjustments in who does what and how things are done must be made. When family members change and family structure does not, problems may occur.

COMMUNICATION IN FAMILIES: AN OPEN SYSTEMS PERSPECTIVE

Communication, or the transmitting of information, concerns the patterns of message sending and receiving among family members and between family members and the environment. *Communication* has been defined as all verbal and nonverbal behavior within a social context (Satir, 1967). Watzlawick, Beavin, and Jackson (1967) say that all human behavior is communication. There is little question that communication is complex or that it occurs on many levels at once. Gestures, manner, dress, tone of voice, facial expression, body posture, silence, and even inactivity communicate as surely as words. In an Open Systems Theory perspective, families are viewed as communication systems, as living systems that maintain relationships internally and with their environments through the sending and receiving of messages (Janzen and Harris, 1980, p. 15). This section of Chapter 6 defines healthy communication and reviews a number of family problems associated with communication irregularities.

What Is Healthy Communication?

Healthy communication is identified in research studies by contrasting communication styles, patterns, and content of problem and nonproblem families (Alexander and Parsons, 1977; Haley, 1980). There is a growing consensus that some kinds of family communications contribute to health and others to pathology (Minuchin, 1974). Healthy communications are clear (their meaning is easy to discern), congruent (they communicate information on an implicit level that is congruent with information communicated on the explicit level), and consistent (parents who forbid an action forbid it repeatedly, over time). Healthy communications are logical and coherent; comments of later speakers relate to, and build on, those of earlier speakers. Healthy communication allows all members a chance to speak, reasons are given for directives, and statements to family members are supportive, positive, and nondefensive (Reiss, 1971; Singer, 1974; Hetherington and Martin, 1979). One hundred percent of family communications do not have to be healthy for a family to be healthy. (Some inconsistency, lack of clarity, dissimulation, and so on occurs in any family.) When unhealthy communications are predominant, however, problems—particularly with children—may develop.

The Double-Bind Phenomenon

The "double-bind phenomenon" is a communication problem that has been observed in families of schizophrenics. A double-bind communication gives two incompatible messages at once. The recipient is not allowed to challenge or discuss the message and is also prevented from bowing out. As a result, the recipient is placed in a double-bind with two ways to lose and none to win. Double-bind phenomena, as described by Watzlawick, Beavin, and Jackson (1967, p. 212), occur under three conditions.

1. Two or more persons are involved in an intense relationship that has a high degree of survival value for one or more of the participants.
2. In this context, messages are given that assert opposing commands; that is, assertions are mutually exclusive, which means neither assertion can be obeyed without disobeying the other.
3. The recipient of the message is prevented from commenting on it or walking away from it.

An example of a double-bind message between parent and child is as follows. A child asks permission to go camping with friends and the parent says okay. In consenting, however, the parent also says: "But I won't be able to sleep while you're away because you know how much I worry about you. And you know how I need my sleep. But you go ahead. I wouldn't want your friends to think your family kept you from going." On one level, the child is given permission to go but the overlaid message is that she should not. If she goes on the trip, she will feel guilty; if not, she may resent her parent. She has no way to win.

Double-bind communications do not always produce pathology. A typical day of interaction with family and friends may contain many double-bind messages. If they are extensive, however, and are the predominant type of communication between parent and child, they can be destructive.

The Reciprocal Double-Bind

Elkaim (1985, 1986) describes a reciprocal double-bind that marriage partners sometimes fall into. This occurs when each partner gives double-bind messages to the other. Elkaim labels the two messages in a double-bind communication as (1) official program and (2) map of the world. The *official program* is the partner's explicit message. It is the explicit request given by one partner for a change in the other partner's behavior. In the example of Anna and Benedetto, for instance, Anna says: "You don't show me affection; I want you to come closer." Her husband, Benedetto, says: "You always side with your friends against me. Give me more recognition."

The *map of the world* is "the blueprint that each member has drawn up in the course of his or her past and then attempts to use" with his or her spouse (Elkaim, 1986, p. 35). The map of the world reflects the cumulative experience of a subject's life and is brought to bear in the marriage relationship often without awareness. Anna, whose father left his family when she was four years old, is afraid of intimacy because she fears being abandoned. Her map of the world says to Benedetto, "Do not come close because you will abandon me." Because of unloving parents and being forced to leave his beloved grandfather at age 12, Benedetto craves tenderness but fears attachment. His map of the world toward Anna is "I can only be rejected" (Elkaim, 1986, p. 37). Elkaim recommends that family systems therapists use paradoxical assignments with the couple to undermine their map of the world and bring to awareness the double-bind messages they transmit (also see Sluzki, 1978).

Inability to Sustain Family Alliances

Haley (1960; 1980) has identified pathology-producing patterns in families with schizophrenic male sons. Compared to healthy families, these families were unable to form and sustain communication or interactional alliances. *Alliances* are joint actions engaged in by two people who share a common interest or goal not shared by a third person (Haley, 1976, p. 109). Haley found that with mother, father, and schizophrenic son, when one supported another's comment, the third attacked the allying pair. If the son says, "I hate boats. You know I've always feared boats," the allying mother might chime in, "That's true. When you were little, you always cried if we tried to take you on a boat." In affirming the son's claim, the mother formed an alliance with her son. In a healthy family, father might agree or say nothing. In pathological families, father attacks the allying pair until one of them retracts his or her comment. The alliance is destroyed. Father might say, "Oh, malarkey! You're just a crybaby. You're afraid of everything, not just boats." At this point, mother says: "Well, he is afraid of everything; that's for sure," withdrawing support for her son's claim. Families that prevent the formation and sustenance of alliances, or temporary bonding, may produce schizophrenic children.

Coalition Formation across Generational Lines

Coalitions, in contrast to alliances, entail a process of joint action of two persons (or parties) *against* a third. Nuclear families have two hierarchical levels: parent and child. Coalitions across hierarchical levels are those between one parent and child against the other parent. Such coalitions are not destructive if they occur on occasion and if they are acknowledged, but if repeated and unacknowledged, they can be harmful. In the case example of Dibs (see below), each parent formed a coalition with Dibs against the other parent. This was unacknowledged, however, and each parent blamed Dibs for problems with his or her spouse. The parents' conception of Dibs as the source of their problems was a confusion of hierarchical relations (Haley, 1976). Their marital problems were not Dibs' fault, but the parents' belief that they were clouded the hierarchical distinction between parent and child and prevented them from forming an alliance on behalf of their marriage or their children.

Delinquency and Family Communication

Numerous theorists and researchers believe delinquency results from family communication problems (Tolan, Cromwell, and Brasswell, 1986). Minuchin and colleagues' early work (1967) on slum families concluded that delinquent families (families that produce delinquents) were less cooperative and productive than adaptive (or nondelinquent) families. Parents in delinquent families tended to rely heavily on behavior-control statements (such as telling a child to stop a problematic behavior), whereas parents in nondelinquent families explained how problem behaviors were inappropriate and suggested better ways to act. Singer (1974) concludes that children's delinquent behavior is a result of inconsistent messages from parents (one parent says one thing, the other says another) and an absence of consequences for transgression despite a claimed restrictive policy.

Patterson and Brodsky (1976) and Wahler (1980) also focus on family interaction patterns as precipitants of delinquency. They describe the *coercive trap* where parents first punish a child's aggressive behavior by yelling, pleading, or spanking but fail to punish the same behavior when the child exhibits it again. This encourages, over time, an aggressive interaction style within the family that generalizes to other social contexts. Alexander and associates (Alexander and Parsons, 1973; Alexander and Barton, 1976; Parsons and Alexander, 1973; Alexander, Barton, Schiavo, and Parsons, 1976) note three differences between delinquent and adaptive families on the quantity and quality of communication styles: (1) Families of delinquents distribute talking unevenly (one or a few members do most of the talking); (2) conversations in delinquent families are disjointed and disorganized; and (3) adaptive families make more supportive comments to each other. The negative effects of confusing communications and an absence of reciprocal reinforcement of clear, meaningful messages are emphasized.

Psychological Absence of a Family Member

Some families have problems because of the psychological absence of a family member. *Psychological absence* occurs when a family member is neither entirely in nor entirely outside a family system (Boss, 1974, p. 1). The person has not died, deserted, or moved away but is involved with the family on an irregular or unpredictable basis. Psychological absence of a family member, particularly a parent, makes other members uncertain about the family's boundary. Fathers who are totally absorbed in their jobs or who spend weekends and evenings glued to the television may be psychologically absent. This makes other members unsure of the family's membership and hampers attempts to organize or establish family routines. Stress levels and disorganization may be greater in families with a psychologically absent member than in families with a member lost through death or divorce (Boss, 1974). Dibs' father in the case example that follows is psychologically absent. He fails to see himself as an active participant in rearing Dibs, and when Dibs goes for treatment, he sees no reason for participating in treatment himself.

The Therapeutic Task in Family Treatment

Troubled families often engage in unhealthy *sequences* or chains of events—actions, exchanges—that are repeated again and again (Haley, 1976, pp. 105–109). Haley says the goal of therapy is to "change the sequences that occur among people in an organized group. When that sequence changes, the individuals in the group undergo change" (Haley, 1976, p. 105). The therapist's task, according to Haley, is to change unhealthy sequences by intervening in such a way that the family cannot continue them (p. 107). One of Haley's interventive methods is to give a family assignments, to practice outside the therapeutic context, that contradict its unhealthy sequences. Once the sequence is undermined, healthier and more productive patterns can be learned.

QUALITATIVE SYSTEM CHANGE:
THE CASE EXAMPLE OF DIBS

The case example of *Dibs* is about a troubled child, his family, and his play therapist, Virginia Axline (1964). We present the example to illustrate the OST principle of *qualitative change from within*. The story is as follows.

Dibs is the second child (his sister, Dorothy, is considerably older and is away at boarding school most of the time) in a family where both parents are professionals, are highly intelligent, and value intellectual achievement. When Dibs' mother became pregnant with him, his father resented the intrusion of another baby into his marriage and professional life and withdrew attention and affection from both mother and baby. Problems between father and mother came to be interpreted as centering around Dibs. Dibs' response to this, as he became aware, was hostility toward his parents and uncooperative and bizarre behavior that became so extreme his parents believed he was retarded.

Demands by Dibs' mother for intellectual achievement were combined with doubts about his ability to learn, continual questioning and criticism of his behavior, and frequent testing of his intellectual abilities. Dibs acted out at home and at school. At home, his father responded to Dibs' behavior by locking him in his room. At school, Dibs' teachers suggested that the mother seek professional help for him. Mother resisted at first but finally did so, at which time the reader meets Dibs as he enters therapy with the book's author and play therapist, Virginia Axline. Dibs is, at this time, five years old. Both mother and therapist noted that after Dibs' birth and the strain that developed between the parents, the family increasingly withdrew from social contacts and ties with others. As a result, few people, relatives or friends, were intimately involved in the family's routines or life.

Figure 6.1 presents a static view of the relevant systems. The family has four members: mother, father, sister Dorothy, and Dibs (Figure 6.1a). Dorothy is away at boarding school during the week. She is described by her mother as a "perfect child" (Axline, 1964, p. 37) who was sent away so the mother could "concentrate on working with Dibs" (p. 168). On weekends, Dibs behaves hostilely toward Dorothy. She is no ally for him against his parents' rejection and disapproval.

As suggested by Figure 6.1a, Dibs' strange behavior was visible outside the family, primarily to the teachers and children at school. This is important, because the suggestion that Dibs needed professional help came from his teacher (and was told to the mother). The teacher's reaction to Dibs' behavior and suggestion to the mother that he needed help is an example of feedback to the family. Initially it was negative feedback because it led to corrective action to alter Dibs' behavior.

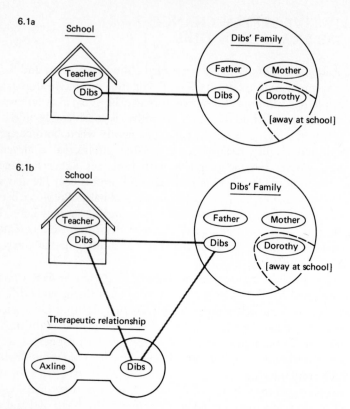

Figure 6.1 A Static View of the Primary Systems in Which Dibs Was Involved Prior To and During Treatment.

Figure 6.1b shows the three social systems in which Dibs was involved after entering therapy: family, school, and therapy. Changes in Dibs' behavior, when they occurred, fundamentally affected his entire family. Dibs' changed behavior set off a new and different set of sequences that allowed the family to "change into a system of greater diversity" or to become less rigidly locked into its old, unproductive narrow sequences (Haley, 1976, p. 105). Dibs' behavioral changes also had an impact on his classroom (and teacher), but the larger size of the school and his less central role in it produced a smaller impact than at home.

The four diagrams in Figure 6.2 show the process that characterized the family at two points in time: the school prior to Dibs' improvement, and the therapeutic system. For convenience, we can begin at point A in Figure 6.2a: The spouses have marital trouble, withdraw from each other, and blame Dibs. This leads to cold, distant behavior on their part toward Dibs (point B). This influences Dibs (point C) to withdraw from his parents, to be hostile

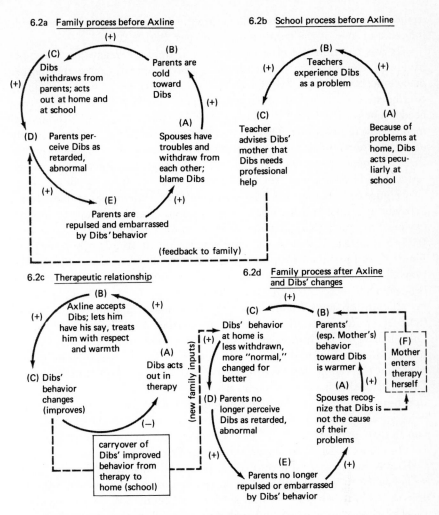

Figure 6.2 Dynamic Conceptions of Processes Involved in Family, School, and Therapy That Affected Dibs and His Family Over Time.

toward them, and to exhibit odd behavior at home and at school (refusing to talk, hiding under tables, etc.). The more Dibs behaves this way, the more his parents view him as retarded and abnormal (point D). When his parents view him as abnormal, they are repulsed and embarrassed by him (point E), influencing them to withdraw from other people (a step in the sequence not represented in Figure 6.2a) and from each other, back to point A. This type of sequence, or cycle of events, is a *deviation-amplifying cycle*. Nothing in the cycle *corrects* it or brings it back to a steady state. It is self-perpetuating and, in the present case, was broken and eventually corrected because of an outside influence on one of the family's members (see Fig. 6.2c).

It was through the observation of, and feedback regarding Dibs' behavior at school (which is outside the family boundary), that the mother made a decision to seek help for Dibs. The sequence-cycle inside the family continued, uninterrupted, until a member of another system suggested a need for help. The family's unhappy situation was maintained although all members were miserable. There is no intention here to suggest that a family or other system is unable to change itself from the inside. Rather, once a pathological sequence of events is entrenched, changing it is difficult and may be easier if an outside agent, such as a counselor or therapist, is allowed in.

Figure 6.2b depicts the relationship of Dibs' experiences at home to his behavior at school and his teacher's perceptions of and reactions to this behavior. The teacher's suggestion to Dibs' mother that Dibs needed help is *feedback* from the school to the family regarding it (the family's) outputs. Figure 6.2c presents a simplified view of Dibs' and Virginia Axline's relationship. This diagram, like 6.2a, has a time dimension to it—thus Dibs' behaviors are represented by two different points: At point A, Dibs begins his relationship with Axline by acting like he does at home and at school (hostile, erratic, nonverbal). Axline, in contrast to Dibs' parents, *accepts* Dibs' behavior, lets him have his say (often through dolls and play characters), and treats him with respect. As a result, Dibs changes (point C). This took time (9 years passed over the course of treatment reported in the book). Dibs' changed behavior was then carried by him from the therapeutic relationship to his home and became a new input for the family. Although Dibs' behavior also changed at school, we deal primarily with the results in his family that involved, first, his mother and, over time, his father.

In Figure 6.2d, Dibs' changed behavior first affected the family at point C: Dibs began to act "more normal" at home. He was less hostile, he looked at and spoke to his parents, and so on. As he did this, his parents were less able to sustain their view of him as abnormal (point D). As this changed, they became less repulsed and embarrassed by him (point E). As a consequence, as suggested in Figure 6.2d, the parents (particularly the mother) no longer viewed Dibs as the sole cause of their marital problems. This led the mother to enter therapy and to recognize that she had taken out on Dibs the strained relationship between herself and her husband: "We blamed Dibs" (Axline, 1964, p. 168). As the parents ceased to blame Dibs for their problems, they behaved more acceptingly and warmly toward him (point B) and this, in turn, reinforced Dibs' new behaviors at home. Again, the cycle is *deviation-amplifying*. This time, however, the sequence is beneficial. It helped Dibs to improve and to be himself and became a freeing experience for the entire family.

Several points can be learned from the Dibs example. First, the family system changed qualitatively—admittedly over a period of years—because one of its members (and a young, small one at that) changed. This affirms the Open Systems principle that system change can come from within. Second, Dibs was able to change his family because he became a member of another system outside the family where he was more accepted and better understood. The changes he was able to make there were transferred to and sustained in his home. Through Dibs, the family was *treated*. The changes in Dibs' family could probably have been made much more quickly if, as urged by most family therapists, all members of the family had gone into therapy together. But some parents, like Dibs' parents (especially his father), are unwilling to do this. The Dibs example suggests that even then, a family can be helped if at least *one* of its members improves his or her behavior. Third, the Dibs example illustrates a principle of Haley's (1976) that deserves emphasis: Change behavior and attitude change will follow. Haley stresses the hazards of sharing insights and perceptions in family therapy. His basic principle is that change in a system's sequences (interaction patterns) will lead to system change and to change in all members of a system. Assisting families *to engage in new behavior sequencing* is a basic goal of family intervention from an OST perspective.

IMPLICATIONS FOR SOCIAL WORK

Practice implications for social work with families are noted throughout Chapter 6. A major point is this: *Troubled families can change for the better.* They can change *if* they alter their internal sequencing from narrow, rigid patterns to flexible, versatile, and complex patterns. Internal change is facilitated by changes in the family's linkages or ties with other systems and persons outside its boundaries. If Dibs had not been in school and if his teacher had not suggested that he needed help, his mother might not have sought it. Dibs' relationship with Axline gave him an accepting context and allowed him to change. He changed his family by transferring his new behaviors with Axline to his home.

Three implications of Chapter 6 are emphasized. First, the behavior of family members is most appropriately viewed *as a family output* rather than the output of individual family members. This suggests that social workers view the family system as a primary target of intervention or policy directive. Viewed in isolation, the behavior of individual members may fail to make sense or may be misunderstood.

Although families are small, intimate social systems, they are also linked to other institutional contexts, including education, religion, work, the economy, medical care, the military, law enforcement, crime and the courts, the welfare system, and so forth. Thus, a second implication of Chapter 6 is that problem diagnosis (and policy analysis) should begin by attending to the *totality of the social context* in which families are lodged rather than to internal family patterns and dynamics. Reasons for this are numerous but the primary one is efficiency. Much can be learned about a family—and much can be done to assist it—by focusing on its linkages with other systems. Irresponsible or antisocial behavior by a family member may stem from hunger brought about by too little money. Uncleanliness may be a result of substandard housing and plumbing; idleness to lack of transportation and employment opportunities; school absence to lack of clothing, acceptance by teachers, and so forth. Understanding of the inclusive context prior to initiation of particular actions can improve a practitioner's effectiveness.

A third point to be emphasized here is that a family counselor or therapist should have a primary goal of *assisting troubled families to change their interaction sequencing*. This reflects appreciation of the systemic nature of family relationships and rests on the assumption that changes in interactional patterns *between* family members will lead to changes *in* individual family members (Haley, 1976). It also suggests that it is more efficient to change behaviors and let attitudes follow than to assume that changed attitudes (e.g., insights, understanding, etc.) will produce changed behaviors. Haley (1976) argues, from a systems perspective compatible with OST, that providing family members with insights regarding their behaviors sometimes causes them to become more stubbornly committed to unproductive sequences. He suggests that the primary responsibility of therapists is to help a family change its behavioral sequencing by intervening in such a way that the family is forced to change. Everything else—including attitudes, feelings about self, regard and support for others—will follow.

Families are special systems because of their child-rearing and socialization functions and their provision of opportunities for intimacy within and across generational lines. Families provide our most enduring and long-term relationships. They predate us in time and memory, and they have claims on us until we die. An Open Systems Theory perspective will, it is hoped, foster greater appreciation of families' extensive openness and ties to their social, economic, political, and cultural environments.

Chapter 7

Small Groups as Open Systems: A Cognitive Map of Groups

INTRODUCTION

Small groups are the building blocks of larger social systems such as organizations and communities. Social workers' involvement in groups is extensive and includes participation in service units, staffing and management teams, committee meetings, task forces, and treatment groups (Alissi, 1980). Understanding of the form and dynamics of small groups is therefore useful. Chapter 7 presents an Open Systems Theory perspective of small groups. An OST perspective focuses attention on three levels of group reality: (1) the individual in a group, (2) the group as a unit, and (3) the group in relation to its environment.

Kurt Lewin, one of the founders of social psychology, argues that groups have realities of their own, independent of those of individual members.

> There is no more magic behind the fact that groups have properties of their own, which are different from the properties of their subgroups or their individual members, than behind the fact that molecules have properties which are different from the properties of atoms or ions of which they are composed. (Lewin, 1947, p. 8)

As noted in Chapter 6, families are a special type of small group. All of us spend time in groups in order to work, play, worship, volunteer, find support, and so on. Despite their pervasiveness, groups as social systems are not well understood. Chapter 7 presents *a cognitive map of small groups*. It depicts

159

small groups as emergent social systems with unique properties and attempts to increase awareness of their dynamics, form, utility, and potential for development and change.

What Is a Small Group?

Small groups as distinctive social systems are defined by five qualities: (1) a limited plurality, (2) commonality, (3) interaction, (4) interdependence, and (5) organization and structure (Theodorson and Theodorson, 1969, p. 176).

1. *Limited plurality* refers to numbers: Small groups are social systems with three or more but fewer than 50 members (O'Connor, 1980). (Dyads as two-person systems are normally excluded from the definition of small groups.) Many group workers view seven members as the ideal treatment group size.
2. *Commonality* refers to mutually shared norms, a mutually shared identity, and mutual feelings of belonging or unity among group members. Members of a group may not like each other, but they have some common information, experiences, and identification. They *know* about some of the same things and they know they belong to a common system.
3. *Interaction* refers to communication among and joint activities of group members. A group's boundary can be identified by observation. Noticing who interacts with whom can be used to determine who belongs or does not belong to a group. Interaction occurs normally around a group's purpose such as recreation for play groups, informal visiting for peer or social groups, tasks for work groups, and so on.
4. *Interdependence* refers to the mutual influence that group members have upon one another. The component parts of groups are interrelated; they influence each other. Global properties and processes such as norms, goals, and events are created by group members through interaction, and they affect members' relationships with each other. Group morale affects members' behaviors and feelings about themselves and the group (Yalom, 1985; Whitaker and Lieberman, 1964; Bion, 1961). Events are mutually, and reciprocally, related rather than independent and linear (Maruyama, 1963).
5. *Organization and structure* refer to the patterned statuses, roles, activities, and practices that emerge in groups as a result of interaction over time. An early student of small groups describes the emergence of organization and stucture as follows.

> In the beginning of the process of group formation, those activities which make it a cultural product are experienced as spontane-

ous performances of voluntarily cooperating individuals. But as the group is formed and its makers become members, such activities are normatively standardized and systematized until they come to be regarded as group institutions, the whole system of which constitutes the dynamic organization of the group. (Znaniecki, 1939, p. 809)

Natural vs. Contrived Groups

Groups can develop naturally or they can be contrived or created deliberately. *Natural groups* are existential in character and emerge without a specific purpose or mandate. Natural groups have numerous *diffuse* purposes. They develop because of the gregariousness and life situations of their members. Natural groups include family, friendship, peer, ethnic, and neighborhood groups. *Contrived groups*, on the other hand, are created for specific purposes. These can include treatment groups established to provide counseling or support, recreational clubs or associations, work groups, athletic teams, labor unions, community task forces, and so on. Because they are intentionally created, and often time-limited in duration, contrived groups are useful for studying emergent properties and developmental dynamics. This chapter focuses primarily on contrived groups.

Task vs. Treatment Groups

Task groups are oriented primarily to producing a service or product and are concerned only secondarily with members' personal needs or wants. Task groups with which social workers are familiar include: a child-abuse service unit in a state welfare agency; a staff team of social workers, psychiatrists, nurses, and psychologists at a state mental hospital; aides and analysts for a state legislative committee; a management team of a not-for-profit agency for the physically handicapped; and so on. Work groups are social systems with a specific purpose and goals, and they are judged on the basis of realization of collective, or group level, goals. *Treatment groups*, in contrast, are oriented primarily to individual members' needs and wants. Treatment groups' goals are to help members improve their personal condition or skills and their interpersonal relationships. In treatment groups, the group per se is a collective instrument used to facilitate individual member change.

Groups as Inclusive vs. Included Systems

As with families, small groups can be studied as inclusive or as included systems (Olmsted and Hare, 1978, p. 6). As an *included system*, relations between a group and its environment are of primary interest. From this perspective, small groups are viewed as the building blocks of larger social systems such as organizations and communities. Groups are said to serve various functions, or purposes, of the social systems that include them. Research on small groups as included systems focuses on (1) the linkages between groups and their environment; (2) the different types of group that exist (voluntary vs. nonvoluntary; task vs. treatment; natural vs. contrived); and (3) the utility of groups for their members and/or the systems that include them (e.g., the work organization).

As *inclusive systems*, groups are viewed as communication and interpersonal networks. Attention focuses on the dynamics of internal group process and the behavior and social psychology of group members (Hare, Borgatta, and Bales, 1965; Lindzey and Aronson, 1969). Individual and group performance are primary concerns along with the normative patterns that develop, the amount and form of intragroup communication, power and leadership relations, role-related behaviors, and so on. This chapter focuses on groups as inclusive systems. Some attention is given to groups as included systems, however, because social workers can benefit from awareness of the effects of a group's environment—social, cultural, political-economic, resource, and so on—on internal form and dynamics.

OPEN SYSTEMS CONCEPTS AND THEMES

Seven OST concepts or themes guide our discussion of small groups.

Wholeness or Totality

As discussed in Chapter 2, the OST concept of wholeness directs attention to the reality of systemic, in addition to component part, phenomena. The cognitive map of small groups that Chapter 7 presents illustrates in detail the multilevel make-up of social systems. Reducing systemic phenomena to the level of component parts, or subsystems, is viewed as a mistake. Viewing a small group as a totality is the more effective way to understand, and affect, group performance (Fuhriman, Drescher, and Burlingame, 1984).

The Principle of Emergent Characteristics

Through member interaction, system-level phenomena *emerge* in small groups (see Chapter 2). Emergent phenomena are understandings and practices of the *group qua group* such as rules for speaking, goals for the group, ways of achieving tasks, and so on. Our cognitive map of small groups identifies emergent phenomena, called *group structural characteristics*, as one of four major components of small groups. Group leaders are advised to adopt a multidimensional view of groups in operation (Sarri and Galinksy, 1985; Burlingame, Fuhriman, and Drescher, 1984).

Linkages with the Environment

Groups, like all social systems, are located in, and tied to, the environment (Garvin, 1987; Toseland and Rivas, 1984; Balgopal and Vassil, 1983). Individual members have ties with people outside the group. Many groups are located in formal organizations (see Chapter 8) or communities that establish them and provide them with direction, resources, and constraints. Societal conceptions of group legitimacy, form, and process provide groups with the right to exist and a sense of purpose. Concern with a group's linkages to the environment reflects a conception of groups as included systems and emphasizes their dependence on the larger social context from which they obtain members, legitimacy, and resources.

Tendency of System-Level Phenomena to Gain Ascendancy over Component Parts

One OST principle is that, with time, the totality of a system becomes dominant over its component parts (Berrien, 1968). When social systems first develop, component parts tend to dominate. Assertive individuals assigned to a task force may influence the kinds and substance of group goals, procedures, rules, and so on that are established for the group. With the passage of time, however, group-level phenomena—group structural characteristics and group episodes (see group cognitive map, below)—become more influential. When group phenomena gain ascendancy, individual members can still affect a group but they must do so in relation to established group goals, practices, assumptions, and so on. Our discussion of group-development processes illustrates the manner in which emergent group phenomena become dominant over individual members as shapers of group reality.

Negative vs. Positive Feedback: Status Quo vs. Change

As discussed in the Dibs example in Chapter 6, feedback processes can lead to a system's correction toward a prior goal or it can influence a system to pursue a new goal. *Negative feedback* keeps a system on course. It occurs when a system, such as a small group, becomes aware that some actions are contrary to its goals and takes steps to bring the group "in line." This can be viewed as a calibrating process. A task force may spend too much time talking about personalities and too little time planning the new program for abused children. If it reorganizes to spend more time on program planning, this is an example of negative feedback bringing a group into line with its original goal(s). *Positive feedback* leads to the development of new goals. A task force may decide, after reviewing data on the problem, that a prevention program using the media would be more productive than a new treatment unit for abused children and negotiate with the agency or community to change its orientation or goals. Positive feedback has occurred.

Mutual Causal Processes

Small groups (and other social systems) experience many simultaneous mutual causal processes that involve system exchanges, outputs, and feedback. Causal, or influence, relationships among component parts are mutual and reciprocal rather than oneway and linear. A group's component parts affect each other through the activities of group members, individually and collectively (see below). This OST principle contrasts with Western analytical thought that focuses on one-way, straight-line (or linear) rather than mutual (circular or reciprocal) causal influences and relationships.

Systemic Developmental Processes

Social systems go through various processes over time that can be viewed as developmental. *Developmental processes* are a series of stages or phases that succeed each other and are associated with different structures and processes. As noted earlier, system-level phenomena tend to become dominant over individual-level phenomena with the passage of time. Treatment groups are relatively normless in their early stages of formation, and member behaviors are sometimes unpredictable and off-the-point. At a later period, such groups are likely to have an elaborate normative structure where members are clear about appropriate and inappropriate behaviors regardless of whether they comply (Lieberman, Yalom, and Miles, 1973). A good deal of research has been done on the developmental stages of contrived small groups and this material is reviewed below.

A COGNITIVE MAP OF SMALL GROUPS

The primary goal of this chapter is to present a cognitive map of small groups. A cognitive map is a model that identifies a system's component parts, the dynamics among its parts, and its relationship to the environment. Following O'Connor (1980), our Cognitive Map of Groups (CMG) views small groups as open systems (1) with member- and group-level phenomena, (2) characterized by an ongoing process, and (3) located within a social, political-economic, and cultural context that affects both group and member behaviors and goals. Most of this chapter is devoted to the presentation and explanation of our CMG.

Four Component Parts of Small Groups:
Their Relation to Hierarchy and Process

Table 7.1 presents four component parts of small groups relative to a typology of hierarchy and process. We describe each part and follow with a discussion of small group dynamics and the relationships between the parts.

Component Part 1: Member Characteristics

Member characteristics are the properties, or qualities, of individuals who belong to groups. Member characteristics exist at the elemental (individual) level and are relatively constant, that is, slow to change (see Table 7.1). Members differ in terms of their demographic characteristics such as age, race, gender, marital status, religious commitment, ethnic and cultural heritage, and so on. Each has a unique family and developmental biography and a distinctive psychological makeup and style. Feelings of self-concept or self-esteem are examples of member characteristics. Some group members are assertive, loud, garrulous; others are retiring, quiet, shy. Members can differ also in regards to their length of tenure in a group. Some may have belonged to a work group for several years whereas others may have belonged only a few weeks.

Member characteristics affect group process and outcomes. Blau (1977a) claims that, compared to homogeneous groups, heterogeneous groups are more tolerant and accepting of outsiders. Heterogeneous task groups are more innovative and effective than homogeneous groups (Katz, 1982), and mixed-gender groups are more nurturing than all-male groups and more task-oriented than all-female groups (Martin, 1985). A great deal of research shows that the treatment of blacks in mixed-race groups is influenced by the qualities of black members such as knowledge pertinent to the group's assigned task (Cohen and Roper, 1972). Understanding of the significance of member characteristics can help social workers be effective in dealing with groups (Chu and Sue, 1984; L. Davis, 1984; Edwards and Edwards, 1984; Ho, 1984). Group leaders are advised additionally to consider these factors when composing groups (Anderson, 1985).

Component Part 2: Member Behaviors

Member behaviors are the actions of individuals in a group, during group meetings. Member behaviors are an elemental (individual) phenomenon and they involve continuous process or activity (see Table 7.1). Member behavior is necessary for group development. Actions of members (and interaction among members) are the substance of group process. Without member behaviors, individuals remain isolated and a group never forms. As shown in Table 7.1, member behaviors are anything group members actually *do* in group meetings. The significance of individual members' actions for the group as a totality is addressed as part of Component Part 4, Group Episodes.

TABLE 7.1. COMPONENT PARTS OF SMALL GROUPS IN RELATION TO HIERARCHICAL LEVEL, PROCESS, AND GROUP OUTPUTS

	Relative Degree of Process or Activity	
Hierarchical Level	*Relative Constancy*	*Continuous Activity*
Systemic	*Part 3:* *Group Contextual Characteristics* group goals group norms and roles group climate normal round of procedures common understandings, interpretations, perspectives	*Part 4:* *Group Episodes* shared events, scenes, incidents, and happenings collective work activities (instrumental and socioemotional) shared expressions of feelings common experiences
Elemental	*Part 1:* *Member Characteristics* individuals' biographies individuals' demographic characteristics (age, race, gender, marital status, religious affiliation and background) individuals' physical/biological qualities and conditions individuals' opinions, attitudes individuals' self-image, self-esteem individuals' motives, wishes individuals' knowledge, expertise, skills, talents individuals' tenure in the group	*Part 2:* *Member Behaviors* actions of individuals in the group such as speaking, crying, hugging, shouting, taking minutes, listening, offering suggestions, sympathizing, criticizing, agreeing to do tasks, etc.

Group Outputs:
+ Formal Achievement
(exported to
environment)

+ Group Need
Satisfaction
(returns to group)

Member behaviors in task groups are different from those in treatment groups. Behaviors in task groups consist primarily of instrumental work such as planning or problem solving, whereas member behaviors in treatment groups consist primarily of socioemotional expressions of affect or assessments of interpersonal relations. Specialized models have been developed to observe member behaviors in task-oriented groups (Bales, 1950; Benne and Sheats, 1948) and in treatment or growth groups (Carkhuff, 1969; Hill, 1977; Schutz, 1969). Whereas member behaviors occur in a group context, they are expressions of individuals and are not properties of the group per se.

Component Part 3: Group Contextual Characteristics

Group contextual characteristics are the properties of a group as a system that are relatively constant or enduring (Table 7.1). They include the social, relationship, and procedural phenomena that *emerge* through members' individual and interpersonal behaviors. As members interact over time, group contextual characteristics develop, including group goals, rules, and procedures, a common identity, shared standards for assessing both each other's and the group's actions and progress, and so on. Through interaction, individual members tend to become *located* in groups (Cartwright and Zander, 1968). As a result, positions, roles, and patterns of relationship (e. g., leader, follower) are established. The position an individual occupies influences his or her behavior in the group. If a person occupies the position of leader, that person may guide the group through various processes, recognize and reinforce speakers, and try to keep the group on course. Expectations likewise shape the behavior of members who occupy the position of follower in a group. Three contextual characteristics of small groups are: (1) group norms, (2) group climate, and (3) a group's normal round of procedures.

1. *Group norms* are standards for appropriate behavior that are shared by group members. Norms have a *should* quality to them. If a member violates a group norm, other members sanction that person. The deviant may be scolded, ignored, thrown out, reminded of the standard, asked to straighten up, and so on. Norms are generally associated with roles. Certain aspects of the *role of group member* are normative, that is, they are required because of shared expectations for members' behavior, whereas others are not. Members of treatment groups are expected, normally, to maintain confidentiality about comments made by other members. If a member informs nongroup members about what group members say and is caught, she or he may suffer the consequences. The dress style of members during group sessions may be nonnormative, and members may be free to dress as formally or casually as they wish. Dress style in employment contexts is often

normative, however, and employees who dress too casually or unconventionally may be chastised or even fired.

2. *Group climate* is the shared socioemotional atmosphere or mood of a group. Some groups have a warm, close climate whereas others are cool and distant. A group's climate can remain stable or can change with time. Shifts in group climate are often the result of circumstances and events that the group experiences internally or in relation to its environment.

3. A group's *normal round of procedures* refers to the agenda of typical or routine activities that a group follows to accomplish its goals. Different types of groups have different normal rounds of procedures. Task groups may be prescribed by management to do things in a certain sequence and in particular ways. Treatment groups may develop informal routines of turn-taking that require each member to speak once before any member can speak a second time. Task groups may pay little attention to individual members' concerns and concentrate on activities that produce a report or hire a new staff member on time.

Component Part 4: Group Episodes

Group episodes are shared, system-level events, incidents, or happenings that occur in groups that are characterized by continuous activity (Table 7.1). Episodes are like scenes in a play; each has distinctive content and meaning but can be understood fully only in relation to the total "drama" or group context. Episodes are a series of shared events that are more than the discrete acts and behaviors of individual members. Episodes command the attention and participation of group members collectively; all members participate in group episodes as actors or observers. Episodes, in turn, give meaning to members' behaviors and help them interpret and make sense of what is said and done. Group theorists have long recognized the importance of group episodes and have developed frameworks to describe and analyze them. Yalom's (1985) model of a group's *curative factors* reflects an episodic view of group process. Group episodes can be instrumental in assisting treatment group members to grow and change (Long and Cope, 1980; MacDevitt and Sanislow, 1987). Many models of group development focus on group process as a series of episodes (Bion, 1961; Sarri and Galinksy, 1985; Whitaker and Lieberman, 1964).

Work in groups. Work occurs in small groups through the dynamics of group episodes. *Work* is throughput or the processing (transforming, organizing, etc.) of inputs by a system. Members of a committee meet to discuss issues and options in order to produce a report. Events at meetings during which they discuss options and decide among alternatives are group episodes. Treatment group members share their fears, concerns, anxieties, and hopes and in doing this enact group episodes. Work can be relationship-oriented and product- or service-oriented. All groups engage in work that attends to the accomplishment of instrumental tasks, but they engage also in work associated with the socioemotional needs, and qualities, of their members.

Small groups perform work of two primary types: (1) instrumental work and (2) socioemotional work (McGrath, 1984; O'Connor, 1980). Each leads to a particular form of group output. *Instrumental work*, as discussed in Chapter 6 on the family, is throughput activity that produces outputs for exchange with the environment. The products of instrumental work are called Formal Achievements (Berrien, 1968). *Formal Achievements* (FAs) are group outputs associated with official goals. *Socioemotional work* (see Chapter 6) is throughput associated with the affective needs and interpersonal relations of group members. *Group Need Satisfactions* (GNSs) are group outputs associated with socioemotional work (Berrien, 1968).

Table 7.1 shows two types of group outputs that result from group episodes through members' collective work activities. Formal Achievements are exchanged with the environment for new inputs associated with official goal accomplishment, and Group Need Satisfactions return to a group as new inputs.

All small groups engage in both types of work, instrumental and socioemotional, and all small groups produce Formal Achievement and Group Need Satisfaction outputs. Task groups, concerned mostly with instrumental work, emphasize FAs over GNSs, whereas treatment groups, concerned mostly with socioemotional work, concentrate on GNSs. Both types of groups must, however, attend to both types of work. If task groups emphasize instrumental work to the exclusion of socioemotional work, members may become disaffected. They may quit their jobs or, more likely, become alienated from their work and fellow group members. Treatment groups, in contrast, tend to focus on members' socioemotional needs to the exclusion of accomplishing official goals. This can lead to members' enjoyment of the group but failure to resolve problems or dilemmas in their lives.

In general, treatment groups are freer to set their own goals—both instrumental and socio-emotional—than task groups are. Both groups are legitimated by, and dependent on, their environment, however, and if the environment requires a certain amount or form of outputs, groups that ignore this do so at their peril (see section on Environment, below).

LINKING OF COMPONENT PARTS
THROUGH GROUP PROCESS

As shown in Table 7.1, two component parts of groups are relatively constant and slow to change whereas two parts change continuously through ongoing activity. Table 7.2 shows that the relatively constant group parts,

TABLE 7.2. GROUP PROCESS AS THE "TIE THAT BINDS" A GROUP'S COMPONENT PARTS

Hierarchical Level	Relative Degree of Process or Activity[a]	
	Relative Constancy	*Continuous Activity*
Systemic	Group Contextual Characteristics $\longleftrightarrow$	Group Episodes
		$\updownarrow$
Elemental	Member Characteristics $\longleftrightarrow$	Member Behaviors

[a] Arrows indicate the flow of influence, through individual and collective process, from one part to another.

namely member characteristics and group contextual characteristics, are linked to each other through the dynamics of member behaviors and group episodes. Members' characteristics influence their behavior and become inputs to group process in this way. Members' behaviors provide the dynamics of group episodes although group episodes are more than individual members' actions. Through members' behaviors and group episodes, group contextual characteristics are created, modified, responded to, etc. An organization's charge to a task group to produce a report is a group contextual characteristic. Members of the group take this charge, discuss and interpret it, and through collective action they take action to achieve it, modify it, and so on. Over time, group contextual characteristics influence the form and shape of group episodes, and group episodes reciprocally shape the content and substance of group contextual characteristics.

What Is a Successful Group?

Successful groups produce Formal Achievements while also accommodating to members' Group Need Satisfactions. This involves juggling the imperatives of a group's component parts to assure that no one part is emphasized to the detriment of others. As noted earlier, different types of groups call for greater emphasis on some parts than others, but some attention to all parts is necessary for a group to be successful.

As suggested by the dynamics shown in Table 7.2, problems in one component part create problems for an entire group. Members who skip meetings can cause a group to fail. Group norms that belittle the importance of all group members can engender member hostility and withdrawal. Table 7.3 lists the impetus, focus, and examples of productive and unproductive conditions and dynamics for each group component part. Social workers can benefit from understanding the contributions of each part to the success or

TABLE 7.3. IMPETUS, FOCUS, AND EXAMPLES OF PRODUCTIVE AND UNPRO-
DUCTIVE CONDITIONS OR DYNAMICS OF GROUP COMPONENT PARTS

Component Part	Impetus and Focus	Productive Conditions or Dynamics	Unproductive Conditions or Dynamics
Member Characteristics	Static; personal	Aware, open, prosocial individuals	Unaware, closed, antisocial individuals
Member Behaviors	Dynamic; personal and interpersonal	Cooperative, supportive, sensitive, constructive actions by individuals	Uncooperative, hostile, insensitive, destructive actions by individuals
Group Contextual Characteristics	Static; group as a totality	Clear and appropriate goals, norms and roles; a positive group climate; a round of procedures that facilitates the accomplishment of work	Ambiguous or inappropriate goals, norms, and roles; a negative group climate; a round of procedures that frustrates the accomplishment of work
Group Episodes	Dynamic; group as a totality	Collective events that include all members, achieve group goals, and foster members' satisfaction and sense of accomplishment	Collective events that exclude some members, fail to achieve group goals, and foster members' dissatisfaction and sense of failure

failure of small-group activity. We turn now to a review of the contributions of each component part to group success.

Member Characteristics

People join groups for a variety of reasons. They ask: Is this a group I would enjoy? Are this group's goals similar to my own? Can I learn something here? In answering such questions, individuals make decisions on whether to join a group and, if they join, how much to invest in it. Successful groups take individual members' motivations, interests, and simultaneous needs for acceptance and independence into account (see Table 7.3). Effective leaders recognize that members' characteristics affect not only their actions but also their perceptions of others. Gender and race are ascribed personal characteristics that influence group members' perceptions of competence even before interpersonal exhange occurs (Martin and Shanahan, 1983). Knowing this and taking steps to defuse the impact of such characteristics on group process make a group leader more effective.

Members' confidence in and trust of other members are influential member characteristics. Effective leaders attend to members' assessments of group climate and feelings of comfort or discomfort. They take pains to assure that each member feels an integral part of the group and that opportunities to take individual initiative and to be a team player are provided.

Member Behaviors

As noted earlier, without the behaviors of members, a group cannot form. Encouragement of group members' participation is therefore important. Group leaders must take care, however, to assure that members' behaviors are appropriate to the group's purpose and contribute to accomplishment of instrumental and/or socioemotional work (see Table 7.3). Domination of group meetings by one or a few individuals can alienate less active members. Hostile, abusive, or inappropriate behaviors by members can be destructive. In treatment groups where self-disclosure is essential, group leaders attempt to facilitate a *dyadic effect* whereby self-disclosure begets self-disclosure (Gordon, 1985). Encouraging member participation while constraining it to a group's normative purpose(s) requires judgment and skill on a group leader's part.

Group Contextual Characteristics

Group leaders are responsible for assuring that groups have sufficient and appropriate contextual properties to accomplish their work (see Table 7.3). To be effective, many group properties are needed: goals to orient members' participation, rules and procedures for engaging in group work, roles that give members a sense of purpose and a means to contribute, and standards for assessing outcomes such as the quantity and quality of Formal Achievement and Group Need Satisfaction outputs.

As noted earlier, many groups are charged by the environment to perform certain kinds and amounts of work. A staffing team in a social welfare organization may be directed to decide for or against residential treatment for disturbed adolescents. Accepting the charge and having the authority and resources to pursue it are necessary if the group is to fulfill its assignment. Both group leaders and members have a responsibility to assure that these conditions are met.

Group contextual characteristics shape and constrain members' participation. Overly restrictive norms, an inflexible round of procedures, and/or a hostile group climate can hamper group success. Such conditions may stifle both initiative and commitment to the group and its goals and also hinder the group's ability to perform both its instrumental and socioemotional work. Likewise, norms that foster pointless conflict or practices that take a group in too many directions can lead to similar results. Group leaders are encouraged by the Cognitive Map of Groups (CMG) model to shape group contextual characteristics to the group's purpose while maximizing members' participation and positive experiences.

Group Episodes

Group episodes are groups in action. Effective groups have many episodes that involve all members, that are orderly enough for members to make sense of their experiences, and that accomplish essential instrumental and socioemotional work (Table 7.3). In a committee, this involves compliance with norms that direct members' actions toward accomplishment of official tasks (instrumental work) and that view members as valuable group members (socioemotional work). If group episodes are erratic, disorderly, or unrelated to group goals or rules, the group may fail to perform expected tasks and members may become resentful, alienated, and disaffected. Treatment groups benefit from episodes that allow members to express their views openly, to enjoy trust and support from other members, and to identify solutions to personal and interpersonal problems.

Episodes that are unproductive include ritualistic compliance with a group's normal round of procedures without accomplishment of substantively meaningful work. Episodes that suppress conflicts communicate to members that open and honest confrontation of differences is unvalued. Episodes that treat some members as scapegoats or that belittle some members' participation and contributions are unproductive. Group leaders can facilitate the enactment of fruitful and satisfying episodes by adhering to standards that require fairness, openness, and the accomplishment of work.

Conclusions

Process, or the actions and interactions of group members, is the tie that binds a group together—for better or worse. Our discussion of the four component parts of groups relative to productive group functioning suggests two conclusions. First, effective leadership of small groups requires skill and judgment. A leader is responsible for assisting a group to value its members, to allow members to participate fully, to achieve instrumental and socioemotional work, and to require members to behave in respectful and productive ways. Social workers who lead groups, whether task or treatment, can benefit from appreciation of the challenges these entail. Second, successful groups focus on both member-level and group-level phenomena simultaneously. Concern with individual members to the neglect of group-level phenomena or concern with group goals and process to the neglect of individual members is equally ineffective. The interrelatedness of the four component parts assures that unproductive qualities (or processes) in one part will, in time, affect an entire group.

SMALL GROUPS AND THE ENVIRONMENT

Small groups, like all social systems, exist in an environment. Figure 7.1 shows that small groups are located in an immediate and general environment and that inputs from the environment enter groups as member characteristics and as group contextual characteristics. Figure 7.1 shows also that group outputs to the environment have consequences for the group. Some of these outputs, in the form of feedback, return to the group as new inputs.

Immediate and General Environments

The *immediate environment* of small groups is the proximate social system, and/or community, in which they exist. Social welfare organizations are the immediate environment of service units that arrange foster care for children. The social welfare organization, as immediate environment, provides the group with resources, legitimacy, a charge, a timetable for completion of assigned work, and so on (Hasenfeld, 1985). It also provides the group with members—that is, employees who are assigned to the unit for specific purposes—and with clients (children in need of foster care placements). Treatment groups' immediate environment is typically a social welfare organization as well. A mental health center may offer groups for drunk drivers or wife beaters. In doing this, it gives a group legitimacy, a meeting place, links to judges and courts that deal with offenders, provides trained leaders, and sets forth an official mission.

Natural groups with which social workers interact—families, gangs, friendship groups, neighborhoods—have immediate environments too. These consist of both informal social contexts and formal organizations. Natural groups are located in neighborhoods and communities that have qualities (racial/ethnic makeup) and resources (high unemployment) that affect their condition and opportunities. Natural groups are linked also to formal organizations such as schools, churches, factories, welfare agencies, hospitals, and so on.

The *general environment* of small groups is the broader social context within which groups exist. The general environment affects most small groups indirectly through its impact on a locality's economy, resources, culture, ideology, and so on. American society views the rearing of children as the primary responsibility of biological parents. When some parents fail to discharge this duty, society provides legitimacy for a foster care unit of a social welfare organization to intervene. Ideological beliefs and cultural norms and assumptions, in addition to material conditions and resources, comprise the general environment of most small groups.

Environmental Inputs as Member Characteristics and as Group Contextual Characteristics

Inputs from the immediate and general environments enter groups in the form of member characteristics and group contextual characteristics.

Member Characteristics as Inputs

Members' linkages with and experiences of natural and contrived groups on the outside provide small groups with inputs. Reference groups are groups with which a person identifies, regardless of whether or not he or she belongs. These become group inputs if members' identification with them is made known to the group. Family, friendship, religious, ethnic group, work group, and recreational group ties also are potential inputs if members' experiences are brought to the group's attention through individual members' behaviors.

Group Contexual Characteristics as Inputs

Inputs enter groups from the environment through a group's contextual characteristics. Organizations that form groups and charge them with tasks to perform provide inputs regarding a group's purpose, norms, performance standards, and so on. They also provide a group with members, resources, a place to meet, and a timetable. Committees, task forces, service teams, and treatment or counseling groups are affected by inputs from the environment that specify purpose, means, and performance criteria.

The Environment and Group Outputs

Because resources, members, and legitimacy derive from the environment, exchange with the environment is an ongoing activity of all open systems. As noted earlier, and as shown in Figure 7.1, small groups produce two major types of output: Formal Achievements and Group Need Satisfactions. Formal Achievements are exchanged with a group's environment for new resources. Inputs can include new members, released time to work on group tasks, travel funds for committee members to visit mental health centers, and so on. Groups that satisfy their environment's expectations regarding quantity and type of Formal Achievements are more likely to receive new inputs. Groups also emit outputs associated with socioemotional work in the form of Group Need Satisfactions (GNSs). Members who gain satisfaction and feelings of accomplishment and self-respect from group participation are more likely to remain committed to it. The GNS outputs return to a group through their effects on individual members' assessments of the group experience. Moreover, GNS outputs can be positive or negative. Groups that foster intra-

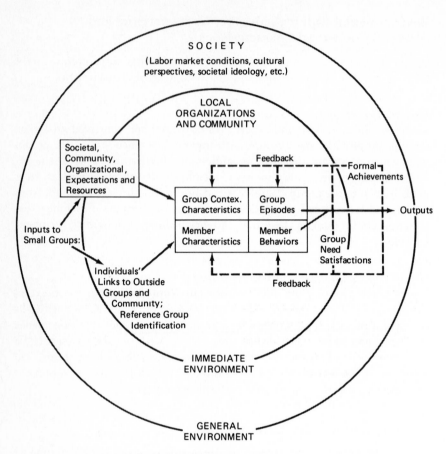

Figure 7.1 Group-Environment Linkages in Relation to Component Parts

group hostility, competition, and resentment reap these as new inputs as sure as groups that foster courtesy, cooperation, and support.

Formal Achievement and Group Need Satisfaction outputs can affect all parts of small groups through the feedback loops that link a group to its environment (see Figure 7.1). Members of a service unit who enjoy each other's company may stay on lunch break after the prescribed lunch-period time. Their enjoyment of each other's company during lunch is a Group Need Satisfaction output. Their delay in returning to work is also, however, a Formal Achievement output. Because of their delay, members may fail to complete assigned tasks. If administrators order workers to return to their desks on time, this is an example of (negative) feedback that corrects members' behaviors. If administration devises new rules about lunch breaks, this can affect a group's contextual characteristics over time. If members meet to discuss their resentment of administration's actions, group episodes are affected by the feedback. And member characteristics can be affected if the reprimand makes them feel ashamed, less confident, or embarrassed about their unit.

Groups are linked to their environment in many ways. The dynamics of input/output and feedback exchange between groups and their environment underscore their open system nature. We explore this further in Chapter 8 on social welfare organizations.

STAGES OF GROUP DEVELOPMENT: GROUP PROCESS OVER TIME

In addition to ongoing internal processes and exchanges with the environment, contrived groups develop in stages over time (Brower, 1986). As members interact, both group and members' goals are interpreted and redefined; norms are created, eliminated, and changed; roles are created and modified; and relationships, including subgroups, emerge and fade (Sarri and Galinsky, 1985). Group processes tend to go through four stages over time. These are (1) origins, (2) emergence, (3) exploration/revision, and (4) work. Little instrumental work is accomplished in the first three stages, during which attention focuses on socioemotional work. Outputs associated with each stage are distinctive, however, as described below.

1. *Origins.* The origins stage of groups occurs prior to the time members first assemble as a group (Sarri and Galinsky, 1985). It consists of actions and events that lead to the creation of a group, including reasons for its creation, the activities of those who create it (such as naming committee members, appointing a chairperson, charging the committee with specific tasks), specification of a meeting place, time, agenda, and so on. The origins stage of groups provides clues about the reasons for a group's creation. Knowledge of this stage can be useful to those who wish to understand why a group proceeds in a particular way.

2. *Emergence.* The emergence stage of groups is the early, formative period during which relatively autonomous individual members interact to form a group. This is typically a time of uncertainty. Members test the waters of group purpose and attempt to establish a direction and form for the group qua group. Episodes in the emergence stage focus on gaining agreement among members as to purpose, structure, goals, rounds of procedure, and so on. Expressions of common identification and purpose are typical (Sarri and Galinsky, 1985). The socioemotional needs of members are attended to as mem-

bers try to assure that they, and others, belong to the group. Members concentrate in this stage on matters of internal concern. This period comes to an end when members have *formed a group*. Groups that successfully complete the emergence stage leave it with a skeletal set of group contextual characteristics—goals, norms, statuses, roles, communication patterns, and so on—in place (Tuckman, 1965; Sarri and Galinsky, 1985). Groups that complete this stage typically have a positive, cheery group climate and relatively satisfied members.

3. *Exploration/Revision.* In the exploration/revision stage, a group's contextual characteristics from the emergence stage are challenged and revised. Tension is high as struggles over control and power emerge. Conflicts arise as members try to resist a loss of influence inherent in the emergence and ascendancy over individual members' preferences, of group contextual characteristics. Goals that were established during the emergence stage are found to be ambiguous, superficial, and conflicting. Members realize that earlier identified roles, statuses, and norms are inappropriate for the group's goals or members' needs. During exploration/revision, groups differentiate and refine earlier roles, norms, goals, rounds of procedure, and so on. When a group's contextual characteristics and episodes are developed enough *for work to be done*, and are acceptable to group members, the exploration/revision stage ends. If this stage is successfully completed, members are committed to at least some common purposes and have sufficient feelings of identification to continue participating in the group. Dropout rates are highest during this stage. Members who have a choice and dislike a group may drop out whereas members who are unable to withdraw (e.g., convicted drunk drivers required to attend treatment sessions) may disengage from personal involvement in the group and attend "in body only."

4. *Work.* The fourth and final stage of group development is the work stage. It is in this stage that groups accomplish work, both instrumental and socioemotional (Tuckman, 1965; Sarri and Galinsky, 1985). Group contextual characteristics and group episodes provide the agenda, structure, and dynamics for members to accomplish instrumental work associated with Formal Achievement output goals and socioemotional work associated with the Group Need Satisfactions of members (Rogers, 1970; Stock and Thelen, 1958). All groups do not develop to the work stage. Groups that reach this stage of development are sometimes referred to as *mature groups*. It is in the work stage that group members cooperate to achieve the group qua group's goals as well as individual goals that are associated with group membership. When a group succeeds in completing this

stage of development, members tend to leave the group with feelings of accomplishment and pride (Bales and Strodtbeck, 1951).

IMPLICATIONS FOR SOCIAL WORK

Chapter 7 contains many implications for social work practice with groups. Our Cognitive Map of Groups draws attention to several points.

1. Small groups should be viewed as existing on two levels simultaneously: individual/member and collective/group. Effective work with small groups requires recognition of this duality and leadership that validates and preserves the integrity of each level (Glisson, 1986).
2. Small groups are linked to the environment in numerous ways. Members bring inputs from the environment through their personal experiences and situations. The immediate and general environments in which small groups exist provide them with legitimacy, members, direction, resources, constraints, and feedback. Positive ties to the environment are necessary if groups are to obtain resources and support.
3. Small groups are composed of four component parts that are mutually and causally related through *process*. Member behaviors and group episodes link the more enduring aspects of groups—namely member characteristics and group contextual characteristics—to each other. Process is the dynamic enactment of group reality. Process engenders contextual characteristics; contextual characteristics shape and constrain process. Small groups provide a useful arena for observing the mutual interdependence of structure and process that characterizes all open systems.
4. Contrived small groups tend to progress through four stages of development over time. If earlier stages are not completed, later ones may fail to develop. Social workers who practice with groups can benefit from realizing that groups, both task and treatment, must successfully deal with emergence and exploration/revision imperatives in order to achieve their work-related goals. Groupwork skills such as facilitator, coach, assessor-interpreter, and guide are useful for practitioners who work with small groups.

Chapter 8

Social Welfare Organizations as Open Systems

INTRODUCTION

The U.S. economy is increasingly dominated by the service sector. Agriculture, manufacturing, and industry were the major employment arenas formerly but services have accounted for most economic growth in the last half of the twentieth century (Schmidman, 1979). Services include financial assistance (banks, savings and loan associations), insurance, entertainment (theme parks such as Disney World; health, sports, and exercise clubs), dining out (restaurants such as McDonald's, Burger King, The Brown Derby), and so on. Social welfare services and benefits are part of the service economy and now account for the largest portion of our nation's gross national product (see Chapter 1, Table 1.4).

How Are Social Welfare Services Provided?

Social welfare services are provided by social welfare organizations (SWOs). Social welfare organizations engage in many activities such as eligibility determination and payment of entitlement and welfare programs such as Aid to Families with Dependent Children (AFDC), Food Stamps, Medicaid, Medicare, and Social Security. They also provide services, information, and surveillance directly to citizens; for example, child and family welfare aid, psychological counseling, detention of juveniles, placement and referral assistance, and so on.

What Are Social Welfare Organizations?

Social welfare organizations are formal organizations legitimated by the state (1) to deliver personal social services, benefits, or goods to citizens, (2) to engage in deviance control on behalf of the state (Kamerman, 1983; Austin and Hasenfeld, 1985), and (3) to promote the public interest or commonweal (Bellah and others, 1985). Government agencies that process AFDC and Food Stamp applications and investigate child abuse cases are social welfare organizations. Not-for-profit agencies that serve crippled children and battered wives or that lobby legislators for better laws are social welfare organizations. And for-profit corporations that provide personal social services (e.g., alcoholism rehabilitation; Austin, 1986) at a cost to client, employer, or insurer are social welfare organizations.

Social welfare organizations are dynamic arenas where social policy and the recipient of social benefits (or control) meet in a formally mediated context (Lipsky, 1980; Prottas, 1979). They are invariably value-based, value-organized, and value-driven (Files, 1981; Martin, 1984). Research indicates that SWOs are seldom highly rationalized around technical-productive goals but tend to operate in variable, ill-defined, and symbolic ways (Jacobs, 1969; Prottas, 1979; Lipsky, 1980; Imershein, Frumkin, Chackerian, and Martin, 1983). Most SWOs are bureaucracies, and people often complain about their inefficiency, insensitivity, and callousness. Such complaints are frequently justified. Social welfare organizations face many contradictory expectations and pressures, however, and only some of their problems are attributable to bureaucracy. To transcend their limitations and be effective, SWOs must contend with the complex social context in which they exist (Patti, 1985).

This chapter describes SWOs from an Open Systems Theory perspective. A conceptual scheme for understanding SWOs is presented in regards to (1) relations with the environment(s), (2) internal structures and processes, and (3) dilemmas associated with a conflictual, sometimes hostile, social, cultural, and political-economic environment. First, we review the OST concepts and themes that are used throughout this chapter.

OPEN SYSTEMS CONCEPTS AND THEMES

Formal Organization

Social welfare organizations are *formal* social systems with legal charters (or incorporation papers) that provide corporate legitimacy. *Formal organization* refers to explicit, in contrast to implicit, status, rules, and procedures. Formal organizations have internal divisions of labor and authority arrangements that prescribe members' relationships to each other. All SWOs, even small ones, are formal organizations. Relations between people in families and friendship cliques are diffuse and implicit. They evolve slowly over time. In formal organizations, relationships are specific, explicit, and susceptible to change as a result of planning or policy decisions. Positions, duties, obligations, rights, relationships, responsibilities, and privileges are spelled out in job descriptions, tables of organization, descriptions of program and agency goals, and so forth. The social welfare organization is the most formally organized of the social contexts reviewed in this book.

Dependence On the Environment

All living systems are dependent on their environments but this is especially true of SWOs. Americans' support for SWOs is ambivalent at best. Many people believe that social problems are the fault of individuals and that any citizen who "really tries" can succeed. Support for welfare benefits, with the exceptions of Social Security and Medicare, is weak. Because of SWO dependence on the environment, external constituents are able to influence SWO goals, priorities, and practices. Resources for SWOs come not from clients or customers but from the government through the actions of legislators, governors, and other officials and their staffs. Because SWOs are unable to increase resources or improve their position by courting recipient support, they are forced to court favor with resource controllers who are located in the environment. Thus, SWOs devote much time, energy, and attention to relations with the environment. Funds for hiring staff, renting buildings, and buying supplies come from external resource controllers as does the organization's legitimacy for engaging in social welfare work.

Enforced Openness

SWOs have less control over their boundaries than do many other types of organizations, resulting in *enforced openness*. Many SWOs are public organizations under the direct control of state, county, or municipal governments. Even if they are private (see below), their funds may be public and their dependence on government may differ little from that of public agencies. Practices of SWOs may be shaped by the actions of governors, legislators, commissioners, and judges as much as by internal priorities or goals. Judges increasingly order SWOs to engage in certain activities in a particular manner and within a particular time period (e.g., each claim of child abuse must be investigated within 24 hours). In private not-for-profit SWOs, reliance on multiple funding sources (a dozen is not unusual even in small agencies) requires mapping (see below) and responsiveness to many external groups. Each funding source may have different accounting procedures, budget cycles, and record-keeping demands. Many SWO administrators spend most of their time on fund-raising and environmental relations. Thus, SWOs lack the luxury of "turning their backs on the environment" (Meyer and Scott, 1983). Some theorists claim that successful SWOs turn their backs on their internal technical core, or core-work activities, and concentrate on the environment. This is because SWO legitimacy comes from the environment. The quality of an SWO's relationship to its institutional environment may affect organizational well-being more than does performance relative to its official mission (Meyer and Rowan, 1977).

Mapping the Environment

Open systems are dynamically interdependent with their environment. *Mapping* refers to efforts to learn about, understand, become like, and/or mirror the environment. Their dependence on the environment—for legitimacy, funds, clients, staff, good will—requires SWOs to study, monitor, and learn about its character and developments. Some SWOs employ lobbyists, liaison staff, researchers, and public relations experts for these purposes. In small agencies, the director often performs the mapping role whereas in large state agencies, entire cadres of staff may work full-time on this task.

Filtering

Filtering occurs at the boundary and consists of selective acceptance of inputs and selective emission of outputs. Individuals are selective as to what they eat and drink and an unwise choice, such as arsenic, can have fatal consequences. Families filter children's inputs such as overseeing the foods they eat or the movies they watch. Social welfare organizations have formal filtering procedures to differentiate eligible from ineligible clients. They also filter information, employees, and resources. Outputs as well as inputs are filtered. Social welfare administrators are selective about their comments to the press, the Kiwanis Club, or legislators. They do not tell all to everyone who happens along. Committees edit their minutes and reports to assure they are worded in acceptable or noncontroversial ways. The filtering process is relatively easy to observe in a SWO because much of it is formalized, that is, explicit and written down.

Generic Subsystems

Subsystems, as noted in Chapter 2, are systems that are embedded in more inclusive systems and are defined by their unique activities. *Generic* means that all (open) systems have them. In this chapter, five types of generic subsystems are reviewed: production, adaptation, support, maintenance, and management. Subsystems are more distinct in SWOs than in less formalized systems. In families or small groups, most subsystem activities are performed by the same individuals, but in SWOs, distinct units, departments, task forces, individuals, and teams perform different activities.

Hierarchy

As noted in Chapter 2, hierarchy refers to successive, more inclusive levels of organization. In bureaucratic SWOs, authority—or the legitimate right to use power (give orders, hire, fire, evaluate, reward)—is hierarchically arranged. Persons in the upper reaches of the authority structure have power over those below. Alternative organizations that attempt to operate democratically reject hierarchy as a threat to equality (Rothschild-Whitt and Whitt, 1986). Hierarchy is, on the other hand, an efficient way to organize the collective efforts of a large number of people (Weber, 1947; Tannenbaum and others, 1974) although it may foster "learned helplessness" (the inability to act independently; Martinko and Gardner, 1982) in organizational members and can be used to control, exploit, and dominate employees (Ferguson, 1984).

Differentiation and Integration

As open systems learn and grow, two opposing processes occur: They become more differentiated and they become more integrated. *Differentiation* consists of division, independence, and the emergence of new parts and activities, whereas *integration* is a progression toward wholeness, dependence, and systematization. In highly differentiated systems that are unintegrated, the parts are independent of each other and change affects only isolated parts. In highly integrated systems, a change in any part affects the others. Differentiation is a consequence of learning (see *negentropy*, below). An infant who can use language to ask for a cookie is more differentiated than one who cannot use language. A family that learns to help an emotionally disturbed child becomes more differentiated by acquiring new knowledge, understandings, and skills and by engaging in new forms of activity. Starting a new program for teenage drug and alcohol abusers makes a SWO more differentiated as it learns about the scope of teenage substance abuse and as it creates organizational positions and arrangements to address the problem.

Without integration, differentiation can be harmful. New employees, programs, goals, and departments must be linked to the larger organization. Willingness to work with other staff and to cooperate in meeting the SWO's overall mandate is necessary if differentiation is to be beneficial. Clarity about each unit's role and its contribution to the overall organization is important. Unless integrated, units may compete with each other for resources and priority. Without a way to coordinate, the SWO may become segmented (Kanter, 1983).

Most SWOs are highly differentiated. They have many—and frequently conflicting—activities, goals, positions, constituents, and rules. Many have multiple departments such as Service to deal with clients, Accounting to maintain financial records, and Housekeeping to clean the building. Some integration is provided by formal structure such as the organization's hierarchy of authority (who reports to whom), procedures for opening cases, and chart of organizational positions and units. Lack of attention to coordination and common purpose and the isolation of individuals and work units can lead to destructive conflict. The optimal amount of SWO integration is unknown. Certain activities seem to call for close integration, such as the work of receptionist, caseworker, and typist/clerk, whereas others may work best if independent, such as a director's public relations activities and caseworkers' contacts with clients.

Loose Coupling and Decoupling

A *loosely coupled* system is one whose component parts and/or subsystems are weakly linked or only somewhat interdependent. (See Chapter 9 on communities for an explanation of linkage.) When parts are *decoupled*, they are independent of each other except that they exist within the same system. Social welfare organizations have many loosely coupled and decoupled parts. For example, documentation of client contacts may be tightly coupled to the budget process because funding rests on a per capita formula whereas exchanges between caseworkers and clients in counseling sessions may be decoupled from administrative control (Lipsky, 1980; Meyer and Scott, 1983). Administrators' relations with external resource controllers are likewise decoupled from the clerical staff's everyday activities.

The existence of loosely coupled or decoupled elements is not a criticism of SWOs. It indicates rather that SWOs are complex social systems with many diverse activities occurring simultaneously. Close linkages of all subsystem activities is unfeasible and, in many instances, undesirable. In relation to previous comments on differentiation and integration, this discussion suggests a paradox. The differentiated parts and activities of SWOs must be integrated enough to achieve the organization's mission, and to survive, but every part and activity need not be linked directly to every other. Integration means that the *total organization* is coherent enough to survive and achieve its ends.

Negentropy (or Negative Entropy)

Negentropy is the accumulation, as opposed to loss, of free and usable energy and information. It results from a surplus of inputs from outside a system's boundary, a capacity to differentiate, utilize, and store these inputs, and an outlet for outputs to the environment. Open systems have the capacity to have negentropy, whereas closed systems do not. Negentropy occurs in open systems through the processes of growth and learning.

Growth is structural or developmental change that occurs from the introduction of maintenance (or matter/energy) inputs (such as staff or financial resources). Growth is similar to a maturational process. Expansion and integration occur at once and appear to follow a predictable pattern. Growth, ironically, narrows the range of inputs to which a system is receptive. For example, a SWO that grows in size (e.g., adds new members) can produce more work (serve more clients) at the same time as its acceptance of clients who fall outside its official mandate may diminish because of an increase of formal rules and procedures that often accompany increases in size (Glisson and Martin, 1980).

Learning is structural change that results from signal (information) inputs. Whereas growth narrows a system's range of acceptable inputs, learning expands it. Learning facilitates greater differentiation and discrimination among inputs, thus allowing open systems to develop new structures, capabilities, and knowledge. Through learning, SWOs can become more knowledgeable and skilled at taking strategic action to improve their status, options, resources, and effectiveness.

As SWOs add more staff, clients, or programs, their ability to survive is enhanced (Heydebrand, 1973). Growth leads to greater internal differentiation, however, and amplifies problems associated with coordination, integration, and control. To respond to the demands of growth, SWOs devise strategies to link diverse tasks and ensure worker commitment to the organization and its mission. One way to maximize learning is to maintain close, responsive contact with the targets of core activity work (Peters and Waterman, 1982). Staff who perform core work activities are a vital resource for SWO learning but one that large state welfare agencies often fail to tap (Prottas, 1979; Fabricant, 1985).

SOCIAL WELFARE ORGANIZATIONS: WHAT ARE THEY LIKE?

Mission and Core Work Activities

The mission of an organization is its official purpose, mandate, and/or aims. It is also a legitimacy claim or a statement of purpose that legitimizes the organization in the eyes of the public by tying organizational goals to societal values. The mission of a child abuse clinic may be to respond to the problem of child sexual abuse. To do this, it may diagnose and treat children who have been sexually abused and counsel parents who sexually abuse their children. It may try to prevent child sex abuse by educating both the public and at-risk children and parents. Legitimacy for such organizations comes from a societal belief that children should not be sexually abused and, if they are, something should be done to help them.

Although SWOs have an official mission that is fairly circumscribed, they serve other purposes as well. In the for-profit sphere, an SWO can make profits for shareholders and owners; in the public and not-for-profit spheres, it provides workers with interesting, clean, and respectable jobs. For those in political, policy-making, or administrative positions, SWOs provide opportunities to make decisions, take interesting trips, have access to others' labor for personal interests and concerns, and so forth. Official mission and the everyday *uses* of social welfare organizations are not always synonymous (Frumkin, Martin, and Page, 1987).

What Are Core Work Activities?

As noted earlier, social welfare organizations are given legitimacy by society and the state (federal, state, and local governments) to engage in certain activities. Many forms and types of activity occur in SWOs, but actions undertaken in accord with the SWO's official mission are called *core work activities*. (Other activities that occur in SWOs are spelled out below in the section on Generic Subsystems of SWOs). Core work activities of SWOs take three broad forms: (1) social benefit and service provision, (2) social control and/or surveillance activities, and (3) social change or public interest (common good) activities (Martin, 1987).

1. *Social benefits and services. Benefits* include cash payment entitlements such as Social Security, Aid to Families with Dependent Children, Food Stamps, public service jobs, employment counseling or referral, and so on. *Services* are provided directly to clients and can include advice, information, counseling or treatment, education or instruction (e.g., how to use birth control, plan meals, balance a checkbook, bathe a child). Services may be voluntarily sought by clients (as in the search for job training or referrals) or imposed by the courts (as in mandatory attendance at driving school for drunk drivers). Social welfare services are rarely paid for by clients who receive them but by the state (government), insurance companies, and/or employers. Citizens who pay insurance premiums to an employer or private insurance company pay only a portion of the actual costs of medical care. When a medical bill is paid, they are recipients of social welfare benefits subsidized by their employer or insurance company.

2. *Social control and surveillance.* A second type of SWO core work activity is social control, protection, or surveillance. When juveniles are a

threat to themselves or society, detaining and monitoring them are social welfare activities. In child abuse cases, removal of a child from its home or family is a form of social control (over the family's rights to the child). When a mentally ill person is committed to outpatient care (court-ordered to remain in the community but to submit to regular therapy and drug prescriptions), mental health counselors who monitor the person's compliance perform a social control function for both client and society (Martin and Pilkenton, 1988). Probation officers who monitor ex-criminals perform surveillance on behalf of the state. Social control is a social welfare activity to the extent it entails a service to society collectively (Austin, 1986; *Time to Care,* 1984). Control may be instituted for the subject's own sake (as in a self-destructive adult or a child who is being abused) or for the sake of others (e.g., preventing a violent person from harming others). To renounce the social control function of social welfare organizations or to view it as improper may be naive but there are many ethical and moral aspects of making decisions for others and controlling them "for their own good" (Austin, 1986; Martin and Pilkenton, 1988).

3. *Social change, public interest, and the common good.* Efforts to improve society's reponsiveness to needs of the citizenry are a third type of SWO core work activity. Clearing houses, public interest organizations, and policy institutes perform social welfare activity when they promote improved services for children, more homes for the indigent, better mental health services for outpatients, free medication for the working poor, and so on. Their aim is to change the public agenda, to affect priorities regarding what is important and who receives scarce resources. Typical tactics are to develop and promote literature, information, legislation, and social policies consistent with their version of the public interest or common good.

Charter or Auspice and Funding

Charter or auspice refers to an SWO's formal, or legal-corporate, status. Charter and auspice concern legal status (relative to the Internal Revenue Service, taxes, and liability), funding sources and arrangements, and corporate purpose. Three categories of SWO charter/auspice are: (1) governmental, (2) private not-for-profit, or (3) private for-profit (Austin, 1986).

1. Governmental (or public) organizations, such as state welfare departments, are chartered by law and supported by public funds (taxes). Their employees are state workers and are protected by career service systems, seniority, and in some states by labor organizations (unions).

Public SWOs face a variety of problems not the least of which are a vulnerability to political influences and a tendency to be overly regulated (Frumkin, Martin, and Page, 1987).

2. Private, not-for-profit organizations are not governmental or public organizations but are legally chartered to perform social welfare work. Not-for-profit SWOs are funded mostly with public funds through contractual arrangements with the state. The term *not-for-profit* means the SWO cannot have shareholders or pay dividends and must reinvest excess funds in the SWO. Many not-for-profit SWOs are financially successful and spend their excess income on additional buildings, staff, equipment, and programs. A board of directors establishes organizational policies, hires and fires the executive director, and is legally liable if things go wrong. Employees of not-for-profit SWOs are often unprotected by career service, seniority, or labor union arrangements. Voluntary organizations, the modal not-for-profit SWO in the past, were staffed by unpaid volunteers and accepted no government funds. Voluntary organizations still exist, but sole reliance on volunteers and a refusal to accept government funds are increasingly rare. Some people argue that private, not-for-profit SWOs are more flexible, innovative, and effective than governmental (public) SWOs (Salas, 1982; Schultze, 1977). Kramer (1981), who has studied nonprofit SWOs, questions this view. He concludes that public SWOs are often more effective. Some not-for-profit SWOs pursue their own goals at the expense of both the client and society. Not-for-profit SWOs that rely solely on public revenues are described by some as quasi-public organizations (Lynn, 1980). Their dependence on public money, regulation by public agencies, and compliance with state regulations make them similar to governmental SWOs.

3. For-profit organizations that provide social welfare services are increasing. For-profit SWOs have stockholders (or private owners), attempt to make profits, and are obliged to provide investors with a return on their investment. Many for-profit SWOs contract with the state, similar to not-for-profit SWOs, to provide services, surveillance, or control. When their budgets consist of public funds (as in contracts with the state), differences between not-for-profit and for-profit SWOs are blurred. Pressures to make a profit can prompt inpatient facilities to seek high bed-counts even if patients could be discharged, to view potential clients as needing their services, and so on. Mechanisms to assure that the public interest is a priority in for-profit SWOs are not yet developed. To be fair, governmental and not-for-profit SWOs do not put the public interest first in all cases either (Kramer, 1985; Frumkin, Martin, and Page, 1987).

Three Types of SWO Environment

Social welfare organizations exist in three different types of environment: institutional, task, and resource. Each type respresents a different reality, and each calls for unique understandings and responses.

1. *Institutional environment.* An institutional environment consists of "the rules and belief systems as well as the relational networks that arise in the broader societal context" (Scott, 1983, p. 14). An institutional environment is ideological or symbolic. It is characterized by values and belief systems rather than by mere technical, factual, or concrete phenomena (Meyer and Rowan, 1977; Meyer, 1978; Meyer and Scott, 1983). There is no consensus on what SWOs should be or do or the kinds of technology they should use. Institutionalized organizations, such as SWOs, are subject to conflicting values, beliefs, pressures, and ideological influences regarding what they are, should be, and should do. This requires them to attend to their institutional environment. Successful SWOs demonstrate compliance with practices that are valued by their institutional environment (Meyer and Rowan, 1977). Competing belief systems exist simultaneously, and SWOs must decide on which to respond to and in what manner. The SWO environment is politicized and is shaped by the swings and vagaries of electoral politics. Themes and values in the institutional environment change as new personalities, events, and fashions become prominent and old ones fade into obscurity.

2. *Task environment.* A second type of SWO environment is the task environment (which is partly institutionalized, that is, characterized by belief systems and values). Task environment refers to aspects of the environment that are essential to the fulfillment of the SWO's official mission (see below; also Hasenfeld, 1983). This consists of other organizations that can refer clients to the SWO, accept clients from the SWO, and provide essential staff and resources. If a battered-women's shelter depends on law enforcement for most of its referrals, law enforcement agencies are part of its task environment. A need for qualified staff makes professional schools a part of the SWO's task environment. A job placement agency depends on employers: Without them, it cannot find clients jobs. Social welfare organizations have many constituents both inside and outside their boundaries (see below). Their task environment is continuously mapped (see below), courted, and negotiated with (Martin, 1980a; 1980b).

3. *Resource environment.* An SWO's resource environment consists of the individuals, groups, and organizations that control resources necessary for SWO survival (Walmsley and Zald, 1973). Resources include funds for staff and physical facilities, the availability of appropri-

ate personnel (professional and nonprofessional), necessary knowledge and information, skills, clients, material, and supplies. As with the institutional and task environments, positive relations with the resource environment facilitate SWO effectiveness and well-being (Martin, 1987).

What Is Bureaucracy?
Is Bureaucracy Antidemocratic?

Like other organizations, most SWOs are formal bureaucracies. Despite popular beliefs that bureaucracy is slow, cumbersome, and recalcitrant, it is the normative way of organizing the collective efforts of paid workers (Perrow, 1983). Many of its qualities are denounced by proponents of organizational democracy, however (Ferguson, 1984). The ideal-type characteristics of bureaucratic organization are contrasted to those of collectivist-democratic organizations in Table 8.1. (*Ideal-type* means that an organization ideally has the qualities listed). This comparison indicates that bureaucracy deviates from the ideal of organizational democracy but it also highlights its utility for organizing work activity.

Bureaucracies and collectivist-democratic (C-D) organizations differ in eight ways (see Table 8.1).

1. *Authority.* Bureaucratic authority is hierarchically organized with persons having more or less authority based on position (or office). Collectivist-democratic organizations view authority as residing in the group as a whole rather than individual offices, and they make decisions by consensus whereas bureaucracies make them on the basis of rules that are implemented by office incumbents.
2. *Rules.* Bureaucracies have explicit, formal rules to guide decisions whereas collectivist-democracies seek to minimize stipulated rules and to maximize ad hoc, individual decisions.
3. *Social control.* Mechanisms to control worker behavior in bureaucracies consist primarily of direct supervision and standardized rules and procedures. In C-D organizations, social control is personalized and moralistic and depends on purposive selection of homogeneous personnel (homogeneous in respect to political beliefs and social values).
4. *Social relations.* Social relations in bureaucracies are ideally impersonal and are based on roles and positions rather than personal characteristics. Collectivist-democratic organizations have as an ideal a community where relations are holistic, personal, and of value in themselves.
5. *Recruitment and advancement.* Bureaucracies recruit and advance

TABLE 8.1. COMPARISONS OF TWO IDEAL TYPES OF ORGANIZATION

Dimensions	Bureaucratic Organization	Collectivist-Democratic Organization
1. Authority	1. Authority resides in individuals by virtue of incumbency in office and/or expertise: hierarchical organization of offices. Compliance is to universal fixed rules as these are implemented by office incumbents.	1. Authority resides in the collectivity as a whole: delegated, if at all, only temporarily and subject to recall. Compliance is to the consensus of the collective, which is always fluid and open to negotiation.
2. Rules	2. Formalization of fixed and universal rules; calculability and appeal of decisions on the basis of correspondence to the formal, written law.	2. Minimal stipulated rules; primacy of ad hoc, individuated decisions; some calculability possible on the basis of knowing the substantive ethics involved in the situation.
3. Social Control	3. Organizational behavior is subject to social control, primarily through direct supervision or standardized rules and sanctions, tertiarily through the selection of homogeneous personnel especially at top levels.	3. Social controls are primarily based on personal or moral appeals and the selection of homogeneous personnel.
4. Social Relations	4. Ideal of impersonality. Relations are to be role-based, segmental, and instrumental.	4. Ideal of community. Relations are to be holistic, personal, of value in themselves.
5. Recruitment and Advancement	5a. Employment based on specialized training and formal certification.	5a. Employment based on friends, social-political values, personality attributes, and informally assessed knowledge and skills.
	5b. Employment constitutes a career; advancement based on seniority or achievement.	5b. Concept of career advancement not meaningful; no hierarchy of positions.

6. Incentive Structure	6. Remunerative incentives are primary.	6. Normative and solidarity incentives are primary; material incentives are secondary.
7. Social Stratification	7. Isomorphic distribution of prestige, privilege, and power; i.e., differential rewards by office; hierarchy justifies inequality.	7. Egalitarian; reward differentials, if any, are strictly limited by the collectivity.
8. Differentiation	8a. Maximal division of labor; dichotomy between intellectual work and manual work and between administrative tasks and performance tasks.	8a. Minimal division of labor; administration is combined with performance tasks; division between intellectual and manual work is reduced.
	8b. Maximal specialization of jobs and functions; segmental roles. Technical expertise is exclusively held; ideal of the specialist-expert.	8b. Generalization of jobs and functions; holistic roles. Demystification of expertise; ideal of the amateur factotum.

Source: Joyce Rothschild-Whitt, "The Collectivists Organization: An Alternative to Rational Bureaucratic Models," *American Sociological Review*, Vol. 44 (1979), Table 1, p. 519.

workers on the basis of "objective qualifications" such as specialized training, formal education, seniority, and/or work performance. Collectivist-democratic organizations prefer to employ friends, persons with similar social and political beliefs, personal attributes, and informal skills. These organizations reject the ideas of career or career advancement.

6. *Incentive structure.* Money is the primary incentive in bureaucracies whereas complying with organizational norms and contributing to a sense of solidarity are primary incentives in C-D organizations. Material incentives are secondary in organizations of this type.

7. *Social stratification.* Different offices in bureaucracies are viewed as meriting different rewards (prestige, privilege, power) and unequal rewards are viewed as justified. For example, a director is paid more than a counselor because, reasoning goes, the director is in charge of the entire SWO and is held responsible for its overall performance. Collectivist-democratic organizations try to operate on strictly egalitarian terms with no one having much more privilege, power, or prestige than anyone else.

8. *Differentiation.* Bureaucracies have an extensive and detailed division of labor. People in each job have specific and generally fixed skills, expertise, and responsibilities. In C-D organizations, in contrast, efforts are made to minimize the division of labor. Jobs and functions are viewed as holistic, are rotated through the staff, and attempts are made to demystify expertise (Thurston, 1987).

In everyday practice, SWOs are only partial bureaucracies. Some aspects of SWOs are highly bureaucratized—with rules and procedures spelled out—whereas others are weakly bureaucratized. As noted earlier, practices such as record-keeping are highly structured whereas others, such as contacts between workers and clients, are highly variable. Some criticisms of bureaucracy are misplaced. Rude behavior, poor responsiveness, and uncaring attitudes are more a product of organizational culture than bureaucracy. Bureaucracy as a particular form of structure and process is a reflection of culture and ideology as much as rational-technical logic or intent (Meyer and Rowan, 1977).

Collectivist-democratic organizations have many problems including the extensive time required to make collective decisions, inefficiencies attributable to rotating jobs, emotional drains of intense interpersonal relationships, and members' discomfort with democratic procedures (Rothschild-Whitt, 1979). Bureaucratic practices may be forced upon C-D organizations by the environment; for example, parents of children in alternative schools may demand formal grades so their children can apply to college (Rothschild-Whitt, 1979, p. 523). If an institutional environment requires certain procedures (records, accounting practices, fire and safety features), C-D organizations that refuse to comply may forego needed resources (Thurston, 1987). Bureaucratic procedures and practices are the easiest route to follow for most SWOs although the costs to employees may, in the long term, be negative (Ferguson, 1984). As organizational forms, both bureaucracies and collectivist-democratic organizations have advantages and disadvantages. To improve the "humaneness" of bureaucracies, many scholars urge that efforts to democratize them be vigilant (Cafferata, 1982; Martin, 1987). To improve productivity and efficiency, collectivist organizations may be advised to bureaucratize selectively (Burt, Gornick, and Pittman, 1983).

Organizational Culture, Symbolism, and Ideology

Organizational research confirms that people seek meaning in their work (Kanter, 1983; Peters and Waterman, 1982; Gold, 1982). They want to feel valued, challenged, important, and a part of something worthwhile. They will work hard for what they believe in. This research has led to a renewed emphasis on the importance of organizational culture, symbolism, and ideology as shapers of workers' behavior and perceptions on the job. Peters and Waterman (1982) view individuals as bundles of inconsistent, or paradoxical, emotions and motives. America's best-run companies are those that understand this and use it to enhance performance. Workers in SWOs often complain about their treatment. They feel like cogs in a machine, as insignificant clerks rather than capable, caring, and intelligent adults (Prottas, 1979; Lipsky, 1980).

Organizational Culture

Organizational culture includes the norms, roles, goals, values, and practices that give a SWO its unique social climate or "personality." Every organization has a unique culture although organizational members may understand this only vaguely. Turner (1986, p. 101) defines organizational culture as "a shared set of meanings which is acquired, demonstrated and utilized in acts of communication within organizations and which serves to create and perpetuate the distinctive social settings of the organizations concerned." Organizational leaders may deliberately attempt to create a culture that emphasizes organizational priorities and values (Peters and Waterman, 1982; Smircich and Morgan, 1982). This can be done, although with difficulty (Turner, 1986), by SWO directors who know what they value, have the skills to put their values into practice, and stick to their convictions (Martin, 1987). Peters and Waterman (1982) describe effective organizational leaders as "obsessed with a few clear values." International Business Machines (IBM) emphasizes customer service as a primary value. An employee who fails to understand this and fails to comply is not around long. Effective social welfare organizations also have clear priorities. An explanation for why some values are important and how one works to achieve them are part of the culture of an effective SWO (Gold, 1982; Sipel, 1984).

Organizational Symbolism

Organizational symbolism is an aspect of organizational culture and includes the rituals, ceremonies, logos, and repetition of exemplary stories in the organization (Turner, 1986). Symbolism develops (emerges) more or less spontaneously over time through social interaction and exchange among organizational members and between members and external constituents. It can be deliberately created by organizational administrators to emphasize certain goals or priorities of the organization. Some of America's best-run companies have awards ceremonies at football stadia, with bands and cheering section, where high performers are applauded as they run onto the field (Peters and Waterman, 1982). The intended symbolism is that honored employees are winners and deserve to be recognized and cheered. Better understanding of symbolism in social welfare organizations is needed. Workers in one state welfare agency say the agency treats them like mushrooms, it "keeps them in the dark [about what is going on] and feeds them s—." Through symbolic actions, SWOs communicate to workers (clients, outsiders) about how they are viewed and valued. Practices such as public scoldings for minor mistakes and emphasis on error avoidance have symbolic as well as practical significance. They communicate to staff that the SWO is concerned with avoiding trouble rather than with meeting clients' needs.

Organizational Ideology

Organizational ideology is a belief system. It includes the beliefs of SWO members about the organization's character, purpose, values, practices, situation, and so on. (Members of SWOs are persons employed by the SWO, including administrators, middle managers, service workers, housekeeping staff and so on. When unpaid workers, or volunteers, perform organizational work, they are considered members also.) Ideology is usually believed as truth. It provides an explanation of things as they are, justification for the status quo, a rationale for what is done and not done, for who is worthy and unworthy, for what is proper and improper. Most accounts of social life, of how it works, have ideological components. Internal accounts of SWO reality in ideological terms is a typical, ongoing activity.

In conversations with outsiders, SWO staff make many ideological statements about their work, including descriptions of intent, practice, and goals. These statements may bear little relation to observed behavior yet staff may be unaware of the divergence. As a belief system, ideology justifies actions, perceptions, cognitions, interpretations, and so forth. The ideology of SWOs partially reflects societal beliefs (Meyer and Scott, 1983). America's ideology about social welfare emphasizes the responsibilities of individuals, rather than the state, for housing, health care, employment, etc. This view influences SWO workers, and even those who sympathize with their clients have ambivalent feelings about them (Prottas, 1979; Martin, 1984). Ideological differences produce conflicts between SWOs and their institutional environment and also between SWO members. A major challenge for SWO staff, particularly directors, is to articulate and promote an ideology that justifies social welfare work—serving the disadvantaged, poor, disabled and so on—as important and worthwhile (Martin, 1987).

Organizational Performance: Service Effectiveness and Organizational Well-Being

Organizational performance and accountability have been public agenda issues ever since the financial crunch of the 1970s. The public is concerned with efficiency and the avoidance of waste. Social welfare policymakers and administrators are committed to performance and accountability but they are committed also to maintaining SWO programs, staff, and budgets and to meeting clients' (or society's) needs (LaMendola and Martin, 1983). Determining good versus poor SWO performance is difficult at best (Martin and Whiddon, 1988). Because many constituents are involved, each expecting different results, the chances for consensus on appropriate SWO performance are slim (Martin, 1980a, b). This suggests that performance should be defined broadly enough to include the interests of multiple individuals and groups. Martin (1987) claims that SWO performance encompasses organizational well-being as well as service effectiveness standards.

Social welfare organization performance can be viewed in terms of two activity realms: (1) core work activity engaged in by SWO members in accord with the organization's official mission, and (2) legitimacy activity engaged in by SWO members (or others on its behalf) to foster organizational well-being. The former concerns service, social control, or social change/public interest activities, whereas the latter consists of conformity to standards and practices that are valued by the organization's primary constituents, especially those in its institutionalized environment (Meyer and Rowan, 1977). Discussions of core work activities focus on effectiveness of work performed or quality of service delivered (Cameron, 1986a; 1986b); Cameron and Whetten, 1983; Martin and Whiddon, 1988). In contrast, discussions of legitimacy focus on compliance with valued themes in the SWO's institutional, task, and resource environments (Meyer, Scott, and Deal, 1981; Hasenfeld, 1983; Gummer, 1984).

Core Work Activities
Core work activities (CWAs) fall into two general groups: (1) actions that assist or control citizens, and (2) actions that foster the public interest or the common good (Bellah and others, 1985). The former concerns work directly

with citizens as clients, and the latter, work with information, ideas, linkages, and relationships. From an Open Systems Theory perspective, core work activities transform inputs (clients, information, data, ideas) into outputs for exchange with the environment (Hasenfeld, 1983). Core work activity in a juvenile detention center includes monitoring and restricting the whereabouts and activities of young people. In a child-advocacy agency, it includes legistlative lobbying, exposure of child care centers that violate health and safety standards, and so forth. A range of SWO core work activities is listed in Table 8.2. These go from eligibility determination for Social Security or Food Stamps to grassroots community organizing to the care and control of the mentally ill.

Performance as service effectiveness focuses on *quality* (Patti, 1985). Quality concerns the degree of excellence, or grade, of service provided. This includes the content of the service, its appropriateness to the problem, whether the right amount is provided, the manner in which it is provided, and so on. Administrators of SWOs are responsible for assuring a high quality

TABLE 8.2. AN ILLUSTRATIVE LIST OF CORE WORK ACTIVITIES PERFORMED BY SOCIAL WELFARE ORGANIZATIONS

1. Eligibility determination—assessing qualifications for income transfers, subsidized housing, Medicaid, Food Stamps, Medicare, Supplemental Security Income, Social Security, etc.
2. Information and referral—informing clients about options, such as Planned Parenthood provides on birth control; referring clients to agencies that can help them.
3. Concrete services—providing transportation, food or clothing, subsidies for rent or utilities, assisting the unemployed to apply for jobs, arranging day care, arranging nursing home placements for the elderly.
4. Case management—securing benefits or services from multiple vendors on behalf of clients; coordinating housing, education, medical care and so forth for a single client.
5. Treatment/casework—advising, comforting, or counseling about problems or concerns.
6. Advocacy—lobbying other professionals or officials on behalf of clients; accompanying rape victims to court hearings; taking the case of the homeless before the city commission.
7. Network building—linking agencies on behalf of a group of clients in order to improve coordination of the service delivery network.
8. Lobbying—appealing to resource controllers for new laws or better funding.
9. Grassroots community organizing—helping citizens organize on their own behalf to provide self-help services, to petition officials for resources, services, rights, and so on.
10. Protective intervention—monitoring and/or removing children, the elderly, the mentally ill, etc., from unsatisfactory living conditions for their own well-being (including the arrangement and oversight of foster care).
11. Supervision, surveillance, and control—detaining dependent or delinquent children in detention centers, control of the mentally ill through medication, legal commitment, and restraint; providing sheltered living quarters for those unable to live on their own such as the developmentally disabled, paroled felons, recovering alcoholics.

of core work activity (Kaufman, 1981; Carter, 1983). It is their responsibility also to assure that core work activities are conducted in normatively and legally appropriate ways. These include record-keeping, documenting, and due-process compliance. These are internal legitimacy activities which, if violated, can threaten organizational well-being.

Legitimacy Activities

Practices that demonstrate compliance with legal statutes or regulations and with values of the SWO's institutional environment are legitimacy activities (J. W. Meyer, 1983a, b). Some of these are mandated by the environment as when legislatures or courts require investigation of reported child abuse cases within 24 hours or mandatory reporting to law enforcement of incest cases. Other legitimacy activities are optional, such as "celebrating rationality in organizational operations" (Meyer and Scott, 1983, p. 212) to gain support from a pro-business society for the SWO's approach to management. Because SWO outputs are often symbolic in nature (Scott, 1983), both types of legitimacy activity affect organizational well-being.

Many legitimacy activities involve external constituents, such as showing compliance with local, state, and federal government laws, rules, and regulations; maintaining positive relations in and with the community; participating in a "web of service network" (Czarniawska, 1985a); developing positive relations with the media; facilitating the work of other SWOs (Molnar and Rogers, 1976; Wiewel and Hunter, 1985); and providing jobs for citizens. These activities affect an SWO's ability to acquire financial resources and community good will, attract and retain qualified staff, and attract appropriate clients. Cameron (1986a) found that effective organizations are able to satisfy many separate constituency groups, even when different constituencies hold contradictory expectations, by performing "in contradictory ways to satisfy contradictory expectations" (p. 550). This suggests that legitimacy demands on SWOs are complex, requiring both skill and judgment on the part of SWO members.

Legitimacy is not only a matter of external relations. Internal practices must also meet legitimacy standards. For instance, core work activities (CWAs) must be performed in legally correct ways, in a timely fashion with required paperwork done correctly. Funds must be spent in accord with their intent; staff must behave ethically and competently; clients must be treated fairly, courteously, and expeditiously (Prottas, 1979; Lipsky, 1980). These activities are aspects of organizational performance and all affect, directly or indirectly, work quality as performed by staff. If an SWO loses financial resources or the public's good will, CWAs may be reduced both quantitatively and qualitatively and staff morale may suffer. SWO directors are responsible for assuring that legitimacy demands, internal and external, are met (Martin, 1987).

Integrative vs. Segmentalist Action in the SWO

Some SWOs use an integrative action approach to problem solving and change whereas others are segmentalist. An *integrative action approach* emphasizes wholeness, eagerness to combine problems with new ideas, and a positive view of change as an opportunity to test limits. "To see problems integratively is to see them as wholes, related to larger wholes. . . ." (Kanter, 1983, p. 27). Integrative thinking actively embraces change and occurs in organizations whose cultures and structures are also integrative, where problems are viewed as part of the whole with implications for organization-wide action. The integrative action approach is consistent with an Open Systems Theory perspective that emphasizes wholeness, interdependence, and the potential for change. *Segmentalism*, in contrast, is an antichange orientation that prevents innovation. It compartmentalizes actions, events, and problems and keeps the pieces isolated from each other. "Companies with segmentalist cultures are likely to have segmented structures: a large number of compartments walled off from one another—department from department, level above from level below, field office from headquarters, labor from management, men from women" (Kanter, 1983, p. 28).

Segmentalist action reflects a rational/analytic approach to problem solving. It views problems as best approached by factoring them into their smallest parts and assigning each part to its logically most appropriate subunit. This, according to Kanter, fragments problems and hinders resolution. Integrative organizations, in contrast, "aggregate subproblems into larger problems, so as to re-create a unity that provides more insight into required action" (1983, p. 29).

WHAT IS AN EFFECTIVE SOCIAL WELFARE ORGANIZATION? FOUR MODELS

As noted above, SWO effectiveness is difficult to determine. Effectiveness is an aspect of organizational performance: How well is the organization doing? Is it doing what it should do? Is it doing it legally, efficiently, fairly? Questions such as "Who wants to know?" "Who benefits from its actions?" and "What is the vested interest of the person asking?" also apply (Scott, 1977).

Four models of organizational effectiveness have utility for understanding SWOs. (Our description of the models relies heavily on Cameron, 1984.) We review them all, rather than only one, to make three points. First, effectiveness lies in the eyes of the beholder. Answers to questions about an SWO's effectiveness are dependent on *who asks the question*. A board member may believe the SWO is doing well if it stays within budget whereas a client may agree only if the service meets her needs. Second, organizations can be effective in some ways and ineffective in others at the same time. An SWO may succeed at meeting service delivery goals but fail to gain needed resources or support from the environment. Third, because each model highlights different phenomena, different models can be used to assess different aspects of performance. No single model is sufficient to gauge the effectiveness of all SWO activities.

The Goal Model

The Goal Model (GM) of effectiveness emphasizes the extent to which an SWO fulfills its official goals. Goals are end-states toward which a system is oriented, and the Goal Model emphasizes systemic outcomes (Campbell, 1977). It is compatible with the current emphasis on SWO accountability. The GM is most useful when goals are clear, consensual, time-bound, and measurable (Cameron, 1984). Problems arise with this model when there is either a lack of consensus on goals or an inability to measure goal accomplishment. This is unfortunately typical rather than exceptional. With multiple and competing constituents, the question of "whose goals?" arises. Should the goals against which effectiveness is judged be those of external resource controllers, SWO administrators, SWO professional staff, clients or whom? Within a single constituency, goals are seldom consensual. Professional staff disagree among themselves over whether changed behavior or greater insight is the appropriate client-change goal (Haley, 1976).

Organizations have stated goals and operative goals (Etzioni, 1969). *Stated goals* are official (ideal) goals that directors articulate at legislative hearings, Kiwanis Club luncheons, and to the public and press, whereas *operative goals* orient the daily routine behavior of staff and administrators. Assessing SWO effectiveness on the basis of stated goals can be a mistake. Stated goals are useful for influencing public opinion, establishing organizational legitimacy and domain, and providing a rationale for securing resources, whereas operative goals are oriented to mundane service, survival and legitimacy purposes such as seeing clients, doing paperwork, complying with legal requirements, and so on. When there is a gap between stated and operative goals, determining which to use to assess effectiveness can be a problem.

Although the GM of effectiveness is imperfect, it can be useful. Performance data on the effects of service can be gathered and used to benefit (Carter, 1983). This requires clear statements about intended outcomes and implementation of a strategy for collecting appropriate data. The "accountability age" demands that the Goal Model of effectiveness be applied to at least some aspects of SWO programs. Establishment of clear, programmatic goals is a joint administrative/professional staff responsibility. Directors who fail to stress service-effectiveness goals may communicate to staff that quality and effectiveness are unimportant. A Goal Model of effectiveness is oriented mostly to internal concerns such as achievement of rationally established, measurable goals.

The System Resource Model

The System Resource Model (SRM) of effectiveness focuses on successful exploitation of the resource environment for scarce resources (Yuchtman and Seashore, 1967). The more resources a SWO gains, the more effective it is. This model is useful when a clear connection between inputs and performance can be shown (Cameron, 1984). The System Resource Model assesses performance on the basis of inputs rather than outcomes and focuses attention on organizational well-being (survival, prosperity) rather than service effectiveness. As noted earlier, survival is problematic for SWOs in a shrinking resource environment with minimal popular support (Thurston, 1987). Resource procurement is a legitimate SWO performance criterion. The System Resource Model of organizational effectiveness focuses on an SWO's ability to procure resources.

Multiple Constituencies Model

The Multiple Constituencies (MC) Model views effective SWOs as those that satisfy, at least minimally, the demands of all strategic constituencies (Cameron, 1984). *Constituencies*, as noted earlier, are groups or bodies that are involved in or served by the SWO. This model is most useful when relations with varied constituents are a concern (Cameron, 1984). Because essential resources and legitimacy lie beyond the SWO's boundary, external constituency demands often receive priority. An MC model of effectiveness is both internally and externally oriented, however, because constituents are located in both realms. Because it facilitates understanding of the SWO as a mix of competing internal and external groups, the Multiple Constituencies Model is reviewed in detail below.

Legitimacy Model

The Legitimacy Model of organizational effectiveness is useful for focusing on ties with the SWO's institutionalized environment (Meyer and Rowan, 1977; Cameron, 1984). *Legitimacy* refers to conformity to institutionalized (normatively accepted) principles, rules, and standards. In this model, SWOs are effective to the extent they engage in normatively correct actions and practices. Determination of what is correct rests in the institutionalized environment (Meyer, 1983a; Meyer and Scott, 1983). The Legitimacy Model therefore focuses attention on the nature, form, content, and extensiveness of a SWO's relations with the environment.

Social welfare organizations are *institutionalized organizations* that develop from institutionalized structures in the environment (Meyer and Rowan, 1977). These structures "define given types of roles and programs as rational and legitimate. These structures in turn encourage the development of specific bureaucratic organizations that incorporate these elements and conform to these rules" (Meyer, Scott, and Deal, 1981, p. 152). From this perspective, the primary concern of an institutionalized organization is to successfully understand and conform to its institutional environment. To do this, the organization "turns its back" on its core work activities, essentially delegating these to professionals who claim expertise and the right to exercise professional authority in organizations of this type. Demonstration of legitimate practices and structures assures organizational survival but not necessarily service effectiveness. The Legitimacy Model is particularly useful for understanding organizational evolution, change, and survival strategies (Cameron, 1984). In summary, the Legitimacy Model of organizational effectiveness is externally oriented. It argues that organizational well-being is a matter of compliance with legitimacy demands from the SWO's institutional environment.

LINKAGES BETWEEN INTERNAL AND EXTERNAL CONSTITUENTS: APPLYING THE MULTIPLE CONSTITUENCIES MODEL TO SWOs

The Multiple Constituencies Model can be used to identify the competing groups and bodies that have a stake in, place demands on, and expect results from SWOs. It is also useful for exploring linkages between internal and external constituents. Following Martin (1980a, b), Figure 8.1 depicts 14 SWO constituents. Many models of organizational structure include only the four or five groups inside the heavy lines shown in Figure 8.1 (Martin and Segal, 1977). This implies, erroneously, that SWOs are closed systems. Rather, as suggested by Figure 8.1, SWOs are open systems with a highly permeable boundary and with ties to many external constituency groups.

Figure 8.1 shows four groups within the heavy lines in a descending order of hierarchical authority: (1) directors and senior administrators including their assistants and advisory staff; (2) middle managers including division, department, and unit heads, and supervisors; (3) core activity workers who deal directly with clients or perform other core work activities (investigating child abuse, lobbying legislators); and (4) clerical and custodial workers (secretaries, receptionists, cleaning staff, food service workers). Beneath the internal constituents are the individual clients, the group whose interests the SWO is mandated, officially, to serve. Location in the hierarchy corresponds roughly with amount of authority (or legitimate power), with direc-

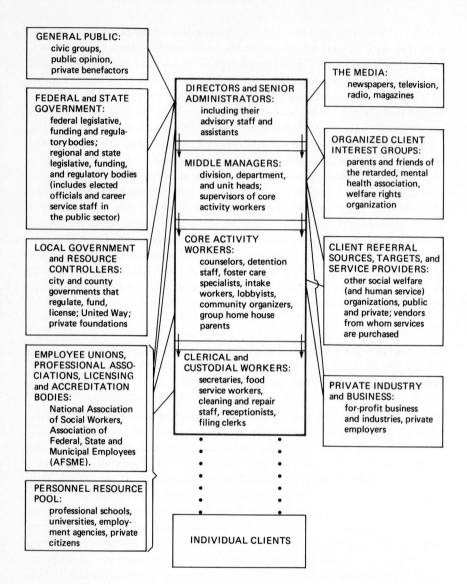

Figure 8.1 The Multiple Constituents of Social Welfare Organizations and Their Cross-Boundary Linkages.

tors possessing the most and clients possessing the least. Because of clients' low power and status, their priorities and goals may receive little emphasis compared to those of more powerful groups (Salaman, 1978; see also Chapter 5).

Clients are shown in Figure 8.1 as external constituents. Opinions vary over whether clients should be viewed as *SWO members* or as *constituents served by the SWO*. This affects where the SWO's boundary is drawn (Bidwell, 1970). A shelter for runaway children cannot fulfill its mission without clients, but clients spend less time than employees in interaction with SWOs and are normally less committed to it. Bidwell (1970) claims that clients should be viewed as external constituents who are served by the organization. Such an orientation highlights the problematic nature of client–SWO relations and mitigates the tendency to assume they can be taken for granted (cf. Mills and Morris, 1986).

Besides clients, nine external SWO constituents are shown in Figure 8.1. These are: (1) the general public, including private citizens, civic groups, churches, private foundations or contributors, and the perceptions and opinions of the public; (2) federal and state government bodies, including legislative, regulatory, and funding agencies; (3) local regulatory and funding bodies, including city and county governments (and their laws, policies, regulations), United Way organizations, etc.; (4) the media, including newspapers, television, radio, and specialized magazines, newsletters, etc.; (5) employee unions, professional associations, licensure and accrediting bodies; (6) other social welfare and human service organizations (public and private), including client referral and placement resources, schools and hospitals, agencies with contractual linkages; (7) private industry and business organizations (of a nonhuman-service variety), including service, retail, manufacturing, construction, and industry; (8) the personnel resource pool, including educational and professional organizations, employment agencies, and private citizens available for employment; (9) organized client groups, such as parents and friends of the retarded, who normally have a goal of improving the status or welfare of particular kinds of clients.

As depicted by the arrows in Figure 8.1, control inside bureaucratic SWOs is exercised from the top down. Power as positionally based authority is concentrated in the hands of a few persons at or near the hierarchy's top (Goldman and Van Houten, 1977). Directors and their immediate subordinates have authority over the entire organization. From their superordinate position, they establish and enforce policies, rules, and procedures for the middle managers, service workers, support staff, and clients who fall under their authority. An unequal distribution of power leads to an emphasis on the goals and objectives of higher-level groups over those of lower ones. If directors lack clear priorities or are unskilled in communicating and reinforcing them, the SWO may have difficulty delivering effective services or performing appropriate legitimacy activities. Lack of vision or commitment on the part of those in power can result in a directionless and ineffective SWO (Martin, 1980b, 1987). Additionally, directors' use of organizational power for purposes other than service effectiveness or organizational well-being can make subordinates resentful, recalcitrant, and uncooperative (Prottas, 1979). Management's treatment of workers can affect the latter's treatment of clients. SWO workers who are treated indifferently can hardly be expected to treat clients, or the public, with sensitivity and care.

Middle managers are staff with supervisory authority who are located at neither the top nor bottom of the authority structure (Shan Martin, 1982). They have less authority than directors and more authority than service workers or support staff. Middle managers link upper administration to core work activities by *supervising the supervisors* of core activity workers; performing planning, evaluation, and staff development tasks; and linking the SWO with its institutional, task, and resource environments. Kerr, Hill, and Broedling (1986) claim that the first-line supervisor who directs and monitors the work of core activity workers has a difficult job. Located close to the worker and far from senior administration, yet neither direct service nor managerial in nature, first-line supervisors are required to face in two directions at once (Imershein, Polivka, Gordon-Girvin, Chackerian, and Martin, 1986). They often identify most with core activity workers but are required by administration to represent organizational/administrative interests to workers rather than workers' interests to administration.

Core activity workers have authority over clerical and custodial staff and over clients. Clerical and custodial workers have minimal authority over clients, and clients have only moral or normative authority. Clients who voluntarily ask for social welfare services have control over whether or not to receive them, whereas involuntary clients—such as delinquents or drunk drivers in court-ordered treatment—lack authority to decide for or against participation (Martin and Pilkenton, 1988). Core activity workers rely heavily on the work of clerical staff yet the latter's contributions are often taken for granted. Secretaries and receptionists can enhance or diminish core activity workers' job performance, and their cooperation is actually problematic (Braverman, 1974). Directors of SWOs are responsible for helping middle managers, core activity workers, and clerical and custodial staff feel useful, important, and a valued part of the organization.

Lines that cross the SWO boundary in Figure 8.1 indicate linkages between internal and external constituents. (Chapter 9, "Communities," provides an explanation of linkages.) Some linkages are reserved for upper administration, but all internal constituents have external ties. Directors represent the SWO to external constituents who have the greatest influence or control over valued resources (Katz and Kahn, 1978). These include legislators, major funders, the media, the general public, regulators, and so on. The media are an increasingly important constituent (Czarniawska, 1985a) and, as a result, some SWOs have employed staff solely to monitor and respond to the media. Community leaders believe that SWOs they know about are effective and those they do not know about are ineffective (Whetten, 1978). Positive coverage in newpapers or television can increase community awareness and, thus, support. Exchanges with the media have many pitfalls, however, and hostile or error-filled exchanges can make trouble for the SWO. Because of this, directors usually reserve this task for themselves or trusted assistants.

Who Selects SWO Directors?

Social welfare organization directors are normally selected by resource controllers external to the organization; thus, ties between directors and powerful external constituents originate in the recruitment and hiring process, if not before (Aldrich and Pfeffer, 1977). Boards of directors—who are unpaid community volunteers—hire directors of not-for-profit SWOs. Governors appoint state welfare directors. Persons selected for such posts often have qualifications, backgrounds, values, and orientations similar to the resource controllers who appoint them (Offe, 1976; Kanter, 1977). Many SWO directors have more in common with external resource controllers than with the SWO's core activity workers or clients (Martin, 1980a, b).

Middle Managers as Linkage Agents

Middle management staff interact with external constituents such as representatives of other SWOs, private industry, the personnel resource pool, organized client groups, and employee unions and professional associations. Except in small SWOs, mid-level staff rarely deal with clients or with the SWO's most powerful external constituents. Mid-level staff interact with the outside around staff recruitment and liaison work with other organizations as directed by upper administration or as needed by core activity workers to conduct their work.

The internal tasks of middle managers include supervision and monitoring of service units and supervisors, program planning and evaluation, oversight of support and clerical staff, documentation of compliance with mandated rules and regulations, report-writing, data gathering and interpretation, and so on. Middle managers link service workers with senior administration through communicating information, decisions, and concerns down and up the authority hierarchy. The necessity to face "both ways"—up and down the hierarchy—makes middle management stressful, particularly for those near the bottom (Kerr, Hill, and Broedling, 1986).

The Linkage Tasks of Core Activity Workers

Many core activity workers perform boundary-spanning tasks in their jobs. Core work activities such as screening applicants for Food Stamps, admitting a child to a residential drug abuse program, or finding a placement for an elderly woman require workers to cross the SWO boundary. Some workers contract with and monitor vendors who provide services to clients. A mental retardation worker may place a client in a small community facility and monitor the placement; arrange and monitor the client's transportation to and from school each week; arrange and monitor health services from a physician. Many core work activity jobs require extensive linkages with the community beyond the SWO's boundary.

Individual clients are dealt with by core activity workers, but organized client-interest groups are dealt with by directors, especially if the group is powerful or well organized. Employee unions (such as the Association of Federal, State and Municipal Employees) and professional associations (such as the National Association of Social Workers) have had dramatic member-ship increases since World War II and, perhaps as a result, are increasingly militant on their members' behalf. Social workers, teachers, and nurses can-not be assumed to be compliant, easy-to-control employees. Executives, boards of directors, and state legislators are increasingly required to take the desires of collectively organized constituents into account as they make decisions on funding, job security, claims of incompetency or misconduct, salary increases, grievance procedures, due process, and termination (John-ston, 1978).

Although links among external constituents are absent in Figure 8.1, the SWO's "web of service network" is normally highly interdependent (Czarniawska, 1985a). Service networks are also highly politicized, and SWO directors who hope to promote service effectiveness and organizational well-being must identify, and understand, the linkages among its external constituencies.

Multiple Constituencies and Organizational Performance: A Dilemma

Expecting SWOs to serve citizens or promote the public interest without regard to organizational well-being is naive. Social welfare organizations are accountable to multiple constituents (or interest groups) that hold conflict-ing, often incompatible, expectations for their performance. Clients expect SWOs to be generous and helpful, whereas legislators require them to re-duce staff error and prevent "welfare cheaters." With different constituencies expecting, indeed, often demanding, different results, organizational per-formance assumes many forms (Cameron, 1984).

Manufacturing and business organizations have an advantage over SWOs. They have many constituents too—wage-earners, managers, directors, stock-holders, customers—but they also have some consensus on performance goals and standards (Walmsley and Zald, 1973; Czarniawska, 1985b). These organizations strive for high sales volumes and profits. If these are reached, all constituents are rewarded through dividends, bonuses, wage increases, and prestige. Labor and management may disagree over how to disburse excess profits, but both generally benefit from a gain as opposed to a loss.

For-profit SWOs are a recent but growing phenomenon in the United States. They provide service for sale to individuals or governments or through third-party contracts with insurance companies and employers. However, the pursuit of profit may undermine commitment to service quality, and more research on for-profit SWOs is needed.

Public and not-for-profit SWOs have few concrete performance criteria. They are established and funded by external constituents (e.g., state legislatures, city or county governments, a group of private citizens, a foundation) for some public benefit purpose. Founding constituents provide direction and resources to the SWO and attempt to secure administrators who will comply with their expectations. Resources are scarce (partly because of a weak political will to fund them), and administrators are encouraged to maximize both productivity (number of persons served) and efficiency (minimize costs per unit of service) and to avoid delay, duplication, and waste.

Per capita funding formulae (e.g., per admission, per unit of service provided) focus attention on client numbers rather than service quality. Administrators of manpower programs view number of client placements (in jobs) as the major *effectiveness* criterion for their agencies (Whetten, 1978). The difficulties of determining service quality encourage the use of quantity indicators as effectiveness criteria (Scott, 1977, p. 83). As might be expected, professionally trained SWO workers prefer effectiveness over efficiency standards. They also prefer autonomy over close supervision, in-depth over problem-specific treatment, and long-term over short-term contact (Whiddon and Martin, 1987; Whetten, 1978). Administrators and professional staff are often at odds over effectiveness standards and criteria.

To please resource controllers and promote organizational well-being (resource procurement, growth), many SWO directors emphasize productivity (quantity of services) and efficiency (more services at less cost). To provide effective service and to assuage professional staff, they stress service quality. These are conflicting goals. Social welfare organization administrators cannot ignore the wishes of resource controllers; thus, concern with quantity, outcome measures, and efficiency is probably inevitable. On the other hand, how can SWOs that fail to provide effective service be justified? Directors of SWOs have little choice but to pursue service effectiveness *and* agency well-being and to solicit constituency support for both (Martin, 1987). Strategies for doing this are identified later.

THE GENERIC SUBSYSTEMS OF SOCIAL WELFARE ORGANIZATIONS

Social welfare organizations vary in size from small two-person clinics to large state agencies with thousands of workers. Regardless of size, all SWOs engage in core work and legitimacy activities. Table 8.3 summarizes the

TABLE 8.3. GENERIC SUBSYSTEMS OF SOCIAL WELFARE ORGANIZATIONS: THEIR TASKS, GOALS, AND METHODS

Subsystem (1)	Tasks (2)	Goals (3)	Methods (4)
I. *Production:* provides service to clients (i.e., processes information inputs to produce outputs for exchange)	Task accomplishment: transformation of raw materials to produce outputs in line with organization's mandate	Service effectiveness; proficiency; productivity; efficiency	Establishes a division of labor; sets up job specifications, standards, and tasks; sets admissions or acceptance criteria for clients (e.g., intake)
II. *Maintenance* of working structure (processes matter/energy inputs including personnel, funds, etc.)	Mediates between task demands and human needs to keep structure in operation (does payroll, bookkeeping, sick leave, etc.)	Maintenance of steady state; aimed at preservation of the system; efficiency; legitimacy compliance	Formulates activities into standard legitimized procedures; sets up system of rewards; socializes new members
III. *Support* subsystem			
A. Production-supportive: procurement of materials and personnel; disposes of product (e.g., placements, referrals)	Transactional exchanges at system boundaries; goal to support productive subsystem	Specifically focused manipulation of organizational environment	Acquires control of sources of supply; creates image of organization
B. Institutional system (lobbies legislators, courts, donors; seeks favorable press)	Obtains social support and legitimacy	Societal manipulation and integration	Contributes to community; influences other social entities

IV. *Adaptation subsystem*	Intelligence gathering, research and development, planning	Pressure for change; organizational learning	Makes recommendations for change to management
V. *Leadership subsystem* (decides/controls; manages; guides; inspires)	1. Resolves conflicts between hierarchical levels	Control	Uses sanctions of authority (sets policies; makes decisions)
	2. Coordinates and directs functional substructures	Compromise vs. integration	Establishes alternative concessions; sets up machinery for adjudication
	3. Coordinates external requirements and organizational resources and needs	Legitimacy and long-term survival: optimization, better use of resources, development of increased capabilities	Increases volume of business by adding functions; controls environment through absorbing it or changing it; restructures organizaton

Source: Adapted from Katz and Kahn (1978, Table 1, p. 84).

tasks, goals, and methods of five generic SWO subsystems. These subsystems are fluid in structure and are identified, as all subsystems are, by their activities, by what they do. Over a period of time, an individual may perform work associated with two, three, or all five subsystems. (The content on five generic subsystems draws heavily on Katz and Kahn, 1978.)

The SWO *production subsystem* (Table 8.3) performs core work activities. In SWOs that provide social benefits, production activities include determining clients' eligibility for benefits. In SWOs with social control core work activities, detaining delinquents, monitoring the community-placed mentally ill, and removing a child from an abusive home are production activities. In social change/public interest SWOs, production work is lobbying legislators for new resources for children, securing better laws for prosecuting wife-beaters, more funds for the frail elderly, and so on. In SWOs that deal with clients, the production subsystem selects and processes or tranforms clients (Hasenfeld, 1983). From an Open Systems Theory perspective, the production subsystem selects, admits, and processes SWO clients (as inputs) to produce outputs for exchange with the environment (see columns 1 and 2 of Table 8.3).

It is tempting to equate the SWO with its production subsystem. Production subsystems reflect an SWO's official mandate and are the part of SWOs with which the general public is most familiar. The public assumes, for example, that the predominant activity of a mental health center is counseling or psychological treatment. For a production subsystem to discharge its responsibilities, however, many other organizational activities must have occurred. Production subsystems depend on the efforts and successes of the four other subsystems.

The *maintenance subsystem* (Table 8.3) undergirds the production subsystem by assuring sufficient and proper staff to conduct core work activities. The maintenance subsystem processes employment papers for new personnel, maintains personnel records, socializes new members, develops personnel manuals, maintains files and records of client service, issues payroll checks, pays insurance premiums, does bookkeeping, accounts for financial resources, and so forth. The maintenance subsystem mediates between the core work demands of the production subsystem and the human needs of workers to keep the structure in operation (Katz and Kahn, 1978). Job titles of employees who operate mainly in this subsystem are personnel directors (now called human resource officers), clerks, receptionists, typists, bookkeepers, and accountants.

The *support subsystem* performs two functions (Table 8.3). First, it supports the production subsystem. It identifies and procures material resources (finances, facilities), qualified personnel, and appropriate clients for the successful functioning of the production subsystem. It also establishes community linkages with other organizations—SWO and non-SWO alike—to ensure the production subsystem's ability to refer, place, or discharge clients, to dispose of SWO outputs. Second, the supportive subsystem promotes legitimacy for the SWO among external constituents. It strives to create and sustain a favorable image in the eyes of significant reference groups outside the SWO. Its goals are to convince outsiders of the SWO's legitimacy in exchange for good will, valued resources, positive media coverage, prestige, qualified staff and clients, and so on. As suggested by the description, actors in this subsystem deal primarily across the SWO boundary. Actors at several levels of the organization's internal hierarchy may engage in supportive activities. The quest for funding and legitimacy belongs usually to senior administrators, but supervisors may do most of the recruitment of service worker personnel, and core activity workers may negotiate client recruitment, referral and placement, or discharge linkages.

The *adaptation subsystem* (Table 8.3) tries to anticipate the future so SWO leaders can be responsive to developments in the organization's institutional, task, and resource environments. Its goal is to assure a stable present and promising future and to avoid costly errors. The adaptation subsystem identifies possible changes in direction, emphasis, programs, funding, and so on that may affect organizational well-being. Because they are more frequently in touch with powerful external constituents, SWO directors and their assistants perform most adaptation subsystem activities. Large and relatively well-off SWOs (such as state welfare agencies) may develop specialized units that work full-time on intelligence gathering, gathering research on future developments, and planning for the future. Small SWOs usually lack such units, and senior administrators perform these activities, typically on an ad hoc or informal basis (Martin, 1987).

The *leadership subsystem* (Table 8.3) is concerned with the integration, coordination, and control of internal processes and with assuring organizational survival and well-being vis-á-vis the external environment. The leadership subsystem monitors and integrates activities of the other four subsystems and uses hierarchical authority to make and enforce decisions that affect the total organization. Actors in this subsystem represent the organization to the outside world, build linkages with external constituents, and attempt to manipulate the environment to assure long-term survival and prosperity. Leadership subsystem actors set and enforce policies and rules, grant and deny merit raises, decide on new directions and programs, and make hiring and termination decisions on personnel.

The leadership subsystem is responsible for assuring the effective performance of all five SWO subsystems. If paychecks are issued later, problems in the maintenance subsystem may be the cause, but the leadership subsystem will be held accountable by both boards and resource controllers. The leadership subsystem is the eyes, ears, and brains of the organization as a totality. It must assure that each subsystem performs its tasks and exchanges with both other subsystems and with the environment in order to fulfill the SWO's mission and comply with legitimacy demands. Leadership activities are performed by all persons in positions of authority in the SWO. Those nearer the power apex make more decisions that affect all organizational members, but all workers make leadership decisions as they interact with peers, subordinates, clients, and external constituents.

Two Models of Subsystem Interdependence

Models A and B in Figure 8.2 show two perspectives on the role of the leadership subsystem. Model A, the Wheel Model, illustrates the coordination, integrative, and linkage functions of the leadership subsystem. The Wheel Model consists of a circle with leadership as the hub and the other subsystems aligned around it. All subsystems are linked through their association with leadership although they may be linked directly as well. The Wheel Model represents the leadership subsystem's integrative rather than control or authority roles. Arrows from the leadership, adaptive, supportive and productive subsystems to the environment reflect *the extensive openness of SWOs*. Four of five subsystems relate directly to the environment, and many of their activities, as reviewed above, are oriented toward compliance with legitimacy expectations and demands. Only the maintenance subsystem is oriented primarily to internal process. The tasks of the maintenance subsystem are to facilitate the operation of the other subsystems and in this way contribute to organizational success.

Model B, the Pyramid Model (Figure 8.2), illustrates the authority, power, and control functions of the leadership subsystem and the hierarchical structure of bureaucracies. As indicated by its location, the leadership subsystem has more authority than other subsystems. Located nearby are the support and adaptation subsystems whose tasks, as noted earlier, are often performed by senior administration. At the base of the pyramid are the production and maintenance subsystems. Again, arrows across the SWO boundary indicate linkages with the environment.

Professional vs. Bureaucratic Authority

Despite the leadership subsystem's authority over the whole, the SWO production subsystem is buffered from leadership control by *professional authority*. As discussed in Chapter 5, professional training, credentials, and expertise pose a rival to hierarchical authority. Professional social workers argue that leadership authority should not interfere with the professional–client relationship and that they must have the autonomy and discretion to perform their work as they see fit (Whiddon and Martin, 1987; Buffum and Ritvo, 1984; Anderson and Martin, 1982). Professionally educated social workers

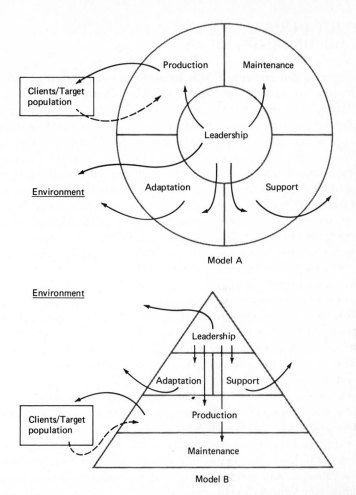

Figure 8.2 Wheel and Pyramid Models of Generic Subsystems Showing Linkages with the Environment and Internal Authority. Model A: Wheel Model Emphasizing Coordination and Linkage. Model B: Pyramid Model Emphasizing Authority and Control.

are, however, being replaced by less educated technicians and paraprofessionals. This is due partly to the scarcity of professionally trained workers who want to work with severely disturbed clients, at night and on weekends, or for relatively low pay. As a result, bureaucratic authority may increasingly intrude into the worker–client relationship. Workers who are not professionally trained are less able to resist bureaucratic authority than are professionals.

CONFLICT IN SOCIAL
WELFARE ORGANIZATIONS

As with other social systems, SWOs are suffused with conflict. Conflicting expectations from multiple constituents produce differences inside the SWO, between inside and external groups, and among external constituents. An SWO director has little constituency consensus upon which to base decisions or justify a course of action (Czarniawska, 1985a). Constituents shown in Figure 8.1 occupy different social locations and have different interests and priorities. Secretaries' working hours are highly regulated and they have few holidays. An increase in their vacation times may inconvenience professional staff. If secretaries demand a change, professional staff may sympathize with them but nevertheless oppose them on *practical* grounds (Martin, 1984).

Conflicts often reflect advantages, or disadvantages, associated with location in the SWO. Location influences members' perceptions and interpretations of the SWO, including the goals they pursue, perceptions of appropriate means for pursuing goals, perceptions of equity, and fairness about the distribution of resources such as earnings, power, benefits, and privileges. Members in different locations therefore see and experience SWOs differently, and SWO reality (Smircich and Morgan, 1982) is a continuously constructed phenomenon that reflects the SWO's highly open, fluctuating character. Only the absence of conflict from such a setting would be surprising.

Conflicts within SWOs take many forms. Supervisors may admonish employees over sloppy record-keeping, workers may refuse to complete paperwork or cooperate with each other, and clients may refuse to deal with certain workers or claim that policies are unfair. Conflicts can occur within one hierarchical level or between different levels. They can be interunit, interdepartmental, and interorganizational in addition to interpersonal. Work units may fight each other over office space. One SWO may compete with another for scarce resources.

Workers in all organizations want more control over their work than they have (Greenberger and Strasser, 1986; Bartolke, Eschweiler, Fleschenberger, and Tannenbaum, 1982). As suggested by the Multiple Constituencies Model, different constituents have different stakes in the organization and may become hostile when expectations are unmet. The unequal distribution of power across both hierarchical and subsystem lines generates conflict. Effective SWO leaders try to develop a collective sense of commitment and ensure that interpersonal conflicts do not become solidified along work unit, department, and programmatic lines. If this occurs, the SWO may become divided and segmentalized with a reduced capacity to learn and adapt (Kanter, 1983).

Three factors that cause conflict among SWO staff who perform core work activities are: (1) ineffective supervision, (2) oppressive paperwork demands, and (3) turf and professional rivalry differences.

1. *Ineffective supervision.* Core activity workers have definite opinions about the type of supervision they prefer. They desire precise job descriptions but also maximal freedom to execute their work (Buffum and Ritvo, 1984; Whetten, 1978). Those SWO workers who have as much (or more) discretion as they desire perform a higher quality of work than those with too little (Whiddon and Martin, 1988). Effective supervisors seek a balance in their relations with subordinates between leeway and direction, freedom and guidance. Ineffective supervision is a major source of frustration, dissatisfaction, and anger among core activity workers in many types of organizations (Mowday, Porter, and Steers, 1982; Smith, Organ, and Near, 1983; Kerr, Hill, and Broedling, 1986).

2. *Oppressive paperwork demands.* A growing problem for core activity workers is paperwork. Some state welfare workers resist opening new cases because of the paperwork involved, and 50 percent or more of service workers' time is estimated to be devoted to paperwork (Martin, 1987). As the trend of contracting services to the private sector increases, state welfare workers spend more time doing paperwork and less time dealing with clients (Austin and Hasenfeld, 1985). This frustrates workers who enjoy client contact and who resent the inability to use their professional knowledge and skills. Today, SWOs have begun hiring technicians and paraprofessionals to perform core work activities that are mostly paperwork. For this and other reasons, future state welfare agencies may have few professional social workers except at supervisory and administrative levels (Frumkin, Martin, and Page, 1987).

3. *Turf problems and professional rivalries.* Employees with low status and limited opportunity for advancement sometimes engage in turf-guarding (Kanter, 1977). *Turf-guarding* is the protection of one's interests and territory against presumed intruders, irrespective of costs to others. Controlling subordinates or maintaining the unit's supplies or space become priorities, with little concern for how this affects service delivery or employees. Turf-guarding is a problem in SWOs where resources are scarce and opportunities for advancement are limited.

Turf conflicts also develop between professional groups. When physicians, nurses, psychologists, and social workers are employed in one organization (such as a mental hospital or mental health clinic), conflicts emerge over who is allowed to do what. Psychiatrists guard the right to do therapy, thereby frustrating clinically trained social workers, nurses, and psychologists. Nurses may be skilled at diagnosis or treatment but denied the opportunity because of professional boundaries that reserve these activities to physicians. Problems for professional social workers can be acute when a director of a multidisciplinary organization is in a different profession or discipline; for example, medicine or psychology. They may be unable to utilize their professional knowledge and skills. This occurs often in Veterans Administration hospitals where social workers want to provide primary care (such as individual counseling, group treatment, and so on) but physicians, who are typically in charge, view them as placement agents who are responsible for finding nursing or foster-home placements for patients ready for discharge.

LEADERSHIP AND THE SWO DIRECTOR

One responsibility of SWO leaders is to create meaning for SWO members and constituents. An effective leader, according to Weick (1976), is one who *punctuates* the ongoing flow of organizational activities to help participants see their experiences as purposeful, meaningful, and worthwhile (also Smircich and Morgan, 1982). Two factors are necessary for leadership that succeeds in creating meaning and fostering service effectiveness: (1) a vision of purpose and (2) the use of positive political skills. (Material in this section draws heavily from Martin, 1987).

A Vision of Purpose

Conflicting expectations of multiple constituents and an absence of consensus on mandate and purpose create a contradictory context. There is no way to please all constituents all of the time and only limited ways to please any of them, ever. The SWO director can respond reactively on a case-by-case basis to the most influential constituent(s) of the day or he or she can promote a proactive vision of the SWO and *sell* it to as many constituents as will *buy*. Without visionary, proactive leadership, SWOs tend to become segmentalized and oriented toward the status quo.

One SWO vision of purpose is that of service effectiveness (Patti, 1985). This vision focuses attention and energy on the *quality of core work activities*. Most people value excellence, and most employees seek meaning in their work (Peters and Waterman, 1982). If service effectiveness is to become the goal and standard, the SWO director needs a concept of how staff—receptionist, clerk, aide, professional social worker, accountant, evaluation researcher, senior administrator—should behave: what they should do, how they should do it, and why. Martin (1987) argues that three conditions are required for a director to implement a vision of purpose. (1) The director must have a clear vision of purpose; (2) must be personally committed to implementing the vision; and (3) must have the skills to implement the vision.

1. *A clear vision of purpose: service effectiveness.* To work, a vision of purpose must be clear. Clarity implies purity, transparency, unmistakability. If an SWO is to succeed in directing its energy and resources to a particular vision of purpose, all SWO constituents must have a pure, unmistakable understanding of it. To illustrate, we use Patti's service effectiveness concept as an example. Patti (1985) argues that emphasizing service effectiveness communicates that an SWO is committed to excellence and will be satisfied with nothing less. All subsystems are expected to support the work of the production subsystem, which, it is recalled, performs the SWO's core work activities. External constituents can be asked to support the service effectiveness vision. If paperwork prevents workers from doing their best, directors can show how to reduce it and lobby resource providers for change. Each funder can be informed about the demands of other funders and their time and energy costs. A vision of service effectiveness can be used to unite multiple and diverse SWO constituents. Few of us can resist a challenge to do well, to help, and to serve to the best of our ability.

In addition to goals, a vision of purpose indicates how to implement. Organizational symbolism, metaphors, and exemplary behaviors and actions are useful here. Peters and Waterman (1982) describe the for-profit corporation's use of stories to communicate important organizational values and goals. Slogans such as "we love to help," "service is our number one value," or "people are our biggest asset" can be employed. Directors provide guidance on SWO values and priorities by focusing on particular behaviors and goals. A director of an old people's home in England chastised a staff member for stopping an elderly resident, Mr. Jones, from going for a walk. Even though Mr. Jones has memory lapses, the director said Mr. Jones could go out if he wished.

> Never again say to Mr. Jones or any other resident [that] they cannot got for a walk. If they lived in their own homes, they could go for a walk when they liked. If Mr. Jones goes walking and gets lost, we'll go find him. Getting lost is a part of life and not the worst thing that can happen. Far worse is having Mr. Jones think he has to get permission to go for a walk. (Martin, 1979)

Word of this conversation spread quickly and the director's views on residents' rights became widely know. Elderly residents were to be treated as independent, responsible adults, not as children in need of constant supervision or control. Such incidents, and the stories they generate, communicate a vision and help to socialize staff about service effectiveness.

2. *Commitment to the vision.* Having a vision is not enough. For a vision to work, SWO directors must commit to it and be willing to withstand pressures to pursue other ends. Without commitment, legal and accountability standards and pressures from important constituents will become top priorities. Constituents may fail to support a director's vision of purpose, particularly in the early stages. The temptation to abandon the vision in favor of easier and smoother paths will be great for directors who are less than fully committed.

3. *Skills to implement the vision.* In addition to clarity and commitment, SWO directors need the skills to implement. Communication skills are needed to explain and win support for the vision. Behaviors that are consistent with the vision and support staff in their efforts to work out the details are essential. Implementation skills can be learned through workshops, short courses, and formal training on organizational culture, symbolism, negotiation, and the communication of meaning. Skills such as decision making, planning, analysis, and supervision are important too, of course (Glisson, 1981). If directors focus solely on rational planning and technology, however, workers may become maintenance-oriented, cautious, and subservient to powerful constituent pressures and demands (Peters and Waterman, 1982).

Ten Action Strategies for SWO directors are shown in Table 8.4. (These are taken from Martin, 1987.) Some strategies concern core work activities and their effectiveness, and others concern organizational legitimacy. Action Strategies VI through X focus on service effectiveness. Of particular importance, Action Strategy VIII encourages directors to emphasize vision and inspiration over supervision and control, and Action Strategy IX highlights the importance of basic values. Behavioral skills to put these strategies into practice can be acquired through special courses and workshops in addition to reading the literature (e.g., Resnick and Patti, 1980).

Positive Political Skills for the SWO Director

Positive political skills are techniques for using power affirmatively. They include campaigning, lobbying, bargaining, negotiating, caucusing, collaborating, and winning votes (Kanter, 1983, p. 216). Positive leaders sell

TABLE 8.4. ACTION STRATEGIES FOR SWO LEADERS TO MAXIMIZE SERVICE EFFECTIVENESS AND ORGANIZATIONAL WELL-BEING

I. *Tie organizational mission to environmental values.* Legitimacy is enhanced if the SWO demonstrates compliance with valued norms in its institutional environment (e.g., shows efficiency in using public funds).

II. *Choose action over analysis.* Choose a course of action or change based on values, priorities, and preferences and build support for that option from the ground up. Avoid excessive analysis of all possible choices. Action over analysis promotes effectiveness and proactivity.

III. *Maintain good (positive, cooperative, honest, frequent) relations with one's "web of influence."* Frequent contact and communication with all constituents in the SWO's institutional environment helps to legitimate the SWO. Visibility is interpreted as effectiveness.

IV. *Use power to help others.* The use of positive political skills by SWO leaders is helpful in marshaling resources and support for both effective services and legitimacy.

V. *Continually educate your constituents.* SWO leaders must assume that all constituents, internal and external, must be convinced and won over to important values and priorities.

VI. *Demonstrate good service delivery and the support of clients.* Emphasis on quality and effectiveness of core activity work requires close and responsive contact with clients. This enhances SWO legitimacy as well.

VII. *Translate symbols into action, action into symbols.* Board policies and social legislation must be interpreted into specific actions that SWO staff can implement. SWO directors are responsible for this. They must also interpret actions of staff (and clients) so that policymakers can see the significance and value of what they do. This affects both effectiveness and legitimacy.

VIII. *Emphasize vision and inspiration over supervision and control.* A proactive vision of service effectiveness and efforts to inspire staff foster outstanding staff performance and service effectiveness. Emphasis on control communicates a lack of trust and back of confidence.

IX. *Highlight basic values and stand by time.* The SWO that tries to do everything does nothing. Emphasis on a few basic values contributes to a sense of direction and understanding of what is most important.

X. *Control essential accountability practices tightly; protect worker discretion in core work activities.* SWOs must show compliance with regulatory and legal mandates such as appropriate handling of cases or use of resources of funds. Beyond this, core activity workers must be allowed the freedom to conduct their work so it accords with their best judgment. Greater discretion contributes to a higher quality of work among social service staff.

Source: P. Y. Martin, "Group Sex Composition in Work Organization: A Structural-Normative Model." In *Administration in Social Work*, Vol. 11 (3/4), in press, The Hayworth Press, NY (1987).

their ideas rather than give orders. A definition of politics as behind-the-scenes chicanery is rejected in favor of positive political skills that affirm proactive, prosocial attempts to win over others to one's view, to develop support for an idea, and to gain cooperation and compliance through persuasion and influence rather than power and control (Kanter, 1983; Block, 1987).

Research on SWO directors and business managers reveals that they allocate time differently. Business managers spend more time on internal affairs, mostly motivation and supervision of staff, whereas SWO directors spend more time on planning and intergovernmental relations or negotiation (Files, 1981). Directors of SWOs spend 39 percent of their time on planning, 26 percent on intergovernmental relations/negotiation, and 12 percent on staff motivation and supervision. Comparable percentages for business managers are 17 percent, 12 percent and 29 percent, respectively (Files, 1981). Files concludes that business managers specialize in staff supervision, whereas SWO directors specialize in planning and intergovernmental relations/negotiation. Moreover, SWO directors are more externally oriented (Meyer and Scott, 1983) and more political. Negotiating, bargaining, coalition building, planning and goal-setting are essential leadership skills. Skills such as these are required inside the SWO and with the environment.

Organizational innovators who use political skills in a positive way have been described as *corporate entrepreneurs* (Kanter, 1983). Corporate entrepreneurs are "the people who test limits and create new possibilities for organizational action by pushing and directing" innovation in the organization (Kanter, 1983, p. 210). An SWO director's ability to implement a vision of purpose requires entrepreneurial know-how and skill (Martin, 1987; Czarniawska, 1985b; Brunsson, 1985). Power is defined as "the capacity to mobilize people and resources and to get things done" (Kanter, 1983, p. 213). Organizational power derives from three basic commodities that can be turned into action: (1) information (data, technical knowledge, expertise, political savvy); (2) resources (funds, space, time, staff, supplies); and (3) support (backing, endorsement, approval, legitimacy) (Kanter, 1983, p. 216). These commodities are turned into power by corporate entrepreneurs in three ways: problem definition, coalition building, and mobilization. *Problem definition* refers to convincing others in the organization to perceive and define a problem (or goal) in a particular way; *coalition building* is gaining support for the perception/definition among a wide range of relevant organizational members; and *mobilization* is gaining official support, including resources to turn the dream into a reality.

Peers and subordinates, and constituents on the outside, may be easier to sell a new idea or project to than one's superiors (Kanter, 1983). One way to gain the approval of superiors is to demonstrate that significant organizational constituents have already *bought in* on the idea. Buying in (or as Kidder, 1981, describes it, "signing on") is a promise of support from organizational constituents for an innovation or change. To succeed at implementing a vision of purpose that makes service effectiveness the top priority, an SWO director must get many contituent groups to *buy in*. This may be difficult, but the use of positive political skills can help. Social workers' distaste for the twin topics of power and political skills is a result of viewing power as control rather than influence, of domination rather than facilitation (making things happen; cf. Kanter, 1977). Positive political skills allow an SWO director to use power to promote a vision of purpose that, in the present example, emphasizes service effectiveness above all else.

STAFF PERFORMANCE, AUTONOMY, AND PARTICIPATION

Staff performance is the lifeblood of social welfare programs. Plans for benefits, services, laws, and entire social welfare programs come to nought if designated staff fail to enact prescribed roles and tasks. The cooperation and commitment of core work activity staff determine service delivery outcomes. Administrators and policymakers of SWOs must understand workers' standards for assessing performance and the conditions they perceive as necessary for effective service. Research by Whiddon and Martin (1988) addresses these points.

Staff Performance Quality

Quality of staff performance concerns the degree to which SWO staff behaviors reflect (1) mastery of the technical and operational demands of the job and (2) a prosocial view of organizational behavior (Martin and Whiddon, 1988). Technical and operational demands consist of accurate knowledge of the regulations and procedures that workers are required to follow. This includes compliance with laws, rules, and procedures; arriving at work on time; keeping up with paperwork; being proactive rather than reactive in completing work, and so on (Martin and Whiddon, 1988). A prosocial view of organizational behavior consists of "acts such as helping, sharing, donating, cooperating, and volunteering" (Brief and Motowidlo, 1986, p. 710).

Prosocial organizational behavior is behavior that is "(a) performed by a member of an organization, (b) directed toward an individual, group, or organization with whom he or she interacts while carrying out his or her organizational role, and (c) performed with the intention of promoting the welfare of the individual, group, or organization toward which it is directed" (Brief and Motowidlo, 1986). Quality of worker–client relations is critical in service organizations (Smith, Organ, and Near, 1983; Schneider, Parkington, and Buxton, 1980). Staw, Bell, and Clausen (1986) conclude that the primary product of service organizations is *affect* or the communication to customers (clients) that they are valued and the organization cares or that they are not valued and the organization is indifferent. Clients of social welfare organizations appreciate courteous, caring treatment although they do not always receive it (Prottas, 1979). Martin and Whiddon (1988) urge that prosocial behavior be required of all SWO staff as a minimal behavioral standard.

Table 8.5 shows a Staff Performance Scale that can be used by SWO staff to assess the technical, operational, and prosocial aspects of their work. Developed after talking with service workers and first-line supervisors, the scale has high validity and reliability (Whiddon, 1982; Martin and Whiddon, 1988). Research shows, furthermore, that workers with greater discretion in their jobs report that their service units perform a higher quality of work.

Worker Autonomy, Participation, and Performance

Studies of social welfare organizations report that job autonomy, or discretion, is important to core activity workers. Workers with greater autonomy are more satisfied with their work and their supervisors (Buffum and Ritvo, 1984). They are also more committed to the organization (Glisson and Durick, 1987). More importantly, workers with more autonomy believe they perform a higher quality of work (Whiddon and Martin, 1987). The SWO workers with *more autonomy than they desire* report the highest quality of work. Having too little autonomy, on the other hand, is related to lower work quality.

Holland (1973) and Holland and others (1981) found that participation by mental-hospital workers in program planning and execution is associated with positive behavior toward residents (cf. Martin and Segal, 1977). This suggests that more autonomy leads to superior staff performance, which, in turn, contributes to outstanding service quality and favorable client outcomes. The evidence that such a causal sequence is cumulative underscores the need for SWO leaders to emphasize staff autonomy and discretion as a means of fostering excellent service. Participation in organization-wide decisions is of less concern to core activity workers than is job discretion (Holland and others, 1981; Whiddon and Martin, 1987).

Worker participation in SWOs is a complex issue. Kanter (1983) notes that corporations that encourage worker participation and collaboration are seldom permissive. Organizations that allow greater participation demand more also. Autonomy communicates respect to workers for their abilities and skills, but it also requires more responsibility and initiative.

Peters and Waterman (1982) report that excellent American companies have to *force authority and decision making down* the authority hierarchy. Workers readily relinquish freedom to superiors who want to take it (Smircich and Morgan, 1982) because bureaucratic structure legitimates this arrangement. Encouragement of worker autonomy requires a vision of purpose that makes workers responsible for SWO goal accomplishment. Decentralization of decision making to core activity workers—who know most about core work functions—requires work and commitment of leaders. Leaders who need power and enjoy control are unlikely to make the effort. Bureaucratic hurdles

TABLE 8.5. WHIDDON'S STAFF PERFORMANCE SCALE. A MEASURE OF SOCIAL SERVICE WORKERS' QUALITY OF WORK PERFORMANCE (DIRECT SERVICE STAFF VERSION)[a]

Instructions: Circle the response that most closely reflects the situation *in your unit.*

In general, the direct staff in my unit:

	SD	D	N	A	SA[b]
1. are energetic in their jobs.	1	2	3	4	5
2. try to find the best alternatives in offering services to clients.	1	2	3	4	5
3. fail to use the supervisory relationship to its fullest advantage.	1	2	3	4	5
4. do required assignments, such as federally required paperwork, late or inaccurately.	1	2	3	4	5
5. seem unfamiliar with state and federal laws that affect their clients.	1	2	3	4	5
6. take pride in their individual work.	1	2	3	4	5
7. work cooperatively with other staff.	1	2	3	4	5
8. deal straightforwardly and openly in supervision.	1	2	3	4	5
9. seem satisfied to just "go by the book" in offering services to their clients.	1	2	3	4	5
10. take the initiative and are self-starters in their work.	1	2	3	4	5
11. demonstrate knowledge of and make use of departmental regulations.	1	2	3	4	5
12. demonstrate knowledge of and make use of professional skills necessary for working with their clients.	1	2	3	4	5
13. take pride in the work of their unit.	1	2	3	4	5
14. are not concerned about being present on the job when they are supposed to be.	1	2	3	4	5
15. seldom work independently but wait to be told what to do.	1	2	3	4	5
16. demonstrate inflexibility in dealing with their clients.	1	2	3	4	5
17. seem interested in giving an extra effort in doing their jobs well.	1	2	3	4	5
18. seldom make use of other community resources when these might be appropriate for their clients.	1	2	3	4	5
19. seem to do as little as possible in fulfilling the requirements of their jobs.	1	2	3	4	5
20. act as advocates for clients within the parameters of the regulations and laws.	1	2	3	4	5

[a] Nine items are worded negatively and require reverse scoring. The negatively worded items are: 3, 4, 5, 9, 14, 15, 16, 18, and 19.

[b] Response scale: SD = strongly disagree, D = disagree, N = neutral, A = agree, and SA = strongly agree.

Source: Beverly Whiddon, "The Effect of Congruence on the Relationships Between Participation/ Job Discretion and Staff Performance." Unpublished Ph.D. Dissertation (Tallahassee: Florida State University, 1982).

in segmented, noninnovating organizations discourage job discretion and autonomy at the core work activity level (Kanter, 1983). Mid-level administrators in organizations of this type find that efforts to enhance work quality by increasing worker discretion are fruitless.

IMPLICATIONS FOR SOCIAL WORK

Strategic implications for SWO administrators and staff are noted throughout Chapter 8. Social welfare organizations are depicted as dynamic, complex, and conflictual arenas of social interaction and exchange. Understanding the mutually dependent relationship of SWOs and their environments is perhaps the most important point of Chapter 8. Social welfare organizations are profoundly affected by their institutional, task, and resource environments although they influence these environments also. Though it may be difficult, SWO leaders can sell a vision of purpose that emphasizes service effectiveness to SWO constituents, many of whom are outside the organization's boundary.

Social welfare organizations are a paradoxical mixture of (1) a fragmented political arena suffused with inconsistencies, contradictions, and conflicting interests, and (2) an organized system with interrelated parts that mesh into a dynamic whole. In the hands of powerful constituents, SWOs (and other organizations) are tools for achieving numerous ends besides their official purpose (Martin, 1987). Social welfare organizations provide jobs (and other resources) for educated, middle-class citizens in addition to services, benefits, and control to clients. In seeking to understand SWOs, this should be kept in mind. Most SWOs attempt, nevertheless, to fulfill their official mission. Appreciation of their multiple uses, conflictual and contradictory environments, and multiple constituency character—both internal and external—helps in comprehending the seemingly irrational actions that SWOs sometimes take.

Leadership is an activity, not a person or position, and should not be equated with any one person. Any SWO member with a vision of purpose, who is committed to its implementation and who employs positive political skills, can be a leader. This is easier for senior administrators although Kanter's research (1983) shows that lower-level workers can lead as well. Core activity workers can utilize positive political skills to improve quality and implement change at the service-delivery level. If SWOs are political entities as well as *legal-rational tools* for achieving goals, this holds promising potential. Positive political skills can be used to improve quality, especially in SWOs that are committed to quality and that accept innovation as a way to learn and improve.

Chapter 9

Communities as Loosely Coupled Systems

INTRODUCTION

Chapter 9 is about communities. Communities are complex arenas of social interaction that include an array of people, groups, and organizations performing many diverse activities. As depicted in Chapter 9, communities are loosely coupled, or linked, systems that include many other systems and that have extensive ties with their environment. Chapter 9 is oriented to helping the reader (1) conceptualize and understand communities, and (2) identify strategies to promote citizen empowerment, locality development, social planning, and social action for purposes of social change at the community level. We begin with a review of the Open System Theory concepts and themes that undergird our conceptualization of community.

OPEN SYSTEMS CONCEPTS AND THEMES

Seven Open Systems Theory concepts, or themes, form the conceptual framework for our discussion of community. These are: (1) linkages, (2) relative strength of linkages, (3) boundary, (4) levels of inclusiveness, (5) direction of influence, (6) social systems as occupiers of concrete time and space, and (7) diverse and conflicting interests.

Linkages

Linkages are ties or connections between systems and/or the component parts of systems. The concept of linkages is employed to describe and assess the current and historical features of American communities. A major point of this chapter is that communities have changed, and they have less local control over their destinies than they formerly had. One reason is that linkages with external groups and organizations have increased and strengthened while linkages at the local level have decreased and weakened.

Horizontal linkages occur among peer systems or systems that lack authority or power over one another. For example, public schools that share curriculum materials or substitute teachers are linked horizontally. *Vertical linkages* occur between systems with unequal power, that is, between a system with greater authority or power and one with less authority or power. In vertical linkages, a subordinate system is subject to the authority/power of the superordinate system. County school boards that hire principals and oversee testing and instructional standards of all county schools are linked vertically to the schools they oversee and the schools are linked vertically to the school board.

Community linkages vary also in regards to whether they remain inside a community's boundary (see below) or span its boundary. Linkages that remain inside the boundary are called *internal linkages* whereas linkages that span the boundary are called *external linkages*.

Relative Strength of Linkages

Relative strength of linkages concerns the degree to which community systems or component parts are interdependent upon each other. Degree of interdependence can range from complete independence to minimal interdependence to moderate interdependence to great interdependence. In OST terms, this concerns the extent to which community elements are tightly versus loosely coupled. As indicated in the title of Chapter 9, we view communities as loosely coupled systems. Community elements vary, however, in the degree to which they are coupled with other elements. Individuals and families may be linked with local government loosely through paying taxes or parking fines or through driving on city streets and playing in city parks, whereas organizations such as police departments or restaurant owners have direct ties to city hall. The former are a subdepartment of city government, whereas the latter have to secure a license and pass sanitary inspections to remain in operation. Recognition that some community systems are tightly coupled to other systems, both internal and external to the community, whereas others are loosely coupled, can be used by social workers to understand community processes and to conceptualize community practice.

Boundary

As defined in Chapter 2, a system's *boundary* refers to its limits, or to an area or region, that sets it off from other systems and from its environment. Communities, like families and social welfare organizations, have boundaries. Community boundaries are sometimes difficult to identify because American communities are highly linked to their environments and have many ties with organizations and individuals on the outside. A community's boundary is not, furthermore, necessarily synonymous with geopolitical bounds such as city limits or county lines. The concept of boundary nevertheless indicates that communities occupy concrete geographical space—that is, they are located in a particular place and this place can be identified on a map—and we concur in this.

Levels of Inclusiveness

As noted in Chapter 6 on families and in Chapter 7 on small groups, some social systems are inclusive and some are included. Communities are *inclusive systems* to the families, businesses, firms, governments, churches, schools, and welfare agencies that are located in them and are *included systems* relative to the economic, social, political (e.g., state and national governments), legal, and cultural systems in which they are located. We argue below that American communities are weak inclusive systems today compared to the nineteenth century. The emergence of national chain retail stores and restaurants, a strong federal government, the regionalization of banks, financial institutions, and utilities, and so on, has led to diminished control by local communities over many organizations and services that are located within their boundaries.

Direction of Influence

Direction of influence concerns the form of influence that occurs between community elements and between a community and its environment. Influence flows in two major directions: horizontal and vertical. *Horizontal influence* occurs when one system, or part, affects another without the use of authority or power. An elementary school principal who successfully lobbies a fellow principal to share the former's art teacher or school van has used horizontal influence. Horizontal influence occurs between peers, that is, parties that are more or less equal relative to authority or power (see Chapter 5 on the professional–client dyad). *Vertical influence* occurs between parties that have an authority or power relation to each other. When the U.S. Department of Health and Human Services (DHHS) issues regulations for the awarding of Food Stamps, and the local Food Stamps Office is required to comply, authority flows in a *vertical-down direction*. If the local Food Stamps Office petitions DHHS to change a regulation and is successful, this is a *vertical-up flow of influence*. Vertical influence always concerns, by definition, elements that are linked via authority arrangements. Vertical influence therefore involves relations among or between nonpeer systems (or elements). A community's power structure can be identified by attending to vertical linkage patterns among community elements and between communities and their environments.

Social Systems as Occupiers of Concrete Space and Time

As noted in Chapter 2, this text is concerned with *concrete social systems*. Communities are loosely coupled social systems that occupy concrete, or real, space and time. Our conception of communities views them as geographic locales, or areas, where people live, where families, neighborhoods, and formal organizations are located, and where networks of cross-cutting linkages exist among various types of systems. Communities can be observed and studied at one point in time—such as today—and over time, such as from prior centuries to the present.

Diverse and Conflicting Interests

Social systems that are highly open, loosely coupled, and characterized by a multitude of different types and forms of activity are likely to experience *conflicts*. Modern communities are this way. As noted in Chapter 1, Americans are a diverse mixture of ethnic, cultural, religious, and social class groups, and American communities are often divided along these and related lines. Residents are divided by neighborhood into affluent, middle class, working class, poor, shanty, or slum. Business interests conflict with labor interests. Poles disagree with Greeks. Protestants differ from Catholics; Jews or Baptists differ from Presbyterians. Working-class residents may feel their neighborhoods are healthy and viable whereas developers may try to condemn their neighborhoods in order to put up new office buildings or high rises. Hispanics may feel that Spanish should be an official language in schools, whereas others may insist on English. And so on. American communities are typically factionalized, that is, riddled with diverse and conflicting interests and interest groups.

DOES COMMUNITY STILL EXIST?

Some argue that communities no longer exist (cf. Bernard, 1973). This claim stems from recognition of the negative impact of the industrial revolution, modernization, and urbanization on aspects of traditional community life.

For many, the concept of community suggests a picture of villages or small towns and face-to-face interaction. Today's communities are clearly different from those of yesteryear. Industrialization and urbanization have reshaped community life, and technological changes associated with modernization have diminished the importance of locale. A previous weeklong or daylong journey now takes hours and minutes, thus expanding life beyond town boundaries. Living in one city and working in another is not uncommon. Innovations and developments in the mass media have increased extralocal awareness. Radio, television, syndicated news services, and national publications provide the same information to all geographic regions. Local and regional differences in culture, values, and life styles tend to become homogenized into a *mass culture* (Martin, Wilson, and Dillman, 1988). People are less identified by or with locale (Vidich and Bensman, 1977).

Communities have grown in scale also. As noted in Chapter 1, most Americans live in metropolitan areas. Urban sprawl is pervasive and the boundary of one community blurs into the next. Isolation and anonymity are common in large cities where many people pass each other en route to work but know their neighbors only by sight, seldom by name. Intimacy and informality and a commonality of thought, sentiment, and values associated with small towns are problematic in cities (Simmel, 1977).

Although communities are not the center of social life today as they were for our ancestors, they have not disappeared. People reside in particular neighborhoods, shop in neighborhood stores, visit friends in the hospital, work in factories and offices, and patronize local businesses such as insurance companies, banks, and real estate agencies. Their children attend schools. They are members of local groups such as parent-teacher associations, neighborhood associations, charity agency boards, labor unions, and recreational clubs. They play and recreate in parks, movies, bars, athletic teams, and restaurants (Bernard, 1973). It is through these activities that they interact with fellow residents and develop social networks of friends, acquaintances, colleagues, and allies. These daily rounds of collective activity are the dynamics and substance of community life.

There is some evidence that Americans' interest in their communities is on the increase (Naisbitt, 1982). Citizens are organizing to protect their community's *quality of life*. Awareness of the physical environment's fragility has prompted efforts to protect the quality of water, land, and air. Self-help and consumer-advocacy groups provide opportunities for social and political participation as they organize to control and shape events in their communities (Naisbitt, 1982). Increased opportunities for personal and familial cultural enrichment are emerging as well.

Community organizations provide basic services such as police and fire protection, animal and pest control, public libraries, utility services such as water, electricity, garbage collection, and sewage disposal. Although the number, size, and type of organizations that provide services differ from one locale to the next, most communities have formal and/or voluntary organizations to provide them. To pay for these services, governments levy taxes on property and sales. Governments also regulate and attempt to control various individuals, groups, and organizations in the locale. Government rules and guidelines are usually formalized into written laws, regulations, and codes, and citizens are often included in shaping them.

Besides its formally organized aspects, much of community life is *existential*, that is, involving informal daily routines of waking, bathing, dressing, eating, walking or driving to work or school, talking, sharing, cooperating, shopping, eating, discussing, arguing, and so on. Residents interact routinely in families, kin groups, friendship cliques, cultural and ethnic groups, work groups, and with neighbors. Such interactions and dynamics form the essence of *communal* life and occur parallel to more formally organized social, political, economic, and cultural activities and events.

Despite their changed character, communities do exist. They are, furthermore, important to the people who live in them. Communities are localities where people live; communities are social contexts where many formally organized and informally organized activities occur; communities have governments, special interest groups, families, businesses, schools, welfare agencies, hospitals, and so forth. For social workers who are committed to community development and enhancement, understanding of communities is essential. Social work's commitment to community and community practice is reviewed next.

SOCIAL WORK'S HISTORY OF COMMUNITY INTERVENTION

Social work has a long history of community involvement and a heritage that commits it to community development and reform. Social work's philosophical foundations are inherent in, and expressed through, its involvement in community work (Harrison, 1987). Social work emerged as a profession early in the twentieth century as part of the Progressive Era and adopted the humanism and spirit of reform characteristic of that time.

Community organization practice was common in the early days of social welfare work. Much of this work was informal and guided by practicality and common sense rather than scientific principles or technology. It was nevertheless based on the conception of individuals and families as embedded in community and of community as a resource and a locus for social action and collective activity (Lubove, 1972). Early community practice developed in two prototype social welfare organizations associated with nineteenth-century attempts to address poverty and other problems of the urban poor: (1) charity organization societies and (2) settlement houses. Charity organization societies (COSs) were umbrella organizations at the local level which coordinated and rationalized the activities of independent, voluntary philanthropic organizations. The latter provided services and benefits directly to the poor (Chambers, 1963, p. 367). Settlement houses were neighborhood centers established (primarily in cities) to promote communication across social classes, ages, and ethnic groups, to teach self-help, to provide education, referral services, and information, and to encourage and organize for political action. COSs and settlement houses embodied different philosophical approaches to social welfare community work. The COSs were concerned with coordination and integration of philanthropic work from above, whereas settlement houses were concerned with citizen initiatives, collective action, and organization from below.

Charity Organization Societies

Based on a similar organization in London, the first charity organization society in America was founded in 1877 in Buffalo, New York, by well-to-do citizens interested in coordinating and rationalizing private philanthropy for the urban "worthy poor" (Garvin and Cox, 1987). The social and economic chaos that followed the Civil War and the social problems of European immigrants who flooded to the United States during this period led to the emergence of private philanthropic agencies that attempted to help the urban masses. In an effort to reduce demands on a few philanthropists, to reduce duplication of effort, and to meet ever-increasing needs, charity organization societies (COSs) were established to "make broad studies of social and economic problems and [to] recommend specific remedial measures" (Murphy, 1954, p. 35; see also Garvin and Cox, 1987). Leaders in this movement were generally upper-class philanthropists who believed that economic and social problems resulted primarily from flawed character and who were suspicious of public efforts to help the poor.

The COS movement established several precedents for the later emergence of community organization practice in social work. The COSs attempted to engage in cooperative planning among charitable organizations, to ameliorate various social problems, to create new agencies, and to reform old ones (Garvin and Cox, 1987, p. 33). They also developed some of the earliest forms of social-survey techniques, an important early example of which occurred in Pittsburgh in 1922 (Watson, 1922), for purposes of learning about the housing conditions, wages, working conditions, and so on of the urban poor. The COS leaders tried to secure reforms in tenement housing codes, to develop antituberculosis associations, to obtain legislation to support juvenile court and probation workers, to establish day-care programs for children, and to cooperate with police to control beggars and vagrants (Garvin and Cox, 1987; Watson, 1922). Contrary to the settlement house movement, however, COSs took action *for the poor* rather than viewing the poor as able to take action for themselves. The COS successes at community-wide planning and interorganizational coordination nevertheless provided a model for community intervention that the social work profession subsequently adopted.

Settlement Houses

The settlement house movement, like that of COSs, was based on a British precedent. It began in the United States in 1886 in New York City with the founding of a Neighborhood Guild that was intended to foster neighborhood organization and civic renaissance (Davis, 1977). Jane Addams founded Hull House in Chicago in 1889, and by 1910 more than 400 settlements were operating in the United States (mostly in the North and Midwest). These settlements, or neighborhood centers, were invariably located in poor sections of cities, and a primary purpose, early on, was to "restore communication between the college educated and the working class and to help improve conditions in the cities" (Davis, 1977, p. 1267). Contrary to the thinking of COSs, the root causes of social problems were believed to lie in environmental conditions, not in individual character. Thus, settlement house workers, in contrast to COS leaders, were typically middle class, were critical of the social order, and were identified with, rather than patronizing of, the poor (Garvin and Cox, 1987).

Settlement houses attempted to provide services to neighborhood residents. These included kindergartens, clubs and recreational programs for children, evening schools for adults, and public baths and art exhibitions (Garvin and Cox, 1987, p. 35). They laid great stress on social reform, and services were often viewed as experiments that, if successful, could serve as models for other neighborhoods and communities. Settlement house leaders worked for legislative and administrative reform at the local, state, and national levels. A major emphasis in all of their activities was education of all kinds and participation and organization of the poor on their own behalf (Garvin and Cox, 1987). Contrasting the COS and settlement house movements, Kramer and Specht (1983, p. 3) conclude: "Whereas the charity organization movement represented the community's attempt to help the individual adjust to social situations by use of scientific helping processes, the settlement movement represented the community's desire to adjust society to better meet people's needs." Both of these orientations were adopted by the social work profession in its conception of, and interventions in, the community.

Summary

The Charity Organization Society and settlement house movements of the nineteenth century left a legacy that social work, as it became formally organized in the twentieth century, adopted. From these precedents, community organization practice evolved in three directions: (1) social planning, (2) locality development, and (3) organization for social action and change (Rothman and Tropman, 1987). *Social planning* concerns efforts to rationalize and coordinate formal organizations for a variety of purposes including meeting citizens' needs, improving service to the poor or disadvantaged, preventing welfare clients from falling through the cracks, and so on. *Locality development* aims at increasing citizen participation in community activities, fostering participation and democratic decision making of all community residents, promoting education about community organization and the political process, and encouraging and developing indigenous leaders. *Organization for social action and change* is concerned with helping citizens to organize themselves for purposes of gaining new resources, electing representatives to political office, changing legislation, and so on.

WHAT IS A COMMUNITY?

Table 9.1 summarizes five different conceptions of community. The fifth, or Existential Model, incorporates elements from the other four and is the model we favor. Of the five, the Existential Model places greater emphasis on natural groups such as families, kin, neighbors, and friends in their daily living routines. As shown in Table 9.1, four of the models view communities as occupying a concrete geographical locale—that is, an area of land that can be shown on a map. These same four models view formal organizations as essential component parts of communities. The Common Sentiments Model is the only model that claims a community can exist independently of a concrete geographic locale. Concern with shared identification, values, and commitment is important, however, and aspects of this model are incorporated in the Existential Model. As indicated in Table 9.1, each model holds different implications for the community organization practitioner.

As noted in Table 9.1, a *System of Systems Model* of community views a local community as consisting of its formal organizations and the relationships among them (Sanders, 1975). Local government is viewed as the coordinator or hub of community organizations, including schools, businesses, hospitals, churches, factories, social welfare organizations, and so on. This model does not disavow natural or existential systems such as families and neighborhoods but it does not focus on them. A System of Systems Model draws attention to relationships among formal organizations including

TABLE 9.1. FIVE MODELS OF COMMUNITY IN TERMS OF FOCUS, TERRITORY, AND COMMUNITY PRACTICE ORIENTATION

Model	Focuses attention on:	Conceives of community as a territory or geographic locale?	Orients community practitioner toward concern with:
System of Systems (Sanders)	Formal organizations with local government as hub or coordinator	Yes	Building interorganizational linkages among formal organizations and government in a geographic area
Functional Subsystems (Warren)	Institutional activity networks; existential systems as well as formal organizations	Yes	Establishing linkages among formal organizations and natural groups (e.g., families); linking networks to each other in a geographic area
Interactional Field (Long)	Geographic locale as site of overlapping but quasi-independent institutional games (e.g., banking, education, welfare)	Yes	Fostering linkages within and between institutional games in a geographic area
Common Sentiments (Nisbet)	Common (shared) values, feelings of identification, commitment, and attachment	Not necessarily	Promoting/developing feelings of common values and commitments among members of a community (e.g., all social workers in the U.S.; all residents in an area)
Existential (Gottschalk)	Existential (or natural) groups such as families, neighborhoods, ethnic groups as well as formal organizations and institutional activity networks	Yes	Promoting linkages among and between existential and formal systems and fostering feelings of common identification and commitment in a geographic area

cooperation and sharing as well as conflicts 'and disagreements. Inter-organizational planning and coordination are common goals of community practitioners who employ this model.

The *Functional Subsystems Model* (Warren, 1963) views a community as a set of institutional activity networks that perform functions associated with daily life in a locality. From this perspective, community is the organization of social activities in a locale and it is also an interorganizational field or a place where formal organizations interact with each other (Warren, 1970). Five primary types of activities, or functions, occur in a community: (1) production/distribution/consumption of goods and services necessary for daily living; (2) socialization of community members; (3) social control to induce conformity to norms; (4) social participation opportunities for members of formal organizations and informal groups; and (5) mutual support in the form of health and welfare services. The Functional Subsystems Model focuses attention on linkages among community elements and can be used by practitioners concerned with social planning, locality development, and/or social action oriented to social change.

The *Interactional Field Model* views a community as a geographic locale where numerous and diverse "institutional games" are played simultaneously (Long, 1958). As described by Long (1958, pp. 252–53):

> [S]tructured group activities that coexist in a particular territorial system can be looked at as games. . . . [T]here is a political game, a banking game, a contracting game, a newspaper game, a civic organization game, an ecclesiastical game, and many others. Within each game there is a well-established set of goals whose achievement indicates success or failure for the participants, a set of socialized roles making participant behavior highly predictable, a set of strategies and tactics handed down through experience and occasionally subject to improvement and change, an elite public whose approbation is appreciated, and finally a general public which has some appreciation for the standing of the players.

The Interactional Field Model of community directs attention to formal organizations and activities, but it does not rule out the participation and significance of existential groups such as families and neighborhoods. Similar to the Functional Subsystems Model, this model focuses attention on processes that link organizations—and existential groups—to each other and can be used to promote social planning, locality development, and social action.

The *Common Sentiments Model* of community (Nisbet, 1966) defines community differently from the other models shown in Table 9.1. In this view, community "encompasses all forms of relationship which are characterized by a high degree of personal intimacy, emotional depth, moral commitment, social cohesion, and continuity in time. . . . Community is a fusion of feeling and thought, of tradition and commitment, of membership and volition"

(Nisbet, 1966, p. 47). From this view, a community exists because of values, sentiments, feelings of identification, and commitment that are held in common by a collective of individuals. This can occur in a locality, such as a town or city, but it can also occur independently of locale. In this view, all social workers, all single parents, or all rape survivors can form a community. The defining quality is that the members share common sentiments that unite them.

Community practitioners who employ a Common Sentiments Model are concerned with promoting common values, identification, and commitments among community members. None of the three traditional goals of community organization practice is inherent in the Common Sentiments Model. If interorganizational planning, locality development, or social action activities are undertaken, however, common sentiments, values, and identification are likely to emerge as by-products. On the other hand, common sentiments may be necessary before citizens can be persuaded to engage in joint planning, development, or social-action activities. In short, feelings of identification and commonality are probably important correlates of successful community intervention.

The Existential Model of community includes aspects of the other models in Table 9.1 and adds to them. Gottschalk (1975, 1978), building on Hillery (1968), identifies seven characteristics of communities as existential systems. He emphasizes that communities are places where people live, where many activities occur at once, and where families and neighborhoods are as essential as formal organizations.

1. *Communities satisfy daily needs.* Communities are networks of relationships through which residents satisfy their daily needs. Through these networks, goods and services are produced, distributed, and consumed; citizens are socialized and controlled; and members participate with each other and provide mutual support (Warren, 1963). The community is the "smallest unit of social structure which can maintain itself" (Bertrand, 1972, p. 150) and is a social system that satisfies members' existential needs for food, shelter, work, education, and recreation.

2. *Communities have many diffuse goals.* Unlike formal organizations such as social welfare organizations (Chapter 8) or businesses, communities have many diffuse goals. Communities at the level of inclusive system have few specific goals but rather reflect the diverse, often contradictory, goals of the groups and organizations that are located within their boundaries. Communities are loosely coupled systems and seldom have, or pursue, specific goals that are endorsed by all, or even most, community elements.

3. *Communities occupy geographic territory.* Whereas geography alone does

not define community, the Existential Model views a community as occupying concrete geographic territory. Communities as geographic territories often have legal and political boundaries that define them as townships, municipalities, or counties. Legal and political boundaries are *part of a community* but should not be viewed *as the community*. The Existential Model views the mass of people who occupy a common geographic territory and who interact around satisfying daily needs as community members, regardless of whether they reside inside official city or county limits.

4. *Communities include many formal and natural systems.* Communities are composed of formal organizations such as local governments, businesses, industry, schools, and welfare agencies, but they also contain many natural groups such as families, neighborhoods, friendship cliques, ethnic groups, religious enclaves, social classes, and so on. The Existential Model, unlike the System of Systems Model, does not focus primary attention on a locality's formal organizations.

5. *Community members are aware of common membership.* Community members are aware of a common, or shared, membership in or association with a locality (Bernard, 1973; Nisbet, 1966). They *can* share feelings of pride in aspects of a locality such as its natural beauty, its athletic teams, its performing arts groups, its community festivals, and so on. They can also share feelings of resentment and dissatisfaction over community conditions or activities. Regardless of their sentiments, community residents are aware that community conditions and events affect them in one way or another. Whereas Nisbet emphasizes a commonality of values and commitment, the Existential Model claims only that community residents have certain self-identifications about place and membership in common. They *can* hold common values and commitments but this is not necessary for them to be considered members of the community.

6. *Communities are inclusive systems.* Communities include many forms and varieties of social systems inside their boundaries. Because of this, they contain many naturally occurring, or existential, elements such as individuals, families, small groups, neighborhoods, and many formal elements such as social service networks and school systems. To succeed at community organization practice, understanding of this is required. Compared to other social systems with which social workers normally interact, communities are the most inclusive.

7. *Communities contain families.* The Existential Model of community requires the presence of families. Families, as defined in Chapter 6, are residents of a common household who are related by blood, marriage, or adoption. Most of us think of children when families are

mentioned. The requirement of families means that religious orders, mental hospitals, prisons, boarding schools, and similar residential organizations are not defined as communities. Focusing on families underscores the importance of natural, or existential, groups as component parts of communities. Gottschalk (1975, 1978) views this as useful to counteract the focus on formal organizations, and interorganizational linkages, of the System of Systems, Functional Subsystems, and Interactional Field models.

ARE COMMUNITIES SYSTEMS?

Communities are complex, diverse, loosely coupled, continually changing, and inclusive phenomena. They are not as tightly coupled as families, work groups, or social welfare organizations. Their boundaries are frequently difficult to identify. We might ask, then, whether communities are legitimate or bona fide social systems. The answer is yes. Communities, defined according to the Existential Model, satisfy the OST definition of system as explicated in Chapter 2. Communities are *organized* through the orderly activities and routines engaged in by their component parts and subsystems. Through their actions, these parts affect each other, thus making them *interdependent*. Relationships occur in a specific *physical space* and take place in real *time*. And communities have *boundaries*. When viewed as loosely coupled networks of local elements, communities qualify as bona fide social systems.

A TYPOLOGY OF COMMUNITY LINKAGES

Communities can be viewed as linkage networks. A *network* is a system of relationships. Individuals and families participate in kinship, friendship, school, work, and recreational networks. Formal organizations, including social welfare organizations, participate in networks that link them to resources, elites, clients, employees, other local organizations, and organizations beyond the community's boundary. To understand the changes that have occurred in American communities over the past century, we identify six types of linkages.

Table 9.2 presents a typology of community linkages based on form and dynamics and on whether the community's boundary(ies) is (are) spanned. The column axis in Table 9.2 presents form and dynamics in three categories: (1) inclusive system to included component part, where authority (or power) is exercised; (2) included part to inclusive system, where influence is exercised; and (3) peer to peer where cooperation and collaboration occur. The row axis in Table 9.2 indicates whether a relationship spans a com-

TABLE 9.2. TYPOLOGY OF COMMUNITY LINKAGES BASED ON BOUNDARY SPANNING AND FORM (AND DYNAMICS) OF THE RELATIONSHIP

Is (Are) Community's Boundary(ies) Spanned?	Form (and Dynamics) of Relationship		
	Inclusive to included (authority is exercised)	*Included to inclusive (influence is exercised)*	*Peer to peer (collaboration and cooperation occur)*
No	Internal, vertical-down linkage	Internal, vertical-up linkage	Internal, horizontal linkage
Yes	External, vertical-down linkage	External, vertical-up linkage	External, horizontal linkage

Source: Adapted from Warren (1963) and Gottschalk (1975, 1978).

munity's boundary. The cells in Table 9.2 identify six types of linkages, as follows.

1. *Internal, vertical-down linkages* occur inside a community's boundary and involve the exercise of authority by a superordinate body over a subordinate element. If a city planning office makes rules on land-scaping that developers are required to follow, this is an example of an internal, vertical-down linkage. The city office has the authority to require developers to abide by their rules or be denied building permits, occupancy permits, and so on. Internal, vertical-down link-ages occur any time a community-based system with authority in-structs another part of the community over which it has authority to engage in certain procedures, to avoid certain practices, and so on.

2. *Internal, vertical-up linkages* occur in a community when a subordi-nate subsystem (or part) is able to influence—through persuasion, lobbying, and so forth—the superordinate (or inclusive) system to whose authority it is subject. Neighborhood associations that in-fluence decisions by city planning offices have effected an internal, vertical-up linkage.

3. *Internal, horizontal linkages* occur between peer systems, that is, sys-tems without an authority relation to each other. These consist of cooperative/collaborative relations where two or more similar, or similarly interested, groups or organizations cooperate for mutual advantage. Local realtors and homebuilders may cooperate to share information on changes in the city's tax code, believing that their combined efforts to understand or oppose it are superior to each alone.

4. *External, vertical-down linkages* span a community's boundary and involve the exercise of authority. State governments establish laws that affect local communities. Federal social welfare programs make regulations that affect service delivery at the community level. As suggested below, external, vertical-down linkages are much more prevalent in American communities today than they were a century ago.

5. *External, vertical-up linkages* span a community's boundary and involve the exercise of influence. When community welfare offices suggest a policy that leads to a change in statewide procedures, an external, vertical-up linkage has been affected. A group of local voters who influence an elected representative's vote in Washington, D.C. on an issue of local concern also constitutes an external, vertical-up linkage.

6. *External, horizontal linkages* occur between peer systems in two (or more) communities. If two local governments cooperate to establish a regional hospital, airport, or planning council, an external, horizontal linkage occurs. Neither community has power, or authority, over the other. Collaborative projects between schools, law enforcement agencies, battered-women's shelters, and businesses in different communities are also external, horizontal linkages.

Figure 9.1 illustrates the six linkages for two local communities and their external environments. Whether a particular linkage is external or internal depends on the *focal system, or system of reference*, from which the linkage is examined. Because our focus is on local communities, the community is the focal system throughout the ensuing discussion.

Community X is set off from Community Y, and other external systems, by its boundary. As noted earlier, a community can have more than one boundary—and these do not necessarily coincide. These can include a governmental boundary determined by municipal, county, and/or state statute; a residential boundary associated with where citizens' residences are located; and/or a natural terrain boundary such as that provided by rivers, mountains, and so on. As illustrated in Figure 9.1, internal linkages remain inside Community X's (or Y's) boundaries. When power is exercised by a local authority to a local subordinate, the linkage is internal, vertical-down; this is shown in Figure 9.1 as an arrow going from local government to local homebuilders. An internal vertical-up linkage is represented by the arrow going up from neighborhood association to local government. The horizontal linkage between local homebuilders and neighborhood association is indicated by a dashed-line with a two-headed arrow to show that their relationship does not entail authority and is reciprocal rather than one-way.

Community X's external linkages are represented by arrows that span its

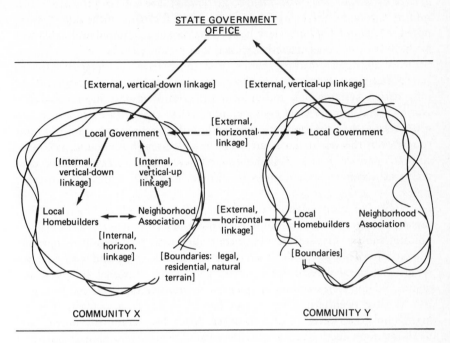

EXTERNAL ENVIRONMENT:

including federal government, national retail chains,
national television networks, etc.

STATE GOVERNMENT
OFFICE

[External, vertical-down linkage]   [External, vertical-up linkage]

[External, horizontal linkage]

Local Government   Local Government

[Internal, vertical-down linkage]   [Internal, vertical-up linkage]

Local Homebuilders   Neighborhood Association   [External, horizontal linkage]   Local Homebuilders   Neighborhood Association

[Internal, horizon. linkage]   [Boundaries: legal, residential, natural terrain]   [Boundaries]

COMMUNITY X   COMMUNITY Y

Figure 9.1 Community Linkage Typology: With Local Community(ies) as the Focal System (or System of Reference).

boundaries. When Community X's local government is instructed by the federal government to enforce affirmative action policies, this is an external, vertical-down linkage between federal government and local government. When a local government influences state or federal regulations, this is an external, vertical-up linkage (see Fig. 9.1). Linkages between local governments (or homebuilders) of Community X and Community Y are external horizontal linkages. These are, like internal horizontal linkages, represented by dashed-lines with two-headed arrows.

CHANGES IN AMERICAN COMMUNITIES: NINETEENTH TO TWENTIETH CENTURIES

The linkage typology can be used to understand changes that American communities have experienced over the past century. The Great Change, as described by Warren (1963), is a loss of local autonomy and control and an increase in external control over local affairs. In the linkage typology, American communities have experienced *a decrease in internal linkages, down and up, and an increase in external linkages, particularly external, vertical-down*. Community autonomy and control have diminished for many of the same reasons noted in Chapter 1. Our society has become urbanized; population and capital have become concentrated; national and regional chains of retail stores, utilities, hospitals, realtors, banks, and so on have proliferated. Modern transportation, telephones, mail service, news media, and computerized information systems link individuals and groups almost instantaneously. National and international credit systems allow charge cards issued in any given state to buy vacations, clothes, and meals in every other state and most countries of the world. Local areas are linked through economic, political, cultural, and social ties. Telephone, credit card, and home mortgage payments are made to organizations in distant cities and, frequently, in other states.

Table 9.3 summarizes Warren's Great Change thesis of American community change. Local communities in the nineteenth century were geographically and socially isolated. They controlled their own resources, options, and citizens. They had few contacts with the outside world and were relatively unaffected by external phenomena and events. Internal linkages predominated and were far more frequent and extensive than external linkages. By the later twentieth century, this had changed. Local communities are highly linked to external organizations. They have minimal control over local resources including, frequently, water, electricity, natural gas, and

TABLE 9.3. SUMMARY OF WARREN'S (1963) GREAT CHANGE MODEL OF AMERICAN COMMUNITIES, NINETEENTH TO LATE TWENTIETH CENTURIES

Century	Characteristics of community in regards to local autonomy and control, predominant linkages, and strength of ties to the environment
Nineteenth Century	(a) Community autonomy and control over local resources, citizens, options, formal organizations, and so forth, were high.
	(b) Internal linkages—vertical-up, vertical-down, and horizontal—were more prevalent than external linkages.
	(c) External linkages—vertical-up, vertical-down, and horizontal—were weak.
Late Twentieth Century	(a) Community autonomy and control over local resources, citizens, options, formal organizations, and so forth are moderate to low.
	(b) Internal linkages—vertical-up, vertical-down, and horizontal—are no more prevalent (and possibly less prevalent) than external linkages.
	(c) External linkages—particularly vertical-down—are strong.

so on. They have many contacts with external organizations and are highly, and quickly, affected by phenomena and events in distant places. Most retail establishments are national chains and locally owned "mom and pop" groceries and restaurants are increasingly rare. Retail establishments and multinational corporations have expanded beyond national boundaries, furthermore, into most countries of the world.

Another view of changes in American community life from the nineteenth century to the twentieth century is illustrated in Table 9.4. Nineteenth-century communities, the majority of which were rural, are said to have been characterized by face-to-face relationships reflecting informality, intimacy, concern for the total person, personal encounters, relations based on family and community, a concern with the sacred, and emphasis on generalized cooperation and expressiveness. In short, relations were holistic. Urbanization and modernization brought with them different forms of interpersonal relations. These include, as shown in Table 9.4, an emphasis on formality rather than informality, a sense of anomie rather than intimacy, concern with roles rather than the total person, encounters based on office or title rather than personal qualities, relations organized by bureaucratic rather than familial or communal standards, emphasis on the secular rather than the sacred, cooperation based on contract rather than general cooperation, and an emphasis on instrumental rather than expressive aspects of relationships.

TABLE 9.4. FORM AND CONTENT OF INTERPERSONAL RELATIONS IN RURAL AND URBAN COMMUNITIES: AN IDEAL TYPE

Form and content of interpersonal community relations	Type of Community	
	Rural	Urban
A. Community relations are:	Personal	Official
	Informally organized	Formally organized
	Based in familial and communal organizations	Based in bureaucratic organizations
	Concerned with the total person	Concerned with particular roles
	Focused on general cooperation	Focused on specific cooperation (e.g., legal contracts)
	Concerned with socioemotional or expressive issues	Concerned with instrumental issues
B. Values tend to be:	Sacred	Secular
C. Individuals experience community life as:	Intimate, supportive	Isolated, anomic

Source: Adapted from Tonnies (1957).

The qualities listed in Table 9.4 suggest that community life in the late twentieth century is less personal and intimate than formerly, that it is lonelier, more segmented, and more formalized. Those who lament changes over the past century must guard against falling prey to romanticized notions of small-town caring and intimacy, however. The tyranny of conformity, reputation, and gossip that small-town residents often held over each other should not be forgotten. Depictions of modern, urban life as devoid of informal, intimate, personal, cooperative, and similar qualities are, furthermore, only partly true (Naisbitt, 1982; Stack, 1974).

LINKAGE DEVELOPMENT AS A RESPONSE TO COMMUNITY PROBLEMS

The linkage typology of communities and community change can be used to conceptualize community problems and identify strategies for improving the quality of community life. Our conceptualization is based on the assumption that community residents, especially those who are disadvantaged, can benefit from more and/or different linkages in their communities. We believe also that social welfare organizations, and citizens' action groups, can benefit from more effective community linkages. Throughout, we assume that citizen empowerment and internal control of community affairs are important goals of social work community practice. We begin with a brief overview of problems associated with the modern community and follow it with suggestions for community organization practice.

Community Problems from a Linkage Perspective

Community problems can be viewed in terms of three types of linkage deficiencies: (1) linkages among community peers, (2) authority linkages in the community, and (3) authority linkages between a community and its environment. We review each of these below.

Linkages among Community Peers

Modern communities are criticized for isolating citizens from one another. Large size makes personal contacts with more than a small percentage of residents impossible. Because of life styles that influence them to associate with acquaintances from work, church, and neighborhood, citizens in different life circumstances have little contact with or awareness of people who differ from themselves. Citizens who are materially advantaged, those in the middle and upper classes, are isolated from the poor and disadvantaged. Separation contributes to a lack of awareness by each group of how others live and it encourages, particularly among the more affluent, misconceptions of the conditions and options that the poor and the disadvantaged face.

For similar reasons, disadvantaged citizens are frequently unaware of, and unlinked to, services and benefits that exist in a community. If they do not know that emergency aid for utility bills or rent payments is available, they cannot apply. Even if aware, they may lack the know-how, or courage, to apply. They may lack a means of transportation to visit application offices. Finally, social welfare organizations (SWOs) that provide services and benefits to the disadvantaged are frequently unlinked to each other (Martin, Chakerian, Imershein, and Frumkin, 1983). They may be unaware of their sister agencies' resources, policies, and services or, if aware, may lack knowledge of how to help citizens obtain them.

Authority Linkages in the Community

Disadvantaged citizens are rarely organized among themselves sufficiently to influence community decisions. Decisions at the community level are often made by *Community Decision Organizations (CDOs)*, that is, community-level organizations "that are legitimated to represent the interests of the community in some segment of broad community concern" (Warren, 1970, p. 141). Examples of CDOs are community welfare councils, urban renewal authorities, antipoverty organizations, housing authorities, chambers of commerce, federations of churches, county health and welfare departments, boards of education, and so on. Administrators and staff of these organizations are typically well-educated, middle-class citizens who, even when acting on behalf of the disadvantaged, are not actually *of them*. Decisions and other actions are taken with minimal participation of a community's disadvantaged such as its poor, physically disabled, mentally ill or handicapped, racial and ethnic minorities, and homeless.

Additionally, social welfare organizations (SWOs) at the local level are frequently ineffective in their dealings with local political and decision-making processes. Their free-standing status gives them leeway and autonomy but it can also lead to their exclusion from planning, resource allocation, and related decisions.

Authority Linkages between a Community and Its Environment

Citizens and community SWOs are frequently excluded from actions by external authorities even though these actions affect the community. Decisions at state and federal levels on social policies, resource distribution, and rule and regulation specification are typically made with minimal input from local communities. This can lead to resource distribution that fails to help and policies that are inappropriate for community residents, programs, and priorities.

Linkage Development Strategies to Enhance Community Empowerment and Control

Based on problems such as those just cited, linkage strategies that can be employed to enhance citizen empowerment and community reform are identified. As shown in Table 9.5, we identify three types: (1) strategies to enhance community peer relations, (2) strategies to enhance internal authority relations, and (3) strategies to enhance local autonomy and self-determination.

I. *Strategies to enhance peer relations in the community.* Four strategies are suggested for improving peer relations in the community. Two are aimed at fostering interpersonal and intergroup linkages among individuals, families, neighborhoods, and friendship groups: (a) social networking and (b) locality development. A third strategy focuses on coordination and

---

TABLE 9.5. COMMUNITY PRACTICE STRATEGIES FOR CITIZEN EMPOWERMENT AND COMMUNITY REFORM

I. Strategies to Enhance Peer Relations in the Community
   A. Social networking: Link citizens to each other and help them organize for mutual aid
      1) Directly link individuals and families to other individuals and families
      2) Establish and facilitate social-support groups
      3) Identify and encourage natural helpers
      4) Develop a pool of volunteers
   B. Locality development: Organize citizens from diverse community groups to cooperate and jointly resolve local problems
   C. Service-delivery system/network development: Link separate social welfare organizations to each other
   D. Case management: Link citizens to needed services and resources
II. Strategies to Enhance Internal Authority Relations
   A. Grass-roots organizing: Help citizens organize collectively to affect community decisions and events
   B. Social planning: Help social welfare organizations, related organizations, and service-delivery networks apply rational-technical planning methods to improve responsiveness to citizens and effective and efficient use of resources
III. Strategies to Enhance Local Control and Self-Determination
   A. Form a partnership with external organizations: Proactively lobby external authorities regarding conditions and priorities at the community level
   B. Engage in political activity: Take direct, organized action to shape and influence community priorities and events
      1) Elect supportive public officials
      2) Develop coalitions for political action
      3) Lobby legislators
      4) Educate the community
      5) Engage in political protest
      6) Conduct action research
      7) Advocate with the criminal-justice system
      8) Serve as a social watchdog

integration of formal organizations, primarily social welfare organizations: (c) service-delivery system/network development. The fourth strategy aims at linking disadvantaged residents to community resources: (d) case management.

A. *Social networking.* Social networking consists of interventions that link individuals and natural groups to each other. It tries to increase options and resources by helping citizens rely on each other for assistance and support. The prototypes of social networking were neighborliness and mutual aid. Community practitioners can contribute to the growth and spread of social networking in four ways (see Froland, Pancoast, Chapman, and Kimboko, 1981).

1. Directly link individuals and families to other individuals and families. Community practitioners can help individuals and families by linking them with other residents through introducing them to each other, encouraging them to call upon one another, and arranging meetings at which mutual interests, needs, and resources are discussed.

2. Establish and facilitate social-support groups. Community practitioners can organize, sponsor, and serve as a general resource person for mutual support groups around specific topics or needs. These can include Parents Anonymous for parents who have abused their children, Alcoholics Anonymous for problem drinkers, Parents Without Partners for single-parents, and so on.

3. Identify and encourage natural helpers. By virtue of occupation, residence, and/or personal characteristics (cheerfulness, competence, friendliness), some people are *natural helpers*. Community practitioners can encourage natural helpers to assume a proactive leadership role to assist others in the neighborhood to secure needed support and resources. Typical candidates for natural-helper roles include law enforcement officers, mail deliverers, teachers, physicians, bartenders, recreation leaders, nurses, housing authority staff, children's club leaders, local merchants, and so on.

4. Develop a pool of community volunteers. Many people will volunteer their time and energy if asked in a way that makes sense and is feasible. Community practitioners can promote social networking by developing a pool of volunteers to engage in particular tasks, at particular places and times. People are more likely to volunteer if asked for a specific, time-limited period (e.g., two hours a week from 3 P.M. to 5 P.M.) to perform a particular service—such as watch over elementary school children at the playground after school. Practitioners can facilitate volunteer activities by structuring tasks, recruiting volunteers, developing schedules, and so on.

B. *Locality development.* A locality development strategy involves the organization of citizens from diverse segments of the community—the middle class, the poor, black and white, labor and management—to meet face-to-face and engage in discussion, cooperation, and problem-solving activities. Locality development aims at promoting citizen empowerment and community cohesion so that citizens feel they can, and subsequently do, resolve local problems on their own. Crime, drug abuse, day care, housing, employment, transportation, and recreation are some community problems that are amenable to collective problem solving that locality development strategies promote.

C. *Service-delivery system/network development.* To minimize duplication and unnecessary waste, to maximize the benefits of scarce resources, and to prevent needy citizens from going unserved, social welfare organizations should ideally be linked through a service delivery system or network (Martin and others, 1983). Service-delivery networks can be developed if four conditions are met (Frumkin, 1982): (1) several SWOs with sufficient resources to meet a range of client needs exist in a community; (2) the several SWOs (or their administrators) agree on their respective responsibilities; (3) procedures for coordination are agreed upon; and (4) mechanisms to oversee and manage the network are installed to assure compliance and to correct problems. Community practitioners can promote the develop of service-delivery networks by talking with leaders of a range of SWOs, by arranging meetings so that leaders can identify common goals and procedures, and by securing resources to pay for staff to monitor the system. Martin, DiNitto, Norton, and Maxwell (1984) describe such a service-delivery network in Sarasota, Florida, that was established among hospitals, law enforcement agencies, legal prosecutors, and rape crisis centers to assure that survivors of sexual assault were well served.

D. *Case management.* Case-management strategies are employed by community practitioners to link community residents to the resources and services they need (Siporin, 1975). Case management involves a variety of practice roles and activities such as referral agent, outreach agent, broker, caregiver, data manager, and advocate (Austin and Carragone, 1981; Weissman, Epstein, and Savage, 1983; O'Connor, 1988). Case managers have an easier job of linking clients to resources and services when coordinated service-delivery networks exist but are even more urgently needed when they do not. Compared to disadvantaged clients such as the poor, frail elderly, abused children, disabled, or mentally disturbed, case managers have more knowledge, more contacts, and more entree to community resources. Their linkage of clients to available benefits and services enhances a community by helping it respond to the needs and problems of its least advantaged citizens.

II. *Strategies to enhance internal authority relations.* As shown in Table 9.5, two strategies can help a community enhance the quality of internal authority relations. These are: (a) grass-roots organizing and (b) social planning.

A. *Grass-roots organizing.* Grass-roots organizing is a linkage strategy aimed at helping citizens organize themselves to affect community decisions and activities. Instead of leaving community decisions to local governments and community decision organizations, citizens can organize themselves to take stands, lobby for their views, and participate in the local political process. From the linkage typology, citizens can exert internal, vertical-up influence on community-decider organizations. Community practitioners can facilitate grass-roots organization by doing the following (adapted from Brager, Specht, and Torczyner, 1987). (1) *Socialize citizens:* They can identify common problems and encourage citizens to develop a collective desire for change; (2) *Build a core group:* They can support development of a committed group of activists who are interested in taking action and encourage individuals to assume leadership roles; (3) *Formalize the organization:* They can help citizens' groups establish a structure and agenda, develop ties with allies, and learn tactics for pursuing their aims. Through grass-roots organizing, community practitioners can help citizens organize to assume active rather than passive roles in shaping community life and, through this, can contribute to their empowerment.

B. *Social planning.* Social planning is a strategy aimed at gaining greater resources and leverage for social welfare interests at the community level. If social welfare organizations (SWOs) and proponents plan together in a rational and comprehensive way, their chances for gaining more resources and for using them effectively are enhanced. From our linkage typology perspective, social planning involves cooperative, horizontal relations among peer organizations; internal, vertical-down relations as common goals, plans, and structures shape joint actions; and vertical-up relations as allied organizations interact with other community decision organizations (CDOs) around resource procurement, disbursement, and so on. Social-planning strategies consist of techniques such as survey research, community power studies, analysis of Census and social-problems data, and related technologies that foster rational analysis, problem solving, and decision making. Since ours is an organizational society (Hall, 1987), social planning often involves interorganizational relations and issues. Effective social planning tries to be comprehensive, to apply the latest expertise and technology to community problems and decisions, to rationalize community actions, and to involve clients and client–representatives in planning and decision-making activities (Siporin, 1975; Brager, Specht, and Torczyner, 1987).

III. *Strategies to enhance local control and self-determination.* We assume that, in most cases, the quality of life enjoyed by community residents is greater if decisions that affect them are made at the local level. This is not universally true, however, as evidenced by state and local laws that relegated American blacks to separate and unequal schools, waiting areas, hospital wards, and so on, prior to enactment of the civil rights legislation of the mid-1960s. Federal laws were required to correct this situation at a local level. Enactment of the Social Security Act and many other laws that provide welfare benefits and services are additional evidence that federal decisions bring resources to local communities that would otherwise be absent. These factors notwithstanding, local communities and their citizens can benefit from greater control over their fate. We identify two strategies to enhance community control and self-determination: (a) Partnership with external organizations, and (b) political activity. (See Table 9.5.)

   A. *Form a partnership with external organizations.* Most resources for social welfare services and benefits are provided by national and state governments, not by local communities. Benefits and services are nevertheless provided by community SWOs to citizens who reside inside their boundaries. A partnership between community agencies and CDOs and authorities external to the community requires organization and initiative at the community level. Community practitioners who assist communities to cooperatively plan, develop coordinated service-delivery networks, and maxmize the use of their resources can assist them also in lobbying external authorities to take local circumstances and needs into account. From our linkage typology, partnerships with external organizations are external, vertical-up initiatives. Both SWOs and other proponents of social welfare benefits and services can act, in concert, to influence federal legislation, regulations, appropriations, and so on.

   B. *Engage in political activity.* Political activity refers to electoral politics as well as to interpersonal, group, and interorganizational actions that involve the mobilization and exercise of power or influence. Resources for social welfare benefits and services are not created by magic. They come mostly from governments that levy taxes on citizens and face many competing demands for resources. As noted in Chapter 1, America's social welfare expenditures increased dramatically between the 1960s and the present. Public sentiment seems unfavorable to similar increases over the next generation, however, and requests for more funds by the military, educators, the medical profession, law enforcement and the courts, and environmental protection groups, among others, have increased. Social welfare interests, and citizens in need of social welfare benefits and services, can expect an uphill struggle in the competition for resources for the foreseeable future. Eight political-action strategies have been suggested for community practitioners (Biklen, 1983; Norwick, 1983; Weissman, Epstein, and Savage, 1983).

1. Elect supportive public officials. Community activists can organize citizens and interest groups to elect to local public office candidates who are sympathetic to their concerns. Candidates who endorse social welfare aims are unlikely to forget individuals and groups who supported them as they serve in office.

2. Develop coalitions for political action. Community practitioners can link groups with similar common, or related, interests to increase the clout of both. Tradeoffs or compromises can be effected to assure that each group works for the other's interests as well as its own.

3. Lobby legislators. Practitioners interested in enhancing community interests can lobby state and federal legislators for these ends. They can write position papers that support a particular view, give expert testimony at legislative hearings, and draft legislation for a committee's consideration. Legislators can be educated about a problem and urged, even pressured, to support a community-level position.

4. Educate the community. Community practitioners can help to build support for community issues and needs by appearing on the media, giving talks and workshops, and developing pamphlets to educate residents about local issues.

5. Engage in political protest. Practitioners can organize and participate in shows of political protest when injustices or inequities are perceived. These can be marches on the capitol, midnight vigils at prisons where executions are performed, and so on.

6. Conduct action research. *Action research* is the application of social science research methods for practical purposes such as demonstrating that the teenage pregnancy rate in one part of town is 50 percent or the school dropout rate is very high. Systematically collected and analyzed data can be used to make a case for a particular policy, action, issue, or allocation.

7. Advocate with the criminal-justice system. Practitioners can intervene on behalf of vulnerable, poor, or otherwise disadvantaged citizens to demand that they receive better treatment, that conditions be changed, that services be provided, and so on. Rape crisis counselors who meet rape survivors at hospitals after a sexual assault often advocate on behalf of the victim's need for privacy and sensitive handling during the rape kit exam (Martin, DiNitto, Norton, and Maxwell, 1985).

8. Serve as a social watchdog. A final strategy for community practitioners is that of "whistle-blowing." This consists of bringing
to the attention of officials, the media, or the public the names of
social welfare organizations that are corrupt, unethical, or unfair.
Exposure of illegal or unethical practices can help preserve public
confidence in the integrity of social welfare proponents, service
deliverers, and interests.

IMPLICATIONS FOR SOCIAL WORK

Social work has long been committed to the community. The social work
profession adopted many goals and strategies from the charity organization
societies and settlement houses of the nineteenth century, but it can nevertheless take most of the credit for the development of community organization practice as we know it today (O'Connor and Waring, 1981). If social
workers are to continue contributing to the development of community
organization practice, an ideology of proactive community change and
change-oriented intervention strategies must be more fully developed.

A growing literature urges social work to reject the status quo and commit to community change and reform. Community practitioners are urged to
move from "enabling to advocacy" (Grosser, 1973) and to view fundamental
change of the social environment as a primary goal of community organization practice (Brager, Specht, and Torczyner, 1987). The Code of Ethics
of the National Association of Social Workers (1979) requires that social
workers take action to correct organizational and community obstacles to
client well-being.

Social workers, and the communities they serve, can benefit from becoming more adept at political action. Political action includes not only
electoral politics but advocacy for those who cannot speak for themselves,
lobbying of decision-makers for resources, educating the public, and pro-
testing wrongs. Appreciation of the politics in all social welfare practice
is growing (Hasenfeld, 1980; Martin, 1987; Murdock, 1982; Lee, 1983;
Gummer, 1984). Nowhere is the need for political action more evident than
in communities. Unemployment, inadequate housing, and the need for health
care, transportation, and social services are pervasive. Social welfare administrators can exercise political skills as part of their work both inside and outside of their agencies on behalf of their clients and community (Gummer,
1984, p. 23; also see Chapter 8 in this text on leadership in social welfare
organizations). Community practitioners who neglect politics or lack political skills are tying their hands and "may be short-changing" their clients and
constituents (Rothman, 1974, p. 200). The road to citizen empowerment
and community reform lies through politics, broadly defined (Wildavsky,

1979). Strategies reviewed in this chapter can be used by all social workers, regardless of position or role, to promote citizen empowerment, social planning, locality development, and social change to the benefit of all.

Epilogue

This book demonstrates, we hope, that Open Systems Theory is useful for social work in the latter years of the twentieth century. Along with our students and colleagues, we have spent more than a decade learning, trying to understand, and teaching about OST. To understand fully, we probably have another decade to go. Like the open systems we discuss, our understanding of Open Systems Theory is incomplete, changing, and rife with contradictions. Rather than a final statement, we hope our readers view this book as a work in progress. We invite them to join us in exploring both the potential and the limitations of Open Systems Theory for social work understanding and practice.

Over the past decade, we have made many attempts to apply OST, some to good effect, others less so. The results were consistently exciting, enlightening, and rewarding, however. Failure was often more instructive than was success. We are aware that varied strains of "systems theory" have waxed and waned across the social work horizon. Ecological systems and ecosystems perspectives are enjoying a moment of glory now. Assumptions and concepts from family systems and open systems views of organizations, even though renounced by critics, continue to pervade most scholarship on families and organizations. Equally important, systems theories continue to serve as guides for intervention and practice. Systems theories are employed by social scientists and social-work professionals because they are helpful in conceptualizing, perceiving, understanding, and dealing with the experienced world. We offer our description and application of Open Systems Theory as a complement to other systems theories. Exploration of similarities and differences between approaches will, we believe, enhance the power and utility of all.

References

Adams, B., *The Family: A Sociological Interpretation.* (San Diego, Calif.: Harcourt Brace Jovanovich, 1986).

Aldrich, Howard E., and Pfeffer, Jeffrey, "Environments of Organizations," *Annual Review of Sociology,* vol. 3 (1977), pp. 79–105.

Alexander, J. F., and Barton, C., "Behavioral Systems Therapy With Delinquent Families," in D. H. Olson (ed.), *Treating Relationships* (Lake Mitles, Iowa: Graphic Press, 1976).

Alexander, J. F., Barton, C., Schiavo, R. S., and Parsons, R. V., "Systems-behavioral Intervention with Families of Delinquents: Therapist Characteristics, Family Behavior, and Outcome," *Journal of Consulting and Clinical Psychology,* vol. 44 (1976), pp. 656–664.

Alexander, J. F., and Parsons, R. V., "Short-Term Behavioral Intervention with Delinquent Families: Impact on Family Process and Recidivism," *Journal of Abnormal Psychology,* vol. 81 (1973), pp. 219–225.

Alinsky, Saul., *Reveille For Radicals* (Chicago: University of Chicago Press, 1946).

Alissi, A. (ed.), *Perspectives on Social Group Work Practice* (New York: The Free Press, 1980).

Anderson, Joseph, "Working With Groups: Little-Known Facts that Challenge Well-Known Myths," *Small Group Behavior,* vol. 16, no. 3 (August 1985), pp. 267–283.

Anderson, R., and Carter, J., *Human Behavior in the Social Environment: A Social Systems Approach,* 2nd ed. (New York: Aldine Publishing Co., 1978).

Anderson, W. A., and Martin, P. Y., "Bureaucracy and Professionalism in the Social Services: A Multi-Dimensional Approach to the Analysis of Conflict and Congruity," *Journal of Social Service Research,* vol. 5 (1982), pp. 33–50.

Aptekar, H., *The Dynamics of Casework and Counseling* (Boston: Houghton Mifflin, 1955).

Ashby, R., *Design For a Brain* (New York: John Wiley, 1960).

257

Austin, D. M., "Comparative Analysis of Human Service Programs." Unpublished manuscript (Austin: University of Texas, 1986).

Austin, D., and Caragonne, P., "Comparative Analysis of Twenty-two Settings Using Case Management Components," *Case Management Research Project* (Austin: School of Social Work, University of Texas, 1981).

Austin, D. M., and Hasenfeld, Y., "A Prefatory Essay on the Future Administration of Human Services," *Journal of Applied Behavioral Science*, vol. 21 (1985), pp. 351–354.

Awad, John, "Services Integration in a Large, Complex Human Service Organization: The State of Florida Case." Unpublished manuscript (Tallahassee, Fla: Department of Health and Rehabilitative Services, 1978).

Axline, V., *Dibs: In Search of Self* (Boston: Houghton Mifflin, 1964).

Bailey, R., and Brake, M. (eds.), *Radical Social Work* (New York: Pantheon Books, 1975).

Bales, R. F., *Interaction Process Analysis: A Method for the Study of Small Groups* (Reading, Mass.: Addison-Wesley, 1950).

Bales, R. F., and Strodtbeck, R. L., "Phases in Group Problem Solving," *Journal of Abnormal Social Psychology*, vol. 46 (1951), pp. 485–495.

Balgopal, P., and Vassil, T. *Groups in Social Work: An Ecological Perspective* (New York: Macmillan, 1983).

Barrett-Lennard, G. T., "The Client-Centered System Unfolding," in F. Turner (ed.), *Social Work Treatment: Interlocking Theoretical Approaches* (New York: The Free Press, 1979), pp. 177–241.

Bart, P. B., Freeman, L., and Kimball, P., "The Different Worlds of Women and Men: Attitudes Towards Pornography and Responses to 'Not a Love Story,' A Film About Pornography," *Women's Studies International Forum*, vol. 8 (1980), pp. 307–322.

Bartlett, H., *The Common Base of Social Work Practice* (New York: National Association of Social Workers, 1970).

Bartlett, H., "Characteristics of Social Work," *Building Social Work Balances* (New York: National Association of Social Workers, 1971), pp. 1–15.

Bartolke, K., Eschweiler, W., Fleschenberger, D., and Tannenbaum, A. S., "Workers' Participation and the Distribution of Control as Perceived by Members of Ten German Companies," *Administrative Science Quarterly*, vol. 27 (1982), pp. 380–397.

Bell, D., *The Coming of Post-Industrial Society* (New York: Basic Books, 1973).

Bellah, R. N., Madsen, R., Sullivan, W. M., Swidler, A., and Tipton, S. M., *Habits of the Heart* (Berkeley: University of California Press, 1985).

Benne, K., and Sheats, P., "Functional Roles of Group Members," *Journal of Social Issues*, vol. 4 (1948), pp. 41–49.

Berger, P. L., and Luckmann, T., *The Social Construction of Reality* (New York: Doubleday, 1966).

Berk, S., *The Gender Factory* (New York: Plenum Press, 1985).

Bernard, Chester, *The Functions of the Executive* (Cambridge, Mass.: Harvard University Press, 1938).

Bernard, J., *The Future of Marriage* (New York: World Publishing Co., 1972).

Bernard, J., *The Sociology of Community* (Glenview, Ill.: Scott, Foresman, 1973).

Bernard, J., "The Good-Provider Role: Its Rise and Fall," *American Psychologist*, vol. 36 (1981), pp. 1–12.

Berne, Eric, personal communication, 1962.

Berne, Eric, *Transactional Analysis in Psychotherapy* (Palo Alto, Calif.: Science and Behavior Books, 1970).

Berrien, K., *General and Social Systems* (New Brunswick, N.J.: Rutgers University Press, 1968).

Bertrand, A., *Social Organization: A General Systems and Role Theory Perspective* (Philadelphia: F. A. Davis, 1972).

Bidwell, Charles E., "The Issue of Client Membership in the Context of Schools," in W. K. Rosengren and Mark Lefton (eds.), *Organizations and Clients: Essays in the Sociology of Service* (Columbus, Ohio: Charles E. Merrill, 1970), pp. 32–60.

Biklen, D., *Community Organizing: Theory and Practice* (Englewood Cliffs, N.J.: Prentice-Hall, 1983).

Bion, W. R., *Experiences in Groups* (New York: Basic Books, 1961).

Black, K. N., "What About the Child From a One-Parent Home?" *Teacher* (June 1979), pp. 24–28.

Blau, P. M., "A Macrosociological Theory of Social Structure," *American Journal of Sociology*, vol. 83 (1977a), pp. 26–54.

Blau, P. M., *Inequality and Heterogeneity* (New York: The Free Press, 1977b).

Blau, P. M., *Exchange and Power in Social Life* (New York: John Wiley, 1964).

Block, P. "Empowering Employees," *Training and Development Journal*, vol. 41 (1987), pp. 34–39.

Blugerman, M., "Contributions of Gestalt Theory to Social Work Treatment," in F. Turner (ed.), *Social Work Treatment: Interlocking Theoretical Approaches* (New York: The Free Press, 1979), pp. 273–292.

Blum, D. B., *Life-Span Changes in a Social Movement Organization*. Unpublished Ph.D. Dissertation (Tallahassee: Florida State University, 1982).

Boss, P., "Psychological Absence in the Intact Family: A Systems Approach to a Study of Fathering," paper presented at the National Council on Family Relations Annual Meeting, St. Louis, 1974.

Bott, E., *Family and Social Network* (London: Tavistock Publications, 1957).

Bott, E., *Family and Social Network: Roles, Norms, and External Relationships in Ordinary Urban Families*, 2nd ed. (London: Tavistock, 1971).

Boulding, K., "General Systems Theory: The Skeleton of Science," *Management Science* (1956), pp. 197–208.

Bowen, Murray, *Family Therapy and Clinical Practice: Collected Papers of Murray Bowen* (New York: Jason Aronson, 1978).

Brager, G., and Holloway, S., *Changing Human Service Organizations* (New York: The Free Press, 1978).

Brager, G., Specht, H., and Torczyner, J., *Community Organizing*, 2nd ed. (New York: Columbia University Press, 1987).

Braverman, Harry, *Labor and Monopoly Capital: The Degradation of Work in the Twentieth Century* (New York: Monthly Review Press, 1974).

Briar, S., and Miller, H., *Problems and Issues in Social Casework* (New York: Columbia University Press, 1971).

Brief, A. P., and Motowidlo, S. J., "Prosocial Organizational Behavior," *Academy of Management Review*, vol. 11 (1986), pp. 710–725.

Brower, Aaron, "Behavior Changes in Psychotherapy Groups: A Study Using an Empirically Based Statistical Method," *Small Group Behavior*, vol. 17, no. 2 (May 1986), pp. 164–185.

Brown, R., "Women as Employees: Some Comments on Research in Industrial Sociology," in D. L. Barker and S. Allen (eds.), *Dependence and Exploitation in Work and Marriage* (New York: Longman, 1976), pp. 21–46.

Brownmiller, S., *Against Our Will: Men, Women, and Rape* (New York: Simon & Schuster, 1975).

Brunsson, N., *The Irrational Organization: Irrationality as a Basis for Organizational Action and Change* (Chichester, England, and New York: John Wiley, 1985).

Buckley, W., *Sociology and Modern Systems Theory* (Englewood Cliffs, N.J.: Prentice-Hall, 1967).

Buffum, W. E., and Ritvo, R. A., "Work Autonomy and the Community Mental Health Professional: Guidelines for Management," *Administration in Social Work*, vol. 8 (1984), pp. 39–54.

Burlingame, Gary, Fuhriman, A., and Drescher, S., "Scientific Inquiry Into Small Group Process: A Multidimensional Approach," *Small Group Behavior*, vol. 15, no. 4 (November 1984), pp. 441–470.

Burr, W. R., "Satisfaction with Various Aspects of Marriage Over the Life Cycle: A Random Middle-Class Sample," *Journal of Marriage and the Family*, vol. 32 (1970), pp. 27–29.

Burrell, G., and Morgan, G., *Sociological Paradigms and Organizational Analysis* (London: Heinemann, 1979).

Burt, M., Gornick, J., and Pittman, K., *Feminism and Rape Crisis Centers* (Washington, D.C.: The Urban Institute, 1983).

Cafferata, G. L., "The Building of Democratic Organizations: An Embryological Metaphor," *Administrative Science Quarterly*, vol. 27 (1982), pp. 280–303.

Cameron, K. S., "The Effectiveness of Ineffectiveness," in B. M. Staw and L. L. Cummings (eds.), *Research in Organizational Behavior*, vol. 6 (Greenwich, Conn.: JAI Press, 1984).

Cameron, K. S., "Effectiveness as Paradox: Consensus and Conflict in Conceptions of Organizational Effectiveness," *Management Science*, vol. 32 (1986a), pp. 539–553.

Cameron, K. S., "A Study of Organizational Effectiveness and Its Predictors," *Management Science*, vol. 32 (1986b), pp. 86–112.

Cameron, K. S., and Whetten, D. A., *Organizational Effectiveness: A Comparison of Multiple Models* (New York: Academic Press, 1983).

Campbell, John P., "On the Nature of Organizational Effectiveness," in Paul S. Goodman and Johannes M. Pennings (eds.), *New Perspectives on Organizational Effectiveness* (San Francisco: Jossey-Bass, 1977).

Cannon, W., *The Wisdom of the Body* (New York: W. W. Norton, 1939).

Carkhuff, R., *Helping and Human Relations*, vol. II (New York: Holt, Rinehart & Winston, 1969).

Carter, R., *The Accountable Agency* (Beverly Hills, Calif.: Sage, 1983).

Cartwright, D., and Zander, A., *Group Dynamics: Research and Theory* (Evanston, Ill.: Row, Peterson, 1960; 3rd reprint, 1968).

Cates, J., *Insuring Inequality: Administrative Leadership in Social Security, 1935–1954*

(Ann Arbor, Michigan: University of Michigan Press, 1982).

Chambers, C., "Social Service and Social Reform: A Historical Essay," *Social Service Review*, vol. 37 (March 1963), pp. 367–390.

Chesler, P., *Women and Madness* (Garden City, N.Y.: Doubleday, 1972).

Chesler, P., *Mothers on Trial: The Battle for Children and Custody* (New York: McGraw-Hill, 1986).

Chu, J., and Sue, S., "Asian/Pacific Americans and Group Practice," *Social Work with Groups*, vol. VII (Fall 1984), pp. 23–36.

Clegg, S., and Dunkerley, D., *Organization, Class, and Control* (London: Routledge & Kegan Paul, 1979).

Coburn, Denise, "Transactional Analysis—A Social Treatment Model," in F. Turner (ed.), *Social Work Treatment: Interlocking Theoretical Approaches*, 2nd ed. (New York: The Free Press, 1979), pp. 293–312.

Cohen, Elizabeth G., and Roper, Susan, A., "Identification of Interracial Interaction Disability: An Application of Status Characteristics Theory," *American Sociological Review*, vol. 37, pp. 643–655.

Coleman, J., "Comments 'On the Concept of Influence,' " *Public Opinion Quarterly*, vol. 27 (1963), pp. 63–82.

Coles, J. L., Alexander, J. F., and Schiavo, R. S., "A Developmental Model of Family Systems: A Social Psychological Approach," paper presented at the National Council on Family Relations Annual Meeting, St. Louis, 1974.

Compton, B., and Galaway, G., *Social Work Processes*, 3rd edition (Homewood, Ill.: Dorsey Press, 1984).

Constable, R. T., "Mobile Families and the School," *Social Casework*, vol. 59 (1978), pp. 421–423.

Coser, L. A., *The Functions of Social Conflict* (London: Routledge & Kegan Paul, 1956).

Cott, N., *The Bonds of Womanhood: Women's Sphere in New England, 1780–1835* (New Haven, Conn.: Yale University Press, 1977).

Crossman, M., and Adams, R., "Divorce, Single Parenting, and Child Development," *Journal of Psychology*, vol. 106 (1980), pp. 205–217.

Czarniawska, B., *Public Sector Executives: Managers or Politicians?* (Stockholm: Stockholm School of Economics, 1985a).

Czarniawska, B., "The Ugly Sister: On Relationships between the Private and Public Sectors in Sweden," *Scandinavian Journal of Management Studies*, vol. 6 (1985b), pp. 83–103.

Dahrendorf, R., *Class and Class Conflict in Industrial Society* (London: Routledge & Kegan Paul, 1959).

Daniels, Arlene K., "The Captive Professional: Bureaucratic Limitations in the Practice of Military Psychiatry," *Journal of Health and Social Behavior*, vol. 10 (1969), pp. 255–265.

Davis, A., "Settlements: History," *Encyclopedia of Social Work*, 17th Issue (New York: National Association of Social Workers, 1977), pp. 1266–1271.

Davis, Larry, "Essential Components of Group Work with Black Americans," *Social Work with Groups*, vol. VII (Fall 1984), pp. 97–109.

Degler, C., *At Odds: Women and the Family in America from the Revolution to the Present* (New York: Oxford University Press, 1980).

Della Fave, L. Richard, "The Meek Shall Not Inherit the Earth: Self-Evaluation and the Legitimacy of Stratification," *American Sociological Review*, vol. 45 (December 1980), pp. 955–971.

DeMaris, Alfred, "Predicting Premarital Cohabitation: Employing Individuals vs. Couples as the Unit of Analysis," *Alternative Lifestyles*, vol. 6 (Summer 1984), pp. 270–283.

Deutsch, M., *The Resolution of Conflict: Constructive and Destructive Processes* (New Haven, Conn.: Yale University Press, 1973).

Directors of the Robbins Institute, "An Integrated Psychotherapeutic Program," *Psychotherapy*, vol. 1, no. 1, (Fall 1955).

Dobash, R. E., and Dobash, R., *Violence Against Wives: A Case Against the Patriarchy* (New York: The Free Press, 1979).

Edwards, E., and Edwards, M., "Group Work Practice with American Indians," *Social Work with Groups*, vol. VII (Fall 1984), pp. 7–22.

Edwards, Richard, *Contested Terrain: The Transformation of the Workplace in the Twentieth Century* (New York: Basic Books, 1979).

Elkaim, M., "From General Laws to Singularities," *Family Process*, vol. 24 (1985), pp. 151–164.

Elkaim, M., "A Systemic Approach to Couple Therapy," *Family Process*, vol. 25 (1986), pp. 35–42.

Elkin, Fredrick, *The Child and Society: The Process of Socialization*, 3rd ed. (New York: Random House, 1978).

Elliott, C. C., *Child Stealing in the USA: A National Survey*, Unpublished Ph.D. dissertation (Tallahassee: Florida State University, 1982).

Ellis, Albert, *Reason and Emotion in Psychotherapy* (New York: Lyle Stuart, 1962).

Emerson, Richard M., "Power-Dependence Relations," *American Sociological Review*, vol. 22 (February 1962), pp. 31–41.

Epstein, I., and Conrad, K., "The Empirical Limits of Social Work Professionalization," in R. C. Sarri and Y. Hasenfield, *The Management of Human Services* (New York: Columbia University Press, 1978), pp. 163–183.

Etzioni, A. *An Immodest Agenda: Rebuilding America before the 21st Century* (New York: McGraw-Hill, 1984).

Etzioni, A., *Readings on Modern Organizations* (Englewood Cliffs, N.J.: Prentice-Hall, 1969).

Fabricant, M., "The Industrialization of Social Work Practice," *Social Work*, vol. 30 (1985), pp. 389–395.

Ferguson, K., *The Feminist Case Against Bureaucracy* (Philadelphia: Temple University Press, 1984).

Ferrar, K., "Experience of Parents vs. Contemporary Communal Households," *Alternative Lifestyles*, vol. 5 (Fall 1982), pp. 7–23.

Fieldler, F. E., *A Theory of Leadership Effectiveness* (New York: McGraw-Hill, 1967).

Files, L., "The Human Services Management Task: A Time Allocation Study," *Public Administration Review*, vol. 41 (1981), pp. 686–692.

Finkelstein, N. E., "Children in Limbo," *Social Work* (March 1980), pp. 100–105.

Fischer, J., *Effective Casework Practice: An Eclectic Approach* (New York: McGraw-Hill, 1978).

Fox, Mary Frank, and Hesse-Biber, Sharlene, *Women at Work* (Palo Alto, Calif.:

Mayfield, 1984).

Freeman, J., "The Women's Liberation Movement: Its Origin, Structure, Activities, and Ideas," in J. Freeman (ed.), *Women: A Feminist Perspective*, 3rd ed. (Palo Alto, Calif.: Mayfield, 1984).

Freidson, Eliot, "Disability as Social Deviance," in M. Sussman (ed.), *Sociology and Rehabilitation* (Washington, D.C.: American Sociological Association, 1965), pp. 71–99.

Freidson, Eliot, "Dominant Professions, Bureaucracy, and Client Services," in W. R. Rosengren and M. Lefton (eds.), *Organizations and Clients* (Columbus, Ohio: Charles E. Merrill, 1970), pp. 71–92.

Freidson, Eliot, *Professional Powers: A Study of the Institutionalization of Formal Knowledge* (Chicago: University of Chicago Press, 1986).

Froland, C., Pancoast, D., Chapman, N., and Kimboko, P., *Helping Networks and Human Services* (Beverly Hills, Calif.: Sage, 1981).

Frumkin, M., "A Generic Framework for Assessing Service Delivery Systems: The Mentally Ill, A Case Example," *Administration in Mental Health*, vol. 10, no. 2 (1982), pp. 79–91.

Frumkin, M., Imershein, A., Chackerian, R., and Martin, P. Y., "Evaluating State Level Integration of Human Services," *Administration in Social Work*, vol. 7 (Spring 1983), pp. 13–24.

Frumkin, Michael, Martin, P. Y., and Page, W. P., "The Future of Large State Welfare Agencies," *New England Journal of Human Services*, vol. 7 (1987), pp. 15–23.

Fuhriman, Addie, Drescher, Stuart, and Burlingame, Gary, "Conceptualizing Small Group Process," *Small Group Behavior*, vol. 15, no. 4 (November 1984), pp. 427–440.

Gallup Report, "Religion in America—50 years: 1935–1985," no. 236 (May 1985).

Galper, Jeffry, *Social Work Practice: A Radical Perspective* (Englewood Cliffs, N.J.: Prentice-Hall, 1980).

Garvin, Charles, *Contemporary Group Work*, 2nd ed. (Englewood Cliffs, N.J.: Prentice-Hall, 1987).

Garvin, Charles, and Cox, F., "A History of Community Organizing Since the Civil War with Special References to Oppressed Communities," in F. Cox, J. Erlich, J. Rothman and J. Tropman (eds.), *Strategies of Community Organization*, 4th ed. (Itasca, Ill.: F. E. Peacock, 1987), pp. 26–63.

Garvin, Charles, and Seabury, Brett, *Interpersonal Practice in Social Work: Processes and Procedures* (Englewood Cliffs, N.J.: Prentice-Hall, 1984).

Gasser, R. D., and C. M. Taylor, "Role Adjustment of Single-Parent Fathers with Dependent Children," *The Family Coordinator*, vol. 25, no. 4 (1976), pp. 397–402.

Germain, C., "An Ecological Perspective in Casework Practice," *Social Casework*, vol. 54 (1973), pp. 323–330.

Germain, C., and Gitterman, A., *The Life Model of Social Work Practice* (New York: Columbia University Press, 1980).

Gilder, G., *Wealth and Poverty* (New York: Basic Books, 1981).

Gil, David, *Child Abuse and Violence* (New York: AMS Press, 1979).

Glasser, William, *Reality Therapy: A New Approach to Psychotherapy* (New York: Harper & Row, 1965).

Glasser, P., Sarri, R., and Vinter, R. (eds.), *Individual Change Through Small Groups* (New York: The Free Press, 1974).

Glenn, N., and McLanahan, S., "The Effects of Offspring on the Psychological Well-Being of Older Adults," *Journal of Marriage and the Family* (May 1981), pp. 409–421.

Glisson, C. A., "A Contingency Model of Social Welfare Administration," *Administration in Social Work*, vol. 5 (1981), pp. 15–30.

Glisson, Charles, "The Group Versus the Individual as the Unit of Analysis in Small Group Research," *Social Work with Groups*, vol. 9, no. 3 (Fall 1986), pp. 15–30.

Glisson, C. A., and Durick, M., "Predictors of Job Satisfaction and Organizational Commitment Among Workgroups in Human Service Organizations." Unpublished manuscript (Knoxville: University of Tennessee, 1987).

Glisson, C. A., and Martin, P. Y., "Productivity and Efficiency in Human Service Organizations as Related to Structure, Size, and Age," *Academy of Management Journal*, vol. 23 (1980), pp. 21–37.

Goetting, A., "Parental Satisfaction: A Review of Research," *Journal of Family Issues*, vol. 7, no. 1 (March 1986), pp. 83–109.

Gold, K. A., "Managing for Success: A Comparison of the Private and Public Sectors," *Public Administration Review*, vol. 42 (1982), pp. 568–575.

Goldman, Paul, and Van Houten, Donald R., "Managerial Strategies and the Worker: A Marxist Analysis of Bureaucracy," *The Sociological Quarterly*, vol. 18 (1977), pp. 108–125.

Goode, W. J., *The Family* (Englewood Cliffs, N.J.: Prentice-Hall, 1964).

Goody, J., *Production and Reproduction: A Comparative Study of the Domestic Domain* (New York: Cambridge University Press, 1976).

Gordon, Ronald, "The Self-Disclosure of Interpersonal Feedback: The Dyadic Effect in a Group Context," *Small Group Behavior*, vol. 16, no. 3 (August 1985), pp. 411–413.

Gornick, J., Burt, M. R., and Pittman, K. J., "Structure and Activities of Rape Crisis Centers in the Early 1980s," *Crime and Delinquency*, vol. 31 (1984), pp. 247–268.

Gottschalk, S., "The Community-Based Welfare System: An Alternative to Public Welfare," *The Journal of Applied Behavioral Science*, vol. 9 (March-June 1973), pp. 233–242.

Gottschalk, S., *Communities and Alternatives: An Explanation of the Limits of Planning* (New York: John Wiley, 1975).

Gottschalk, S., "The Community in America," lecture in *General Systems Theory for Social Workers* (Tallahassee: School of Social Work, Florida State University, Fall 1978).

Gramsci, A., *Selections From the Prison Notebooks of Antonio Gramsci*, Quinton Hoare and Geoffrey Nowell-Smith (eds.) (London: Lawrence and Wishart, 1971).

Greenberger, D. B., and Strasser, S., "Development and Application of a Model of Personal Control in Organizations," *Academy of Management Review*, vol. 11 (1986), pp. 164–177.

Grosser, C., *New Directions in Community Organization: From Enabling to Advocacy*

(New York: Praeger, 1973).

Gummer, Burton, "A Power-Politics Approach to Social Welfare Organizations," *Social Service Review*, vol. 52 (1978), pp. 349–361.

Gummer, Burton, "Consumerism and Clients' Rights," in A. Rosenblatt and D. Waldfogel (eds.), *Handbook of Clinical Social Work* (San Francisco: Jossey-Bass, 1983), pp. 920–938.

Gummer, B., "The Social Administrator as Politician," in F. D. Perlmutter (ed.), *Human Services at Risk* (Lexington, Mass.: Lexington Books, 1984).

Habermas, J., *Legitimation Crisis* (London: Heinemann, 1976).

Haley, Jay, "Direct Study of Child-Parent Interactions Workshop, 1959. Observation of the Family of the Schizophrenic," *American Journal of Orthopsychiatry*, vol. 30 (1960), pp. 460–467.

Haley, J., *Problem-Solving Therapy* (San Francisco: Jossey-Bass, 1976).

Haley, J., *Leaving Home: The Therapy of Disturbed Young People* (New York: McGraw-Hill, 1980).

Hall, R. H., *Dimensions of Work* (Beverly Hills, CA: Sage, 1985).

Hall, R. H., *Organizations: Structures, Processes, and Outcomes*, 4th ed. (Englewood Cliffs, N.J.: Prentice-Hall, 1987).

Hamner, T. J., and Turner, P. H., *Parenting in Contemporary Society* (Englewood Cliffs, N.J.: Prentice-Hall, 1985).

Hampson, R. B., and Tavormin, J. B., "Feedback from the Experts: A Study of Foster Care Mothers," *Social Work*, vol. 25, no. 2 (1980), pp. 108–113.

Hare, A. P., Borgatta, E. F., and Bales, R. F., *Small Groups: Studies in Social Interaction*. 2nd ed. (New York: Knopf, 1965).

Harrison, David, and Hoshino, George, "Britain's Barclay Report: Lessons for the United States," *Social Work*, vol. 29 (May–June 1984), pp. 213–218.

Harrison, W. D., "Reflective Practice in Social Care," *Social Service Review*, vol. 61 (September 1987), pp. 393–404.

Hartman, A., "To Think About the Unthinkable," *Social Casework*, vol. 51 (1970), pp. 467–474.

Hasenfeld, Y., *Human Service Organizations* (Englewood Cliffs, N.J.: Prentice-Hall, 1983).

Hasenfeld, Y., "The Implementation of Change in Human Service Organizations: A Political Economy Perspective," *Social Service Review*, vol. 54 (1980), pp. 508–520.

Hasenfeld, Yeheskel, "Organizational Factors in Services to Groups" in M. Sundel, P. Glasser, R. Sarri, and R. Vinter (eds.), *Individual Change Through Small Groups* (New York: The Free Press, 1985).

Hearn, G., *The General Systems Approach: Contributions Toward an Holistic Conception of Social Work* (New York: Council on Social Work Education, 1969).

Heineman, Martha, "The Obsolete Scientific Imperative in Social Work Research," *Social Service Review* (September 1981), pp. 371–397.

Hepworth, D., and Larsen, J. A., *Direct Social Work Practice: Theory and Skills* (Homewood, IL: Dorsey Press, 1982).

Hesselbart, S. C., "An Experimental Look at the Normative Aspects of Adult Male and Female Family Roles," Unpublished manuscript (Tallahassee: Department of Sociology, Florida State University, 1980).

Hetherington, E. M., and Martin, B., "Family Interaction," in H. C. Quay and J. S. Werry (eds.), *Psychopathological Disorders of Childhood*, 2nd ed. (New York: McGraw-Hill, 1979).

Heydebrand, W. F., *Hospital Bureaucracy: A Comparative Study of Organizations* (New York: Dunellen, 1973).

Hill, W., "Hill Interaction Matrix (HIM): The Conceptual Framework, Derived Rating Scales and an Updated Bibliography, *Small Group Behavior*, vol. 8, no. 3 (1977), pp. 251–268.

Hillery, G. A., Jr., *Communal Organization: A Study of Local Societies* (Chicago: University of Chicago Press, 1968).

Ho, M. K., "Social Group Work with Asian/Pacific Americans," *Social Work with Groups*, vol. VII (Fall 1984), pp. 49–61.

Hoeffer, B., "Children's Acquisition of Sex Role Behavior in Lesbian-Mother Families," *American Journal of Orthopsychiatry*, vol. 51, no. 3 (1981), pp. 536–543.

Holland, C., "An Examination of Social Isolation and Availability to Treatment in the Phenomenon of Child Abuse," *Smith College Studies in Social Work*, vol. 44 (1973), pp. 74–75.

Holland, T., Konick, A., Buffum, W., Smith, M., and Petchers, M., "Institutional Structure and Resident Outcomes," *Journal of Health and Social Behavior*, vol. 22 (1981), pp. 433–444.

Hollis, F., *Casework: A Psychosocial Therapy* (New York: Random House, 1972).

Homans, G. C., *The Human Group* (New York: Harcourt, Brace and World, 1950).

Hotvedt, M., and Mandel, L., "Children of Lesbian Mothers," in W. Paul, J. Weinrich, J. Gonsiorek, and M. Hotvedt (eds.), *Homosexuality: Social, Psychological, and Biological Issues* (Beverly Hills, Calif.: Sage, 1982), pp. 275–285.

Hubbell, R., "Foster Care and Families' Conflicting Values and Policies." Family Impact Seminar Series (Philadelphia: Temple University Press, 1981).

Hunt, J. G., and Hunt, L. L., "The Dualities of Careers and Families: New Integrations or New Polarizations?" *Social Problems*, vol. 29 (June 1982), pp. 499–510.

Imershein, A., Frumkin, M., Chackerian, R., and Martin, P. Y., "Organizational Change in Human Services: A Framework for Critical Analysis," *New England Journal of Human Services*, vol. 3 (Fall 1983), pp. 21–29.

Imershein, A. W., Polivka, L., Gordon-Girvin, S., Chackerian, R., and Martin, P., "Service Networks in Florida: Administrative Decentralization and Its Effects on Service Delivery," *Public Administration Review*, vol. 46 (1986), pp. 161–169.

Jackson, D. D., "Family Interaction, Family Homeostasis, and Some Implications for Conjoint Family Psychotherapy," in H. H. Messerman (ed.), *Individual and Family Dynamics* (New York: Grune & Stratton, 1959).

Jacob, T., "Family Interaction in Disturbed and Normal Families: A Methodological and Substantive Review," *Psychological Bulletin*, vol. 82 (1975), pp. 30–45.

Jacobs, Jerry, "Symbolic Bureaucracy: A Case Study of a Social Welfare Agency," *Social Forces*, vol. 47 (1969), pp. 413–422.

Jacobson, D. S., "Stepfamilies: Myths and Realities," *Social Work*, vol. 24 (May 1979), pp. 202–207.

Janchill, M. P., "Systems Concepts in Casework Theory and Practice," *Social Casework*, vol. 5 (1969), pp. 74–82.

Janzen, C., and Harris, O., *Family Treatment in Social Work Practice* (Itasca, Ill.: F. E. Peacock Publishers, 1980).

Johnston, P., "The Promise of Public-Sector Unionism," *Monthly Review*, vol. 30 (1978), pp. 1–17.

Jones, K., and Poletti, A., "The Italian Experience in Mental Health Care," *Hospital and Community Psychiatry*, vol. 30, no. 8 (August 1987), pp. 795–802.

Justice, B., Calvert, A., and Justice, R., "Factors Mediating Child Abuse as a Response to Stress," *Child Abuse and Neglect*, vol. 9 (1985), pp. 359–363.

Kamerman, S. B., "The New Mixed Economy of Welfare: Public and Private," *Social Work*, vol. 28 (1983), pp. 5–9.

Kanter, R. M., *Communes: Creating and Managing the Collective Life* (New York: Harper & Row, 1973).

Kanter, R. M., *Men and Women of the Corporation* (New York: Basic Books, 1977).

Kanter, R. M., *The Change Masters* (New York: Simon & Schuster, 1983).

Katz, D., and Kahn, R. L., *The Social Psychology of Organizations* (New York: John Wiley, 1978).

Katz, R., "The Effects of Group Longevity on Project Communication and Performance," *Administrative Science Quarterly*, vol. 27 (1982), pp. 81–104.

Kaufman, H., *Administrative Behavior of Federal Bureau Chiefs* (Washington, D.C.: Brookings Institution, 1981).

Keffe, Thomas, "Meditation and Social Work Treatment," in F. Turner, *Social Work Treatment: Interlocking Theoretical Approaches* (New York: The Free Press, 1979), pp. 313–332.

Kent, M. O., "Remarriage: A Family Systems Perspective," *Journal of Contemporary Social Work*, vol. 61, no. 3 (1980), pp. 146–153.

Kerr, S., Hill, K. D., and Broedling, L., "The First-Line Supervisor: Phasing Out or Here to Stay?" *Academy of Management Review*, vol. 11 (1986), pp. 102–117.

Kettner, P., Daley, J., and Nichols, A. W., *Initiating Change in Organizations and Communities: A Macro Practice Model* (Monterey, Calif.: Brooks/Cole Publishing Co., 1985).

Kidder, T., *The Soul of a New Machine* (Boston: Atlantic-Little, Brown, 1981).

Kingston, P. W., and Nock, S., "Time Together Among Dual-Earner Couples," *American Sociological Review*, vol. 52, no. 3 (June 1987), pp. 391–400.

Kirkpatrick, M., Smith, C., and Roy, R., "Lesbian Mothers and Their Children: A Comparative Survey," *American Journal of Orthopsychiatry*, vol. 51, no. 3, (1981), p. 545–551.

Klein, N. C., Alexander, J. F., and Parsons, B. V., "Impact of Family Systems Intervention on Recidivism and Sibling Delinquency: A Model of Primary Prevention and Program Evaluation," *Journal of Consulting and Clinical Psychology*, vol. 45 (1977), pp. 469–474.

Koestler, Arthur, "Beyond Atomism and Holism—The Concept of the Holon," in A. Koestler and J. Smythies (eds.), *Beyond Reductionism: New Perspectives in the Life Sciences* (New York: Macmillan, 1969), pp. 192–197.

Kotken, Mark, "To Marry or Live Together?" *Lifestyles: A Journal of Changing Patterns*, vol. 7, no. 3 (Spring 1985), pp. 157–170.

Kramer, R., *Voluntary Agencies in the Welfare State* (Berkeley: University of California Press, 1981).

Kramer, R., "The Future of the Voluntary Agency in a Mixed Economy," *Journal of Applied Behavioral Research*, vol. 21 (1985), pp. 377–392.

Kramer, R., and Specht, H. (eds.), *Readings in Community Organization Practice*, 3rd ed. (Englewood Cliffs, N.J.: Prentice-Hall, 1983).

Krill, Donald, "Existential Social Work," in R. Turner (ed.), *Social Work Treatment: Interlocking Theoretical Approaches* (New York: The Free Press, 1979), pp. 147–176.

Kuhn, T. S., *The Structure of Scientific Revolution*, 2nd ed. (Chicago: University of Chicago Press, 1970).

LaMendola, W., and Martin, P. Y., "The Service Orientation of Social Service Administrators," *Journal of Sociology and Social Welfare*, vol. 10 (March 1983), pp. 40–55.

LaRossa, R., and LaRossa, M. M., *Transition to Parenthood: How Infants Change Families* (Beverly Hills, Calif.: Sage, 1981).

Lathrope, D., "The General Systems Approach in Social Work Practice," in G. Hearn (ed.), *The General Systems Approach: Contributions Toward an Holistic Conception of Social Work* (New York: Council on Social Work Education, 1969).

Laws, J. L., *The Second X: Sex Role and Social Role* (New York: Elsevier, 1979).

Lee, L. J., "The Social Worker in the Political Environment of a School System," *Social Work*, vol. 28 (1983), pp. 302–307.

Leighninger, R., "Systems Theory," *Journal of Sociology and Social Welfare*, vol. 5 (1978), p. 446.

Lewin, K., "Frontiers in Group Dynamics," *Human Relations*, vol. 1, no. 1 (1947), pp. 5–41.

Lieberman, M., Yalom, I., and Miles, M., *Encounter Groups: First Facts* (New York: Basic Books, 1973).

Lincoln, Yvonna, and Guba, E., *Naturalist Inquiry* (Beverly Hills, Calif.: Sage, 1985).

Lindzey, G., and Aronson, E., "The Handbook of Social Psychology," vol. 4, *Group Psychology and Phenomena of Interaction*, 2nd ed. (Reading, Mass.: Addison-Wesley, 1969).

Lippitt, Ronald, Watson, Jeanne, and Westley, Bruce, *The Dynamics of Planned Change* (New York: Harcourt, Brace and World, 1958).

Lipsky, Michael, *Street-Level Bureaucracy: Dilemmas of the Individual in Public Services* (New York: Russell Sage Foundation, 1980).

Litwak, E., "An Approach to Linkage in 'Grass Roots' Community Organization," in F. Cox, J. Erlick, J. Rothman, and J. Tropman (eds.), *Strategies of Community Organization: A Book of Readings* (Itasca, Ill.: F. E. Peacock Publishers, 1970), pp. 127–137.

London, P., *Modes and Morals of Psychotherapy* (New York: Holt, Rinehart & Winston, 1964).

Long, L., and Cope, C., "Curative Factors in Male Felony Offender Groups," *Small Group Behavior*, vol. 11 (1980), pp. 389–398.

Long, N., "The Local Community as an Ecology of Games," *American Journal of Sociology*, vol. 64 (November 1958), pp. 251–261.

Lubove, R., *The Professional Altruist: The Emergence of Social Work as a Career 1880–1930* (New York: Atheneum, 1972).

Lukacs, G., *History and Class Consciousness* (London: Merlin, 1971).

Lynn, L. E., *The State and Human Services* (Cambridge, Mass. and London, England: MIT Press, 1980).

MacDevitt, John, and Sanislow, Charles, III, "Curative Factors in Offender Groups," *Small Group Behavior*, vol. 18, no. 1 (February 1987), pp. 72–81.

Macklin, E. D., "Nontraditional Family Forms: A Decade of Research," *Journal of Marriage and the Family*, vol. 42, no. 4 (1980), pp. 905–922.

MacLaine, Shirley, *Out on a Limb* (New York: Bantam Books, 1983).

Malinowski, Bronislow, *Orgonauts of the Western Pacific: An Account of Native Enterprise and Adventure in the Archipelagoes of Melanesian New Guinea* (London: Routledge and Kegan Paul, 1922).

Main, T. J., "The Homeless of New York," *The Public Interest*, vol. 72 (Summer 1983), pp. 3–28.

Marcuse, H., *One-Dimensional Man* (London: Routledge & Kegan Paul, 1964).

Marglin, S.A., "What Do Bosses Do? The Origins and Functions of Hierarchy in Capitalist Production," in A. Gorz (ed.), *The Division of Labour: The Labour Process and Class Struggle in Capitalism* (London: Harvester, 1976).

Martin, P. Y., "The Dilemmas of Leadership in Small Residential Organizations," Unpublished manuscript (Tallahassee, Fla.: School of Social Work, Florida State University, 1979).

Martin, P. Y., "A Critical Analysis of Power in Professional–Client Relations," *Arete*, vol. 6 (Spring 1981), pp. 35–48.

Martin, P. Y., "Group Sex Composition in Work Organizations: A Structural-Normative Model," *Research in the Sociology of Organizations*, vol. 4 (1985), pp. 311–349.

Martin, P. Y., "Multiple Constituencies and Performance in Social Welfare Organizations," *Administration in Social Work*, vol. 11, (1987), pp 223–239.

Martin, P. Y., "Multiple Constituencies, Dominant Societal Values, and the Human Service Administrator: Implications for Service Delivery," *Administration in Social Work*, vol. 4 (1980a), pp. 14–27.

Martin, P. Y., "Multiple Constituencies, Differential Power, and the Question of Effectiveness in Human Service Organizations," *Journal of Sociology and Social Welfare*, vol. 6, no. 7 (1980b), pp. 801–816.

Martin, Patricia Y., "Women, Labor Markets and Employing Organizations: A Critical Analysis," in D. Dunkerley and G. Salaman (eds.), *International Yearbook of Organization Studies*, vol. 2 (London: Routledge & Kegan Paul, 1980c).

Martin, Patricia Y., "Trade Unions, Conflict, and the Nature of Work in Residential Service Organizations," *Organization Studies*, vol. 5 (1984), pp. 168–185.

Martin, P. Y., Chackerian, R., Imershein, A., and Frumkin, M., "The Concept of 'Integrated' Services Reconsidered," *Social Science Quarterly*, vol. 64 (1983), pp. 747–763.

Martin, P. Y., DiNitto, D., Norton, D. B., and Maxwell, M. S., *Sexual Assault: Services to Rape Victims in Florida 1984: A Needs Assessment Study* (Tallahassee: Florida Department of Health and Rehabilitative Services, 1984).

Martin, P. Y., DiNitto, D., Norton, D. B., and Maxwell, M. S., "Controversies Surrounding the Rape Kit Exam in the 1980s," *Crime and Delinquency*, vol. 31 (1985), pp. 223–246.

Martin, P. Y., and Pilkenton, K., "Mandatory Treatment in the Welfare State: Research Issues," in A. Rosenblatt (ed.), *For Their Own Good? Essays in Coercive Kindness* (Albany, N.Y.: The Rockefeller Institute of Government, 1988), in press.

Martin, Patricia Y., and Segal, B., "Bureaucracy, Size, and Staff Expectations for Client Behavior in Halfway Houses," *Journal of Health and Social Behavior*, vol. 18 (1977), pp. 376–390.

Martin, P. Y., Seymour, S., Courage, M., Godbey, K., and Tate, R., "Corporate, Union, Feminist and Pro-family Leaders' Views of Work-Family Policies," *Gender and Society*, vol. 2 (1988), in press.

Martin, P. Y., and Shanahan, K., "Transcending the Effects of Group Sex Composition in Small Groups," *Social Work with Groups*, vol. 6 (1983), pp. 19–32.

Martin, P. Y., and Whiddon, B., "Conceptualization and Measurement of Staff Performance in a State Welfare Agency," *Public Productivity Review* (1988), in press.

Martin, P. Y., Wilson, K., and Dillman, C. M., "Southern-Style Gender: Trends in Relations Between Men and Women," in J. Himes and A. Ferriss (eds.), *The South Moves into its Future* (Tuscaloosa: University of Alabama Press, 1988), in press.

Martin, S. *Managing Without Managers* (Beverly Hills, Calif.: Sage, 1982).

Martinko, M. J., and Gardner, W. L., "Learned Helplessness: An Alternative Explanation for Performance Deficits," *Academy of Management Review*, vol. 7 (1982), pp. 195–204.

Maruyama, M., "The Second Cybernetics: Deviation Amplifying Mutual Causal Processes," *American Scientist*, vol. 51 (1963), pp. 164–179.

Mayhew, Bruce, "Structuralism vs. Individualism, I: Shadow-Boxing in the Dark," *Social Forces*, vol. 59 (December 1980), pp. 335–375.

Mayhew, B. H., and Schollaert, P. T., "The Concentration of Wealth: A Sociological Model," *Sociological Focus*, vol. 13 (1980), pp. 1–35.

Mayo, E., *The Human Problems of an Industrial Civilization* (New York: Macmillan, 1933).

Mayo, E., *The Social Problems of an Industrial Civilization* (London: Routledge & Kegan Paul, 1949).

McCord, J., "Some Child-Rearing Antecedents of Criminal Behavior in Adult Men," *Journal of Personality and Social Psychology*, vol. 37 (1979), pp. 1477–1486.

McGrath, Joseph, *Groups: Interaction and Performance* (Englewood Cliffs, N.J.: Prentice-Hall, 1984).

Mead, M., *Male and Female* (New York: Dell Publishing Co., 1949).

Meeker, B., and Weitzel-O'Neill, P. A., "Sex Roles and Interpersonal Behavior in Task-Oriented Groups," *American Sociological Review*, vol. 42 (1977), pp. 91–105.

Meyer, Carol (ed.), *Clinical Social Work in the Eco-Systems Perspective* (New York: Columbia University Press, 1983).

Meyer, C., "Direct Services in New and Old Contexts," in A. Kahn (ed.), *Shaping the New Social Work* (Columbia University Press, 1973).

Meyer, C., *Social Work Practice*, 2nd ed. (New York: The Free Press, 1976).

Meyer, J. W., "Organizational Factors Affecting Legalization in Education," in

J. W. Meyer and W. R. Scott, *Organizational Environments: Ritual and Rationality* (Beverly Hills, Calif.: Sage, 1983a), pp. 217–232.

Meyer, J. W. "Conclusion: Institutionalization and the Rationality of Formal Organizational Structure," in J. W. Meyer and W. R. Scott, *Organizational Environments: Ritual and Rationality* (Beverly Hills, Calif.: Sage, 1983b), pp. 261–282.

Meyer, J. W., "Strategies for Further Research: Varieties of Environmental Variation," in J. W. Meyer (ed.), *Environments and Organizations* (San Francisco: Jossey-Bass, 1978).

Meyer, J. W., and Rowan, B., "Institutionalized Organizations: Formal Structure as Myth and Ceremony," *American Journal of Sociology*, vol. 83 (1977), pp. 440–463.

Meyer, J. W., and Scott, W. R., *Organizational Environments: Ritual and Rationality* (Beverly Hills, Calif.: Sage, 1983).

Meyer, J. W., Scott, W. R., and Deal, T. E., "Institutional and Technical Sources of Organizational Structure," in H. D. Stein (ed.), *Organization and the Human Services* (Philadelphia: Temple University Press, 1981).

Miller, B., "Gay Fathers and their Children," *The Family Coordinator* (October 1979), pp. 544–552.

Miller, J., "Living Systems. Basic Concepts," *Behavioral Sciences*, vol. 10, no. 3 (1965), pp. 193–237.

Miller, R. D., and Fiddleman, P. B., "Attitudes of Mental Health Professionals Towards Involuntary Hospitalization and Treatment," Unpublished manuscript (University of Wisconsin Medical College, n.d.).

Mills, P. K., and Morris, J. H., "Clients as Partial Employees of Service Organizations: Role Development in Client Participation," *Academy of Management Review*, vol. 11 (1986), pp. 726–735.

Minuchin, S., *Families and Family Therapy* (Cambridge, Mass.: Harvard University Press, 1974).

Minuchin, S., Montalvo, G. B., Guerney, B., Rosman, B. L., and Schumer, F., *Families of the Slums: An Explanation of Their Structure and Treatment* (New York: Basic Books, 1967).

Molnar, J. J., and Rogers, D. L., "Organizational Effectiveness: An Empirical Comparison of the Goal and System Resource Approaches," *The Sociological Quarterly*, vol. 17 (1976), pp. 401–413.

Mowday, R. T., Porter, L. W., and Steers, R. M., *Employee-Organization Linkages: The Psychology of Commitment, Absenteeism, and Turnover* (New York: Academic Press, 1982).

Murdock, A. D., 'A Political Perspective on Problem Solving," *Social Work*, vol. 27 (1982), pp. 417–421.

Murdock, G. P., *Social Structure* (New York: Macmillan, 1949).

Murphy, C., *Community Organization Practice* (Boston: Houghton Mifflin, 1954).

Nadelson, C. C., and Nadelson, T., "Dual-Career Marriages: Benefits and Costs," in F. Pepitone-Rockwell (ed.), *Dual Career Couples* (Beverly Hills, Calif.: Sage, 1980).

Nader, R., *Ralph Nader Congress Project* (New York: Grossman Publications, 1975).

Naisbitt, J., *Megatrends: Ten New Directions Transforming Our Lives* (New York:

Warner Books, 1982).

National Association of Social Work, *Code of Ethics* (Washington, D.C.: National Association of Social Workers, 1979).

National Association of Social Work NEWS, vol. 28, no. 10 (November 1983).

Nelsen, J. C., "Uses of Systems Theory in Casework I and II: A Proposal," *Journal of Social Work Education* (1972), pp. 60–64.

Nieva, V., and Gutek, B., *Women and Work: A Psychological Perspective* (Praeger: New York, 1981).

Nieva, V., "Work and Family Linkages," in L. Larwood, A. Stromberg, and B. Gutek (eds.), *Women and Work* (Beverly Hills, Calif.: Sage), 1985.

Nisbet, R., "Moral Values and Community," *International Review of Community Development*, vol. 5 (1960), pp. 77–85.

Nisbet, Robert A., *The Sociological Tradition* (New York, Basic Books, 1966).

Norwick, K. P., *Lobbying for Freedom in the 1980's: A Grass-Roots Guide to Protecting Your Rights* (New York: Perigee Books, 1983).

Oakley, A., *The Sociology of Housework* (New York: Pantheon Books, 1974).

O'Connor, G., "Case Management: System and Practice," *Social Casework*, vol. 69, (Feb. 1988), in press.

O'Connor, G., "Counselor Perceptions as an Intervening Variable in the Correctional Process," *Adolescence*, vol. xiv, no. 56 (Winter 1979), pp. 727–737.

O'Connor, Gerald, "Small Groups: A General System Model," *Small Group Behavior*, vol. 11, no. 2 (May 1980), pp. 145–174.

O'Connor, Gerald, and Waring, Mary, "Toward Identifying the Domain of Social Work: A Perspective," *Arete*, vol. 6, no. 4 (Winter 1981), pp. 1–12.

Offe, Claus, *Industry and Inequality*, Translated by James Wickham (London: Edward Arnold, 1976).

Offe, C., *Contradictions of the Modern Welfare State* (London: Hutchinson, 1984).

Okun, Barbara, *Effective Helping: Interviewing and Counseling Techniques* (North Schuate, Mass.: Duxbury Press, 1976).

Okun, Barbara and Rappaport, Louis, *Working with Families: An Introduction to Family Therapy* (North Schuate, Mass.: Duxbury Press, 1980).

Olmsted, M., and Hare, A. P., *The Small Group*, 2nd ed. (New York: Random House, 1978).

O'Neall, Linda, Personal communication, 1972.

Osmond, M. W., "Cross-societal Family Research: A Macro-sociological Overview of the Seventies," *Journal of Marriage and the Family*, vol. 42 (1980), pp. 995–1016.

Palmer, T., "Types of Treaters and Types of Juvenile Offenders," *California Youth Authority Quarterly*, no. 4 (1965), pp. 14–23.

Pappel, C., and Rothman, B., "Social Group Work Models: Possession and Heritage," *Journal of Education for Social Work*, vol. 2, no. 2 (Fall 1966), pp. 66–77.

Pareto, V., *An Introduction to Pareto, His Sociology*, G. C. Homans and C. P. Curtis (eds.). (New York: Alfred Knopf, 1934).

Parsons, B. V., and Alexander, J. F., "Short Term Family Interventions: A Therapy Outcome Study," *Journal of Consulting and Clinical Psychology*, vol. 41 (1973), pp. 195–201.

Parsons, T., and Bales, R. F., *Family Socialization and the Interaction Process* (Glencoe,

Ill.: The Free Press, 1955).

Patterson, G. R., and Brodsky, G., "A Behavior Modification Programme for a Child with Multiple Problem Behaviors," *Journal of Child Psychology and Psychiatry*, vol. 7 (1976), pp. 277–295.

Patti, R., "In Search of Purpose for Social Welfare Administration," *Administration in Social Work*, vol. 9 (1985), pp. 1–14.

Perlman, Helen, *A Problem Solving Process* (Chicago: University of Chicago Press, 1957).

Perlman, R., and Gurin, A., *Community Organization and Social Planning* (New York: John Wiley, 1972).

Perlmutter, Felice D., and Alexander, Leslie B., "Exposing the Coercive Consensus: Racism and Sexism in Social Work," in R. Sarri and Y. Hasenfeld (eds.), *The Management of Human Services* (New York: Columbia University Press, 1978).

Perls, Fritz, *Gestalt Therapy Verbatim* (Lafayette, Calif.: Real People Press, 1969).

Perrow, C., *Complex Organizations: A Critical Essay*, 2nd ed. (Glenview, Ill.: Scott, Foresman, 1979).

Perrow, C., "The Organizational Context of Human-Factors Engineering," *Administrative Science Quarterly*, vol. 28 (1983), pp. 521–541.

Peters, T. J., and Waterman, Jr., R. H., *In Search of Excellence: Lessons from America's Best-Run Companies* (Harper & Row, 1982).

Pincus, A., and Minahan, A., *Social Work Practice: Model and Method* (Itasca, Ill.: F. E. Peacock Publishers, 1973).

Piven, F., and Cloward, R., *Regulating the Poor: The Functions of Public Welfare* (London: Tavistock, 1972).

Piven, F. F., and Cloward, R., *The New Class War: Reagan's Attack on the Welfare State and Its Consequences* (Pantheon Books, 1982).

Pleck, J. H., "Masculinity–Femininity: Current and Alternate Paradigms," *Sex Roles*, vol. 1, no. 2 (1975), pp. 161–179.

Polsky, H., "System as Patient: Client Needs and System Function," in G. Hearn (ed.), *The General Systems Approach: Contributions Towards a Holistic Conception of Social Work* (Council on Social Work Education, 1969).

Prottas, J., *People Processing* (Lexington, Mass.: D.C. Heath & Co., 1979).

Radcliffe-Brown, A., *Structure and Function in Primitive Society* (London: Cohen & West, 1952).

Rapoport, R., and Rapoport, R. N., *Dual-Career Families Re-examined* (New York: Harper & Row, 1976).

Rapp, R., "Family and Class in Contemporary America: Notes Toward an Understanding of Ideology," *Science and Society*, vol. 42 (1978), pp. 278–300.

Regan, M. C., and Roland, H. E., "Rearranging Family and Career Priorities: Professional Women and Men of the Eighties," *Journal of Marriage and the Family*, vol. 47 (1985), pp. 985–992.

Reid, William, *The Task-Centered System* (New York: Columbia University Press, 1978).

Reiss, D., "Varieties of Consensual Experience: II. Dimensions of a Family Experience of the Environment," *Family Process*, vol. 10 (1971), pp. 28–35.

Resnick, H., and Patti, R. (eds.), *Change from Within: Humanizing Social Welfare Organizations* (Philadelphia: Temple University Press, 1980).

Richmond, M., *Social Diagnosis* (New York: Sage, 1917).

Richmond, M., *What Is Social Casework?* (New York: Sage, 1922).

Roethlisberger, F., and Dickson, W., *Management and the Worker* (Cambridge, Mass.: Harvard University Press, 1947).

Rogers, Carl, *Client-Centered Therapy* (Boston: Houghton Mifflin, 1951).

Rogers, Carl, *On Encounter Groups* (New York: Harper & Row, 1970).

Rogers, Mary, "Instrumental and Infraresources: The Bases of Power," *American Journal of Sociology*, vol. 79 (May 1974), pp. 1418–1433.

Rose, Stephen, *The Betrayal of the Poor: The Transformation of Community Action* (Cambridge, Mass.: Schenkman Publishing Co., 1972).

Rosenthal, Douglas, *Lawyer and Client: Who's in Charge?* (New York: Sage, 1974).

Ross, M., *Community Organization Theory, Principles, and Practice*, 2nd ed. (New York: Harper & Row, 1967).

Rosseau, A. M., *Shopping Bag Ladies* (New York: Pilgrim Press, 1981).

Rothman, J., *Planning and Organizing for Social Change: Action Principles from Social Science Research* (New York: Columbia University Press, 1974).

Rothman, J., and Tropman, J. "Models of Community Organization and Macro-Practice Perspectives: Their Mixing and Phasing," in F. Cox, J. Erlich, J. Rothman, and J. Tropman (eds.), *Strategies of Community Organization: A Book of Readings*, 4th ed. (Itasca, Ill.: F. E. Peacock Publishers, 1987), pp. 3–26.

Rothschild-Whitt, Joyce, "The Collectivist Organization: An Alternative to Rational-Bureaucratic Models," *American Sociological Review*, vol. 44 (August 1979), pp. 509–527.

Rothschild-Whitt, J., and Whitt, A., *Work Without Bosses: Conditions and Dilemmas of Organizational Democracy in Grassroots Cooperatives* (New York: Cambridge University Press, 1986).

Ruzek, Sheryl B., *The Women's Health Movement: Feminist Alternatives to Medical Control* (New York: Praeger, 1978).

Salaman, Graeme, "Towards a Sociology of Organizational Structure," *Sociological Review*, vol. 26 (1978), pp. 519–554.

Salas, E. S., *Privatizing the Public Sector: How to Shrink Government* (Chatham, N.J.: Chatham House, 1982).

Sanday, Peggy R., *Female Power and Male Dominance: On the Origins of Sexual Inequality* (New York: Cambridge University Press, 1981).

Sanders, I., *The Community: An Introduction to a Social System*, 3rd ed. (New York: The Ronald Press Co., 1975).

Sarri, R. C., and Galinsky, M. T., "A Conceptual Framework for Group Development," in M. Sundel, P. Glasser, R. Sarri, and R. Vinter (eds.), *Individual Change Through Small Groups* (New York: The Free Press, 1985), pp. 70–86.

Satir, V., *Conjoint Family Therapy*, 2nd. ed. (Palo Alto, Calif.: Science and Behavior Books, 1967).

Scallen, R., An Investigation of Parental Attitudes and Behavior in Homosexual and Heterosexual Fathers. Unpublished doctoral dissertation (Los Angeles: California School of Professional Psychology, 1981).

Scheff, Thomas J., "Negotiating Reality: Notes on Power in the Assessment of Responsibility," *Social Problems*, vol. 16 (1968), pp. 3–17.

Schneider, B., Parkington, J. J., and Buxton, V. M., "Employee and Customer

Perceptions of Service in Banks," *Administrative Science Quarterly*, vol. 25 (1980), pp. 252–257.

Schmidman, J., *Unions in Postindustrial Society* (University Park: Pennsylvania State University Press, 1979).

Schon, D., *The Reflective Practitioner: How Professionals Think in Action* (New York: Basic Books, 1983).

Schutz, W. C., *Joy: Expanding Human Awareness* (New York: Grove Press, 1969).

Schultze, C. L., *The Public Use of Private Interest* (Washington, D.C.: The Brookings Institution, 1977).

Schwartz, Barry, "Waiting, Exchange, and Power: The Distribution of Time in Social Systems," *American Journal of Sociology*, vol. 79 (January 1974), pp. 841–870.

Schwartz, W., "Between Client and System: The Mediating Function," in R. Roberts and H. Northern (eds.), *Theories of Social Work with Groups* (New York: Columbia University Press, 1976), pp. 171–197.

Schwartz, William, "Social Workers in the Group," *Social Welfare Forum* (New York: Columbia University Press, 1961).

Scott, W. R., "Effectiveness of Organizational Effectiveness Studies," in P. S. Goodman and J. M. Pennings (eds.), *New Perspectives on Organizational Effectiveness* (San Francisco: Jossey-Bass, 1977).

Scott, W. R., "The Organization of Environments: Network, Cultural, and Historical Elements," in J. W. Meyer and W. R. Scott (eds.), *Organizational Environments: Ritual and Rationality* (Beverly Hills, Calif.: Sage, 1983).

Sexton, P. C., "The Life of the Homeless," *Dissent* (Winter 1983), pp. 79–84.

Shulman, L. *A Casebook of Social Work with Groups: The Mediating Model* (New York: Council of Social Work Education, 1968).

Shulman, L., *The Skills of Helping Individuals and Groups*, 2nd ed. (Itasca, Ill.: F. E. Peacock Publishers, 1984).

Simmel, G., "The Metropolis and Mental Life," in R. Warren (ed.), *Perspectives on the American Community*, 3rd ed. (Chicago: Rand McNally & Co., 1977), pp. 33–44.

Simon, Herbert, "The Architecture of Complexity," *Proceedings of the American Philosophical Society*, vol. 106, no. 6 (December 1962), pp. 467–482.

Singer, M., "Delinquency and Family Disciplinary Configurations: An Elaboration of the Superego Lacunae Concept," *Archives of General Psychiatry*, vol. 21 (1974), pp. 795–798.

Sipel, G. A., "Putting 'In Search of Excellence' to Work in Local Government," *Public Management*, vol. 66 (1984), pp. 2–5.

Siporin, M., "Situational Assessment and Intervention," *Social Casework*, vol. 53 (Feb. 1972), pp. 91–109.

Siporin, M., *Introduction to Social Work Practice* (New York: Macmillan, 1975).

Skinner, B. F., *Walden Two* (New York: Macmillan, 1948).

Skocpol, T., and Ikenberry, J., "The Political Formation of the American Welfare State in Historical and Comparative Perspective," *Comparative Social Research*, vol. 6 (1983), pp. 37–64.

Sluzki, C., "Marital Therapy From a Systems Theory Perspective," in T. J. Paolino, and B. S. McCrady (eds.), *Marriage and Marital Therapy: Psychoanalytic, Be-*

havioral, and Systems Theory Perspectives (New York: Brunner/Mazel, 1978).

Smalley, R., *Theory for Social Work Practice* (New York: Columbia University Press, 1967).

Smircich, L., and Morgan, G., "Leadership: The Management of Meaning," *Journal of Applied Behavioral Science*, vol. 18 (1982), pp. 257–273.

Smith, C. A., Organ, D. W., and Near, J., "Organizational Citizenship Behavior: Its Nature and Antecedents," *Journal of Applied Psychology*, vol. 69 (1983), pp. 653–663.

Smith, R. E., *The Subtle Revolution* (Washington, D.C.: The Urban Institute, 1979).

Sokoloff, Natalie J., *Between Money and Love: The Dialectic of Women's Home and Market Work* (New York: Praeger, 1980).

Stacey, M., "The Division of Labour Revisited or Overcoming the Two Adams," in P. Abrams, R. Keen, J. Finch, and P. Rock (eds.), *Practice and Progress: British Sociology, 1950–1980*, (London: Allen & Unwin, 1981).

Stack, C., *All Our Kin: Strategies for Survival in a Black Community* (New York: Harper & Row, 1974).

Staw, B. M., Bell, N. E., and Clausen, J. A., "The Dispositional Approach to Job Attitudes: A Lifetime Longitudinal Test," *Administrative Science Quarterly*, vol. 31 (1986), pp. 56–77.

Stein, I., *Systems Theory, Science, and Social Work* (Scarecrow Press, 1974).

Stein, Joan, *The Family as a Unit of Study and Treatment*, (Seattle: Regional Rehabilitation Research Institute, University of Washington, School of Social Work, 1969).

Stock, D., and Thelen, H. A., *Emotional Dynamics and Group Culture: Experimental Studies of Individual and Group Behavior* (New York: New York University Press, 1958).

Streib, G., "The South and Its Older People: Structural and Change Perspectives," in J. P. Himes and A. Ferriss (eds.), *The South Moves into Its Future* (Tuscaloosa, Al.: University of Alabama Press, 1988), in press.

Stuart, R. B., "Behavioral Contracting with the Families of Delinquents," *Journal of Behavior Therapy and Experimental Psychiatry*, vol. 2 (1971), pp. 1–11.

Stuart, Richard, "Behavior Modification: A Technology of Social Change," in F. Turner (ed.), *Social Work Treatment: Interlocking Theoretical Approaches*, 2nd ed. (New York: The Free Press, 1979), pp. 433–448.

Sundel, Marlin, Glasser, P., Sarri, R., and Vinter P. (eds.), *Individual Change Through Small Groups* (New York: The Free Press, 1985).

Tallman, I., "The Family as a Small Problem-Solving Group," *Journal of Marriage and the Family*, vol. 32 (1970), pp. 94–104.

Tannenbaum, A. S., Kavcic, B., Rosner, M., Vianello, M., and Wieser, G. *Hierarchy in Organizations* (San Francisco: Jossey-Bass, 1974).

Theodorson, G., and Theodorson, A., *A Modern Dictionary of Sociology* (New York: Thomas Crowell Co., 1969).

Thompson, Allan, *Dynamics of the Industrial Revolution* (London: Edward Arnold, 1977).

Thorne, B. (ed.), *Re-thinking the Family: Some Feminist Questions* (New York: Longman, 1982).

Thurston, M. A., Strategies, Constraints, and Dilemmas of Alternative Organizations: A Study of Women's Health Centers. Unpublished Ph.D. dissertation (Tallahassee: Florida State University, 1987).

Time to Care (Stockholm: Swedish Center for Policy Analysis and Research, 1984).

Tolan, P., Cromwell, R., and Brasswell, M., "Family Therapy with Delinquents: A Critical Review of the Literature," *Family Process*, vol. 25 (1986), pp. 619–650.

Tonnies, F., *Community and Society*, edited and translated by C. P. Loomis (New York: Harper Torchbook, 1957).

Toren, N., "Semi-Professionalism and Social Work: A Theoretical Perspective," in A. Etzioni, *The Semi-Professions and Their Organization* (New York: The Free Press, 1969), pp. 141–196.

Toren, N., and Kraus, V., "The Effects of Minority Size on Women's Position in Academia," *Social Forces*, vol. 65 (June 1987), pp. 1090–1100.

Toseland, Ronald, and Rivas, Robert, *An Introduction to Group Work Practice* (New York: Macmillan, 1984).

Tuckman, B. W., "Developmental Sequence in Small Groups," *Psychological Bulletin*, vol. 63 (1965), 384–399.

Turner, B. A., "Sociological Aspects of Organizational Symbolism," *Organization Studies*, vol. 7 (1986), pp. 101–115.

Turner, F., "Psychosocial Therapy," in F. Turner (ed.), *Social Work Treatment: Interlocking Theoretical Approaches* (New York: The Free Press, 1979a), pp. 69–90.

Turner, F., "Interlocking Perspectives for Practice," in F. Turner (ed.), *Social Work Treatment: Interlocking Theoretical Approaches* (New York: The Free Press, 1979b), pp. 535–546.

Urban Communes Project, Second Report to Participants (New York: Columbia University Press, 1976).

U. S. Bureau of the Census, *Historical Statistics of the United States, Colonial Times to 1970*, Part I (U.S. Government Printing Office: Washington, D.C., 1975a).

U. S. Bureau of the Census, *Historical Statistics of the United States, Colonial Times to 1970*, Part II (U.S. Government Printing Office: Washington, D.C., 1975b).

U. S. Bureau of the Census, *Statistical Abstracts of the United States, 1982–1983*, 103rd ed. (U.S. Government Printing Office: Washington, D.C., 1982).

U. S. Bureau of the Census, *General Population Characteristics, United States Summary*, Vol. I, PC80-1B1 (U.S. Government Printing Office: Washington, D.C., 1983a).

U. S. Bureau of the Census, *Statistical Abstracts of the United States: 1984*, 104th ed. (U.S. Government Printing Office: Washington, D.C., 1983b).

U. S. Bureau of the Census, *Current Population Reports, Population Characteristics, Series P-20, No. 381* (U.S. Government Printing Office: Washington, D.C., 1983c).

U. S. Bureau of the Census, *Current Population Reports, Population Characteristics, Series P-20, No. 380* (U.S. Government Printing Office: Washington, D.C., 1983d).

U. S. Bureau of the Census, *Supplementary Report, Ancestry of the Population by State: 1980*. PC80-S1-10 (U.S. Government Printing Office: Washington, D.C., 1983e).

U. S. Bureau of the Census, *Current Population Reports, Series P–23, No. 130, Population Profile of the United States: 1982* (U.S. Government Printing Office: Washington, D.C., 1983f).

U. S. Bureau of the Census, *Current Population Reports, Series P-23, No. 131, Voting and Registration Highlights From the Current Population Survey: 1964 to 1980* (U.S. Government Printing Office: Washington, D.C., 1984a).

U. S. Bureau of the Census, *Subject Reports, Vol. 2, PC80-2-4D, Persons in Institutions and Other Group Quarters* (U.S. Government Printing Office: Washington, D.C., 1984b).

U. S. Bureau of the Census, *Current Population Reports, Series P-23, No. 138, Demographic and Socioeconomic Aspects of Aging in the United States* (U.S. Government Printing Office: Washington, D.C., 1984c).

U. S. Bureau of the Census, *Statistical Abstracts of the United States: 1985*, 105th ed. (U.S. Government Printing Office: Washington, D.C., 1984d).

U. S. Bureau of the Census, *Current Population Reports, Series P-23, No. 145, Population Profile of the United States, 1983–84* (U.S. Government Printing Office: Washington, D.C., 1985a).

U. S. Bureau of the Census, *Current Population Reports, Series P-20, No. 398, Household and Family Characteristics: March 1984* (U.S. Government Printing Office: Washington, D.C., 1985b).

U. S. Bureau of the Census, *Current Population Reports, Series P-20, No. 412, Households, Families, Marital Status, and Living Arrangements: March 1986* (Advance Report) (U.S. Government Printing Office: Washington, D.C., 1986a).

U. S. Bureau of the Census, *Current Population Reports, Series P-23, No. 146, Women in the American Economy* (U.S. Government Printing Office: Washington, D.C., 1986b).

U. S. Bureau of the Census, *Statistical Abstracts of the United States: 1987* (U.S. Government Printing Office: Washington, D.C., December, 1986c).

U. S. Department of Justice, Federal Bureau of Investigation, *Uniform Crime Reports: Crime in the United States, 1982* (U. S. Government Printing Office: Washington, D.C., 1983).

U. S. Department of Justice, Federal Bureau of Investigation, *Uniform Crime Reports: Crime in the United States, 1983* (U. S. Government Printing Office: Washington, D.C., 1984).

U. S. Department of Justice, Federal Bureau of Investigation, *Uniform Crime Reports: Crime in the United States, 1984* (U. S. Government Printing Office: Washington, D.C., 1985).

U. S. Department of Justice, Federal Bureau of Investigation, *Uniform Crime Reports: Crime in the United States, 1985* (U. S. Government Printing Office: Washington, D.C., 1986).

U. S. Department of Justice, Federal Bureau of Investigation, *Uniform Crime Reports: Crime in the United States, 1986* (U. S. Government Printing Office: Washington, D.C., 1987).

Vandepol, A., "Dependent Children, Child Custody, and the Mothers' Pensions: The Transformation of State-Family Relations in the Early 20th Century," *Social Problems*, vol. 29 (1982), pp. 221–235.

Verzaro-Lawrence, M., "Shared Childrearing: A Challenging Alternative Lifestyle," *Alternative Lifestyles*, vol. 4, no. 2 (May 1981), pp. 205–217.

Vickery, Anne, "A Systems Approach to Social Work Intervention: Its Uses for Work with Individuals and Families," *British Journal of Social Work*, vol. 4 (Winter 1974), pp. 389–404.

Vidich, A., and Bensman, J., "Small Town in Mass Society," in R. Warren (ed.), *Perspectives on the American Community*, 3rd ed. (Chicago: Rand McNally & Co., 1977), pp. 265–276.

Vinter, R. (ed.), *Readings in Group Work Practice* (Ann Arbor, Mich.: Carlos Publishers, 1967).

Visher, E. B., and Visher, J. S., "Common Problems of Stepparents and their Spouses," *American Journal of Orthopsychiatry*, vol. 48, no. 2 (1978), pp. 252–262.

Visher, E. B., and Visher, J. S., *Stepfamilies: A Guide to Working with Stepparents and Stepchildren* (New York: Brunner/Mazel, 1979).

von Bertalanffy, L., *General System Theory: Foundations, Development, Applications* (New York: George Braziller, 1968).

Wagner, D. G., Ford, R. S., and Ford, T. W., "Can Gender Inequalities Be Reduced?" *American Sociological Review*, vol. 51 (1986), pp. 47–61.

Wahler, R. G., "The Insular Mother: Her Problems in Parent–Child Treatment," *Journal of Applied and Behavioral Analysis*, vol. 13 (1980), pp. 207–219.

Walker, K. E., *Time-Use Patterns for Household Work Related to Homemakers' Employment* (Washington, D.C.: U. S. Department of Agricultural Research Service, 1970).

Walker, K. E., and Woods, M. E., *Time Use: A Measure of Household Production of Family Goods and Services* (Washington, D.C.: American Home Economics Association, Center for the Family, 1975).

Wallerstein, J. S., and Kelly, J. B., "Children and Divorce: A Review," *Social Work*, (November 1979), pp. 468–475.

Walmsley, Gary, and Zald, M. N., *The Political Economy of Public Organizations* (Lexington, Mass.: D.C. Heath & Co., 1973).

Warren, M., "Implications of a Typology of Delinquents for Measures of Behavior Change," *California Youth Authority Quarterly*, no. 3 (1965), pp. 6–13.

Warren, R., *The Community in America* (Chicago: Rand-McNally & Co., 1963).

Warren, R., "The Interorganizational Field as a Focus for Investigation," in F. Cox, J. Erlick, J. Rothman, and J. Tropman (eds.), *Strategies of Community Organization* (Itasca, Ill.: F. E. Peacock Publishers, 1970), pp. 139–151.

Wasserman, Sidney, "Ego Psychology," in F. Turner (ed.), *Social Work Treatment: Interlocking Theoretical Approaches* (New York: The Free Press, 1979).

Watson, F. D., *The Charity Organization Movement in the United States* (New York: Macmillan, 1922).

Watson, R.E.L., "Premarital Cohabitation vs. Traditional Courtship: Their Effects on Sequential Marital Adjustment," *Family Relations*, vol. 32 (1983), pp. 139–147.

Watzlawick, P., Beavin, J. H., and Jackson, D. D., *Pragmatics of Human Communication* (New York: W. W. Norton, 1967).

Weber, Max, *The Theory of Social and Economic Organization*, trans. A. M. Henderson and T. Parsons (New York: The Free Press, 1947).

Webster, M., Jr., and Driskell, J. E., Jr., "Status Generalization: A Review and Some New Data," *American Sociological Review*, vol. 43 (1978), pp. 220–236.

Weick, K. E., "Educational Organizations as Loosely Coupled Systems," *Administrative Science Quarterly*, vol. 21 (1976), pp. 1–19.

Weinstein, Deena, *Bureaucratic Opposition: Challenging Abuses at the Workplace* (New York: Pergamon Press, 1979).

Weissman, H., Epstein, I., and Savage, A., *Agency Based Social Work: Neglected Aspects of Clincial Practice* (Philadelphia,: Temple University Press, 1983).

Werner, Harold D., "Cognitive Theory," in F. Turner (ed.), *Social Work Treatment: Interlocking Theoretical Approaches*, 2nd ed. (New York: The Free Press, 1979), pp. 243–272.

Whetten, D. A., "Coping with Incompatible Expectations: An Integrated View of Role Conflict," *Administrative Science Quarterly*, vol. 23 (1978), pp. 254–271.

Whiddon, B., The Effect of Congruence on the Relationships Between Participation/Job Discretion and Staff Performance. Unpublished Ph.D. dissertation (Tallahassee: Florida State University, 1982).

Whiddon, B., and Martin, P. Y., "Quality of Staff Performance in a State Welfare Agency," Unpublished manuscript (Tallahassee: Florida State University, 1987).

Whitaker, D. S., and Lieberman, M., *Psychotherapy Through the Group Process* (New York: Atherton Press, 1964).

White, L., Booth, A., and Edwards, J., "Children and Marital Happiness: Why the Negative Correlations?" *Journal of Family Issues*, vol. 7, no. 42 (June 1986), pp. 131–147.

Whiteside, M. F., and Auerbach, L. S., "Can the Daughter of My Father's New Wife Be My Sister?" *Journal of Divorce*, vol. 1, no. 3 (1978), p. 271–283.

Wiewel, W., and Hunter, A., "The Interorganizational Network as a Resource: A Comparative Case Study of Organizational Genesis," *Administrative Science Quarterly*, vol. 30 (1985), pp. 482–496.

Wildavsky, A., *The Politics of the Budgeting Process*, 3rd ed. (Boston: Little, Brown, 1979).

Witkin, Stanley, and Gottschalk, S., "Alternative Criteria for Theory Evaluation in Social Work Research," *Social Service Review* (1988), in press.

Wolpe, Joseph, "The Systematic Desensitization Treatment of Neuroses," in J. Fischer (ed.), *Interpersonal Helping: Emerging Approaches for Social Work Practice* (Springfield, Ill.: Charles Thomas, 1973).

Yalom, I., *The Theory and Practice of Group Psychotherapy*, 3rd ed. (New York: Basic Books, 1985).

Yuchtman, E., and Seashore, S. E., "A System Resource Approach to Organizational Effectiveness," *American Sociological Review*, vol. 32 (1967), pp. 189–903.

Znaniecki, F., "Social Groups as Products of Participating Individuals," *American Journal of Sociology*, vol. 44 (1939), pp. 799–811.

Index